TWENTIETH-CENTURY AMERICAN LITERATURE

Texts, Contexts, Themes and Perspectives

TWENTIETH-CENTURY AMERICAN LITERATURE

Texts, Contexts, Themes and Perspectives

DR. SOHAN LAL

Associate Professor, Department of English,
Satyawati College, University of Delhi

B L O O M S B U R Y

NEW DELHI • LONDON • OXFORD • NEW YORK • SYDNEY

BLOOMSBURY INDIA
Bloomsbury Publishing India Pvt. Ltd
Second Floor, LSC Building No. 4, DDA Complex,
Pocket C – 6 & 7, Vasant Kunj,
New Delhi 110070

BLOOMSBURY, BLOOMSBURY QUEST and the Diana logo are
trademarks of Bloomsbury Publishing Plc

First published in India 2026
This edition published in 2026

ISBN: 978-93-69523-31-3
2 4 6 8 10 9 7 5 3 1

Printed in India by Manipal Technologies Limited, Manipal

To find out more about our authors and books, visit
www.bloomsbury.com and sign up for our newsletters

This Book is Dedicated to my parents,
Late Choudhary Ram Rakh Ji
and
Mrs. Keli Devi Ji,
whose values, sacrifices, blessings and unwavering
support remain my greatest inspiration.

Contents

Preface

The 20th century stands as a watershed moment in American history—a century characterized by global wars, social revolutions, rapid technological progress, and deep cultural transformations. Against this backdrop of upheaval and reinvention, American literature evolved from regional storytelling and realist traditions into a powerful medium for experimentation, resistance, and reinvention.

This book, 'Twentieth-Century American Literature: Texts, Contexts, Themes and Perspectives', is both a reflection and a celebration of that transformation. It is not simply a linear survey of literary movements or an annotated chronology of major authors. Rather, it is a thematic journey that explores how literature responded to the profound shifts in American society and, in doing so, shaped the national consciousness itself.

At the dawn of the century, American writers were confronting the spiritual and philosophical crises brought about by industrialization, urbanization, and the devastating trauma of the First World War. The result was modernism, a literary movement that broke with traditional narrative forms and gave voice to a fragmented, often disillusioned inner world. Authors such as T.S. Eliot, William Faulkner, and F. Scott Fitzgerald sought to express the psychological dislocation and loss of certainty that defined the early 20th century.

As the century progressed, new voices emerged from historically marginalized communities. The Harlem Renaissance signaled an unprecedented flourishing of African American cultural and literary expression. Writers like Langston Hughes and Zora Neale Hurston used fiction and poetry to assert a distinct Black identity, resist racial oppression, and forge new aesthetic forms rooted in music, oral tradition, and community experience.

Mid-century America brought with it the paradoxes of postwar prosperity and Cold War paranoia. Amid this tension, the Beat Generation rejected societal conformity, materialism, and war. Writers like Jack Kerouac and Allen Ginsberg infused their work with spiritual yearning, radical politics, and a defiant embrace of personal freedom. Their raw and energetic prose opened the door to broader cultural revolutions.

By the 1960s and 1970s, postmodernism had taken hold, embracing literary self-awareness, parody, and philosophical skepticism. Writers such as Kurt Vonnegut, Thomas Pynchon, and Don DeLillo challenged the very foundations of narrative truth, often employing fragmented structures and metafictional devices. These authors reflected a society saturated by media, haunted by nuclear dread, and unsure of its own reality.

Crucially, this era also saw an explosion of literature that centered race, gender, sexuality, and ethnicity—voices that had long been excluded from the American literary canon. African American writers like James Baldwin, Toni Morrison, and Alice Walker confronted the psychological toll of racism, explored ancestral memory, and reimagined history through a Black lens. Feminist and queer authors such as Audre Lorde, Sylvia Plath, and Tony Kushner foregrounded bodies, identities, and desires that challenged dominant social norms. Meanwhile, ethnic and immigrant writers brought a kaleidoscope of new perspectives—from the diasporic narratives of Maxine Hong Kingston and Sandra Cisneros to the complex legacies of Native American experience in the work of Sherman Alexie.

This book, then, is a literary map of cultural transformation. It traces how American writers responded to themes such as war, alienation, race, technology, gender, and the elusive promise of the American Dream. Each chapter centers on a major movement or voice, contextualizing it within the broader historical moment while also analyzing key texts that define its contours.

Through this approach, the book seeks to answer larger questions:

- How did American literature adapt to the disintegration of old certainties?
- In what ways did writers push the boundaries of form and genre?
- How did underrepresented voices rewrite the national story?
- And what is the legacy of 20th-century literature in our current moment?

The 20th century was a period of conflict and creativity, of rupture and renewal. Its literature offers not just a record of these changes but a means of understanding them—through metaphor, voice, image, and story. In tracing these voices, we discover the literary pulse of a nation both fractured and united by its search for meaning.

This book is written for students, scholars, and general readers who seek to understand not just the "what" of literature, but the "why" and the "how." It is my hope that readers will come away with a deeper appreciation of how 20th-century American literature gave shape to the voices, struggles, and aspirations of a changing nation.

Dr. Sohan Lal
Associate Professor, Department of English,
Satyawati College, University of Delhi, Delhi

Acknowledgements

The writing of 'Twentieth-Century American Literature: Texts, Contexts, Themes and Perspectives' has been an intellectually rewarding journey through the complex landscape of twentieth-century American writing. Engaging with the works of diverse authors and critics has reaffirmed my belief in literature's enduring capacity to illuminate the cultural, social, and political currents that shape human experience. I remain deeply indebted to the many writers and scholars whose works have informed and inspired the reflections presented in this book.

I extend my sincere gratitude to Prof. Subhash Kumar Singh, Principal of Satyawati College, University of Delhi, and to my colleagues and the non-teaching staff of the College for their continued encouragement and support. The vibrant academic environment of the University of Delhi has provided a fertile space for dialogue, inquiry, and reflection.

My thanks are due to my students whose curiosity and thoughtful engagement with literary texts continually renew my own interest in teaching and writing of this book. Their questions and interpretations have often prompted me to revisit familiar works from fresh perspectives.

I also wish to acknowledge the guidance and encouragement of Prof. Balaram Pani, Dean of Colleges, University of Delhi, and Prof. Yogesh Singh, Hon'ble Vice Chancellor, University of Delhi. I am equally grateful to the editors, librarians, and fellow scholars whose insights and assistance have contributed to the completion of this work.

Above all, I owe a profound debt to my family and loved ones for their patience, understanding, and unwavering support throughout this journey. Their encouragement has been a constant source of strength.

I offer my sincere thanks to all who have, in different ways, accompanied me in the completion of this book.

Thank You!

Introduction: The Literary Pulse of a Century

The 20th century stands as one of the most turbulent and transformative epochs in American history. It was a century marked by world wars, civil rights struggles, technological revolutions, economic upheavals, feminist and queer movements, and dramatic shifts in cultural norms. It was also a time when the United States emerged from a provincial literary identity to become a global center of artistic innovation and ideological contestation. American literature, ever sensitive to the rhythms of its time, evolved in profound ways to both reflect and interrogate the rapidly changing realities of the century.

In the early decades, the nation confronted the trauma of industrialization, urbanization, and the First World War. These forces shattered long-held ideals of progress and coherence, giving rise to modernist literature—a movement characterized by fragmentation, introspection, and experimentation. Writers like T.S. Eliot, Ezra Pound, Ernest Hemingway, and William Faulkner broke away from traditional narrative structures and poetic forms, adopting new techniques such as stream of consciousness, nonlinear time, and ambiguous symbolism. Their work signaled a crisis of identity and meaning in an increasingly alienating world.

Simultaneously, the Harlem Renaissance brought forth a cultural explosion that centered African American voices in literature, music, and visual arts. This vibrant movement not only challenged the racial hierarchies of American society but also redefined the literary canon by introducing themes of Black pride, cultural memory, resistance, and artistic freedom. Figures like Langston Hughes, Zora Neale Hurston, and Claude McKay used the written word to illuminate the richness and complexity of African American life, asserting that literature could be both politically charged and aesthetically daring.

By mid-century, the horrors of the Second World War, the existential angst of the atomic age, and the emergence of a hyper-consumerist society spurred a new wave of literary responses. The Beat Generation, led by iconoclasts like Jack Kerouac and Allen Ginsberg, rejected post-war conformity and sought transcendence through spontaneous expression,

Eastern spirituality, and a visceral embrace of experience. Their works, often controversial, challenged literary decorum and opened new spaces for personal, political, and sexual liberation.

As the century progressed, postmodernism emerged as both an extension and critique of modernism. Where modernism mourned the loss of coherence, postmodernism embraced fragmentation, pastiche, irony, and metafiction. Writers like Thomas Pynchon, Kurt Vonnegut, and Don DeLillo blurred the lines between high and low culture, questioned the nature of reality, and played with narrative conventions. In doing so, they revealed the constructedness of all meaning and highlighted the role of media, language, and technology in shaping human experience.

Yet, the story of 20th-century American literature is not solely about stylistic innovation. It is also about the emergence of new voices and the ongoing struggle for representation. The latter half of the century witnessed a flourishing of African American literature beyond the Harlem Renaissance, with authors like Richard Wright, Ralph Ellison, James Baldwin, and later, Toni Morrison and Alice Walker, chronicling the enduring legacies of slavery, segregation, and systemic racism. Their works brought psychological depth and historical consciousness to the portrayal of Black life in America, often centering on themes of double consciousness, cultural memory, and social justice.

Equally important were the contributions of feminist and queer writers, who expanded the literary landscape by foregrounding issues of gender, sexuality, and embodiment. The feminist wave of the 1960s and 1970s inspired groundbreaking work by authors such as Sylvia Plath, Adrienne Rich, Audre Lorde, and Gloria Anzaldúa, whose poetry and prose interrogated patriarchy, redefined womanhood, and reclaimed personal narrative as political testimony. Queer literature, often marginalized and censored, emerged more assertively in the public sphere through the work of writers like James Baldwin, Allen Ginsberg, and later, Tony Kushner and Dorothy Allison, carving space for diverse sexual identities and challenging heteronormative paradigms.

The final decades of the century also brought a surge in immigrant and ethnic American literatures—a mosaic of voices that articulated the complexities of diaspora, assimilation, intergenerational trauma, and hybridity. Writers of Asian American, Latinx, Native American, and Jewish American backgrounds infused the literary canon with stories shaped by displacement and longing, resistance and renewal. Works by Maxine Hong Kingston, Sandra Cisneros, Sherman Alexie, and Bernard Malamud, among others, revealed that the American experience could not be reduced to a single narrative—it was inherently plural, contested, and evolving.

This book, *Twentieth-Century American Literature: Texts, Contexts, Themes and Perspectives*, does not aim to present an exhaustive catalog of all the literary achievements of the 20th century. Instead, it endeavors to chart a thematic and historical journey—one that highlights how literature responded to and helped shape the cultural and political shifts of its time. It seeks to show how American writers grappled with core questions of identity, freedom, justice, belonging, and truth. From the battlefields of Europe to the streets of Harlem, from suburban ennui to cosmic absurdity, from whispered confessions to revolutionary manifestos—20th-century American literature bears witness to the nation's multifaceted journey.

In tracing these voices, this book argues that literature was not a passive mirror of social change but a powerful agent in shaping collective consciousness. Writers did not merely observe history—they intervened in it, challenged it, and reimagined it. The novels, poems, essays, and plays that emerged during this time reveal the emotional and intellectual contours of an America in motion, in conflict, in transformation.

By the century's end, American literature had become a global force, diverse in language and form, and capacious in its vision. It is this richness and complexity that this book hopes to honor, examine, and celebrate.

1

Introduction to 20th Century American Literature

Understanding the Foundations of a Transformative Century

The 20th Century: A Landscape of Change

The 20th century stands as one of the most dynamic and turbulent periods in American history, marked by sweeping transformations in politics, technology, society, and culture. These shifts did not occur in isolation—they fundamentally reshaped the ways Americans understood themselves and their nation. The rise of industrial capitalism, the devastation of two World Wars, the crippling effects of the Great Depression, the ideological tensions of the Cold War, and the digital revolution in the latter part of the century all contributed to a volatile yet creatively fertile landscape. Against this backdrop, literature served as both a mirror and a map—reflecting lived experiences while also charting new paths of understanding, resistance, and expression.

At the turn of the century, American literature remained deeply rooted in the conventions of the 19th century, dominated by realism and naturalism. Writers like Theodore Dreiser, Stephen Crane, and Edith Wharton portrayed the grim realities of industrial life, class struggle, and gender roles, emphasizing the deterministic forces shaping human fate. Yet, as the new century progressed, the certainty and structure of these modes began to fracture. The chaos and trauma of World War I catalyzed a crisis of faith in traditional narratives, giving rise to modernist experimentation. Authors like T.S. Eliot, F. Scott Fitzgerald, Gertrude Stein, and William Faulkner broke away from linear storytelling and objective narration, instead probing the subconscious, the fragmented self, and the instability of language.

The mid-century period saw further ruptures, with post-World War II writers grappling with existential disillusionment, identity politics, and the alienation of modern life. The postmodern era—characterized by irony, intertextuality, metafiction, and skepticism of grand narratives—challenged the very nature of authorship, reality, and representation. Writers like Thomas Pynchon, Kurt Vonnegut, and Don DeLillo questioned not only what stories were told, but how and why they were told.

Simultaneously, the literary canon began to expand in powerful and irreversible ways. Voices long silenced by race, gender, class, and sexuality emerged with force. African American writers such as Zora Neale Hurston, Richard Wright, James Baldwin, and Toni Morrison redefined American identity through the lens of Black experience. Women writers, including Sylvia Plath, Adrienne Rich, and Alice Walker, explored female agency, resistance, and subjectivity in the face of patriarchy. The rise of Chicano/a, Asian American, and Native American literatures further diversified the narrative landscape, insisting on the inclusion of multiple Americas within the American story.

Thus, the 20th century was not merely a backdrop to literary development—it was the very crucible in which new voices, forms, and visions were forged. Literature evolved in tandem with society's upheavals and aspirations, reflecting both the ruptures and the resilience of a nation in flux. As we journey through the key movements and authors of this century, it becomes clear that American literature was—and remains—a vital space for interrogating the promises and contradictions of the American experience.

Breaking with the Past: From Realism to Modernism

As the 20th century unfolded, American literature stood at a crossroads. The late 19th century had been dominated by realism, a literary approach grounded in the careful depiction of everyday life. Realist writers such as Mark Twain, Henry James, and William Dean Howells sought to capture the complexities of human behavior and social structures with precision and nuance. Their narratives emphasized ethical dilemmas, social environments, and character psychology, offering readers a mirror to contemporary American life in all its contradictions.

However, the turn of the century—and especially the catastrophic impact of World War I—shattered the sense of continuity and certainty that realism had relied upon. The mechanized brutality of the war, the collapse of traditional hierarchies, and the accelerating pace of urbanization and industrialization deeply unsettled society. For a new generation of writers, the old narrative forms no longer seemed adequate to express the dislocation, fragmentation, and existential anxiety of the modern condition.

Out of this cultural upheaval emerged Modernism—a revolutionary artistic and literary movement that rejected linear storytelling, fixed meanings, and objective truths. Modernist literature embraced formal experimentation and psychological depth, often favoring ambiguity, stream-of-consciousness narration, and disjointed chronology. Rather than offering clarity or resolution, modernist texts mirrored the fractured reality of postwar life.

Writers such as T.S. Eliot and Ezra Pound led the charge in poetry, stripping verse of its traditional meters and embracing allusion, fragmentation, and intertextuality. Eliot's *The Waste Land* (1922) became emblematic of the movement, presenting a disjointed collage of voices, languages, and cultural references that reflected the spiritual desolation of the modern world. Gertrude Stein pushed prose into the realm of abstraction with her cubist-inspired syntax and focus on repetition and rhythm. Meanwhile, novelists like William Faulkner experimented with multiple narrators and nonlinear timelines in works such as *The Sound and the Fury* (1929), exploring the deep psychological wounds and social tensions of the American South.

These American modernists were heavily influenced by European innovators such as James Joyce, Marcel Proust, and Virginia Woolf, but they also rooted their work in specifically American contexts—grappling with questions of race, region, identity, and memory. Their writing was not meant to comfort; it was meant to confront. Readers were asked to engage actively with texts, to reconstruct meaning from fragments, and to acknowledge the uncertainty at the heart of modern life.

Modernism represented a profound break with the past—not merely a change in style, but a new way of seeing the world. It marked a decisive turn away from external realities and toward the interior life, from narrative clarity to psychological complexity, from societal norms to individual alienation. In doing so, it helped redefine what literature could be: not a window onto the world, but a labyrinth of perception, experience, and interpretation.

Literature and Social Context

Literature is never created in a vacuum. It is in constant dialogue with the society in which it is produced—shaped by historical forces, cultural shifts, and political upheavals. Nowhere is this more evident than in 20th-century American literature, where some of the most significant literary movements and landmark works emerged directly in response to the nation's evolving socio-political realities. Throughout the century, writers both chronicled and critiqued the world around them, bearing witness to change while influencing how that change was understood and remembered.

One of the earliest and most profound examples of this dynamic was The Great Migration, which saw over six million African Americans move from the rural South to urban centers in the North and West between 1916 and 1970. This movement transformed American demographics, labor patterns, and cultural life—particularly in cities like New York, Chicago, and Detroit. The Harlem Renaissance, flourishing in the 1920s and 1930s, was born from this migration. Writers such as Langston Hughes, Zora Neale Hurston, and Claude McKay used poetry, fiction, and essays to explore Black identity, racial pride, and the legacy of slavery and segregation. Their work not only celebrated African American culture but also challenged the dominant literary and social norms of the time.

The economic collapse of the Great Depression in the 1930s inspired a surge of socially conscious literature. As millions of Americans faced poverty, unemployment, and displacement, writers turned their focus toward class struggle, economic injustice, and the resilience of ordinary people. John Steinbeck's *The Grapes of Wrath* (1939) offered a searing portrayal of Dust Bowl migrants and the failures of capitalism, while Richard Wright's *Native Son* (1940) revealed the psychological and structural effects of systemic racism on Black urban life. These works exemplified a broader trend toward realism infused with moral urgency, as writers sought to expose inequality and provoke reform.

In the wake of World War II, American literature became increasingly preoccupied with existential questions about morality, identity, and the role of technology in human destruction. The unprecedented devastation of the atomic bomb, the Holocaust, and the rise of totalitarian regimes forced writers to confront the fragility of civilization and the dark capacities of humanity. Authors such as Norman Mailer (*The Naked and the Dead*, 1948) and Kurt Vonnegut (*Slaughterhouse-Five*, 1969) explored war's absurdities and the psychological scars it left behind, combining satire, surrealism, and bleak irony to capture the disillusionment of the postwar era.

The Cold War further deepened themes of anxiety, surveillance, and ideological conflict in American literature. The climate of fear and suspicion created by McCarthyism and anti-Communist hysteria found expression in novels such as Ray Bradbury's *Fahrenheit 451* (1953) and Arthur Miller's *The Crucible* (1953), both of which used allegory to criticize censorship and political persecution. During this time, the concept of "truth" itself came under scrutiny, with writers questioning the reliability of information, the integrity of institutions, and the very nature of reality—a concern that would persist into postmodern literature.

Meanwhile, the second half of the 20th century witnessed the rise of major social justice movements that expanded the American literary canon and redefined its boundaries. The Civil Rights Movement, Second-Wave Feminism, and the LGBTQ+ rights movement brought new voices to the forefront—voices that had long been silenced or marginalized. Writers such as James Baldwin, Maya Angelou, Gloria Anzaldúa, Audre Lorde, and Tony Kushner wrote boldly about race, gender, sexuality, and intersectional identity, challenging dominant narratives and advocating for inclusion, recognition, and empowerment. Their work was not just literary—it was political, cultural, and deeply personal.

Throughout the 20th century, literature served as a lens through which the complexities of American life could be examined and reimagined. By engaging with social issues—whether racial injustice, economic disparity, war, surveillance, or identity politics—writers transformed the literary landscape, making it more inclusive, more critical, and more reflective of the diverse experiences that define the American story.

The Rise of Marginalized Voices

One of the most transformative developments in 20th-century American literature was the emergence and recognition of voices that had historically been excluded from the mainstream literary canon. While the early decades of the century were dominated by white, male, Eurocentric perspectives, the social and political revolutions of the mid- and late-century created space for new narratives—stories rooted in race, gender, class, ethnicity, and sexuality. These writers not only broadened the thematic scope of American literature but also fundamentally redefined its form, language, and purpose.

The Harlem Renaissance in the 1920s and 1930s marked the first major wave of this transformation. Fueled by the Great Migration and a newfound racial consciousness, African American writers like Langston Hughes, Zora Neale Hurston, and Jean Toomer rejected the assimilationist norms of earlier generations. They celebrated Black culture, language, and history on its own terms. Their literature challenged stereotypes and conveyed the richness of African American life—its rhythms, sorrows, joys, and political struggles. This movement laid the groundwork for later generations of Black writers who would continue to interrogate America's racial hierarchies.

By the 1950s and 1960s, amid the backdrop of the Civil Rights Movement, a new wave of African American literature emerged, marked by a powerful blend of political critique and literary innovation. Writers like James Baldwin, Lorraine Hansberry, and Amiri Baraka addressed the psychological and structural consequences of racism while demanding a reckoning with the nation's violent past. Later, authors like Toni Morrison and Alice Walker delved into themes of generational trauma, gendered oppression, and the importance of historical memory, often centering the lives and voices of Black women—long doubly marginalized in both society and literature.

In tandem, the Second-Wave Feminist Movement gave rise to a powerful body of women's literature that interrogated patriarchy, domesticity, and gender roles. Authors such as Sylvia Plath, Adrienne Rich, Betty Friedan, and later, Margaret Atwood and Toni Cade Bambara, explored the psychic and societal costs of women's subordination. They challenged the private/public divide and exposed how deeply political the personal could be. Feminist literature of this period laid bare the tensions between identity and expectation, repression and resistance.

The latter half of the century also saw the emergence of Latinx, Asian American, and Native American literatures, each bringing distinct cultural histories and linguistic innovations to American letters. Chicano/a writers like Rudolfo Anaya and Sandra Cisneros chronicled the hybrid experiences of living between two cultures, often blending English and Spanish to express bicultural identity. Asian American authors such as Maxine Hong Kingston and Amy Tan confronted the legacies of immigration, assimilation, and intergenerational trauma. Meanwhile, Native American writers like N. Scott Momaday, Leslie Marmon Silko, and Louise Erdrich revitalized oral storytelling traditions and addressed the deep wounds of colonization and cultural erasure.

Simultaneously, **LGBTQ+ writers** began to claim visibility in literature, challenging heteronormative assumptions and offering complex portrayals of queer identity. James Baldwin, who addressed both race and sexuality with remarkable candor, paved the way for others like Audre Lorde, Edmund White, and later, Tony Kushner and Alison Bechdel. Their works did more than depict LGBTQ+ lives—they demanded that such lives be recognized as integral to the American story.

The rise of marginalized voices did more than add diversity to American literature—it reshaped its very foundation. These writers questioned who gets to tell stories, what stories get told, and how literature reflects or resists structures of power. In doing so, they expanded the narrative imagination of the nation, making American literature more inclusive, more honest, and ultimately more human.

Postmodernism and the Questioning of Truth

By the latter half of the 20th century, American literature underwent another radical transformation as the optimism of earlier decades gave way to deep skepticism. The social, political, and philosophical upheavals of the 1960s and beyond—including the Vietnam War, the Watergate scandal, the rise of mass media, and the rapid proliferation of technology—undermined long-held certainties about truth, identity, and meaning. In response, a new literary movement emerged: Postmodernism.

Postmodern literature defied the conventions of realism and the grand narratives upheld by modernist writers. Where Modernism had responded to the fragmentation of the world with formal experimentation and a search for deeper truth, Postmodernism questioned whether any coherent truth could exist at all. The movement was characterized by irony, playfulness, self-referentiality, metafiction, pastiche, and an embrace of ambiguity. It blurred the boundaries between "high" and "low" art, between fiction and reality, and between author and reader.

Authors such as Thomas Pynchon, Don DeLillo, Kurt Vonnegut, Ishmael Reed, and John Barth exemplified postmodern sensibilities. Their works often featured nonlinear plots, unreliable narrators, intertextual references, and absurdist elements. In *Slaughterhouse-Five* (1969), Vonnegut collapsed time and space to explore the trauma of war and the futility of attempting to impose order on chaos. Pynchon's *Gravity's Rainbow* (1973) wove a labyrinthine narrative that fused science, paranoia, and pop culture into a complex meditation on power and control. DeLillo's *White Noise* (1985) satirized consumerism, media saturation, and the fear of death in a world governed by simulations and signs.

A hallmark of Postmodernism was its self-awareness—books that knew they were books, narrators that questioned their own authority, and plots that deliberately subverted reader expectations. This metafictional approach forced readers to engage with the act of storytelling itself, exposing how narratives are constructed, manipulated, and consumed. Writers like John Fowles (*The French Lieutenant's Woman*) and Paul Auster (*The New York Trilogy*) deconstructed the role of the author and the illusion of narrative coherence, challenging readers to rethink the relationship between language and reality.

Postmodernism also responded to the growing sense of cultural relativism and pluralism. In a society increasingly aware of its diversity and its histories of marginalization, Postmodern literature often reflected the idea that there was no single, unified American experience. It embraced multiple perspectives, fragmented identities, and competing truths. This ethos resonated with postcolonial, feminist, and minority writers who questioned dominant cultural narratives and resisted monolithic representations.

Critics of Postmodernism have sometimes accused it of being overly cynical, overly obscure, or politically disengaged. However, many postmodern writers used irony and fragmentation not to escape reality, but to expose its contradictions and challenge systems of meaning and authority. In a world saturated with media, spectacle, and conflicting ideologies, Postmodernism offered a way of understanding how truth could be constructed, manipulated, and contested.

By the end of the 20th century, Postmodernism had left an indelible mark on American literature. It taught readers to question appearances, distrust absolutes, and embrace complexity. While its techniques and concerns continue to evolve in the 21st century, the postmodern impulse—to interrogate truth and redefine narrative—remains a powerful force in contemporary writing.

The Digital Turn and New Media Literatures

As the 20th century drew to a close, a new wave of transformation began to take shape—one not rooted in war or ideology, but in technology. The rise of the internet, personal computers, and digital media revolutionized not only how literature was produced and consumed, but also how stories were conceived, shared, and understood. This period marked what many critics call "the digital turn," where the boundaries of literature expanded beyond the printed page into screens, hypertexts, and virtual spaces.

The digital age fundamentally altered the role of the author and reader. With the rise of blogs, forums, social media, and self-publishing platforms, traditional publishing hierarchies were disrupted. Writers who may have once struggled for recognition in print could now share their work widely and instantaneously. This democratization of literary production allowed for more diverse and global voices to emerge, continuing the expansion of the literary canon that began earlier in the century.

New forms of narrative began to take shape—ones that embraced interactivity, non-linearity, and multimedia elements. Hypertext fiction, pioneered by authors like Michael Joyce (*afternoon, a story*, 1987) and Shelley Jackson (*Patchwork Girl*, 1995), allowed readers to navigate digital stories through clickable links, creating unique narrative pathways with each reading. These works mirrored postmodern concerns with fragmentation and multiplicity, but they also pointed forward, to a future in which literature could be experienced rather than merely read.

Meanwhile, literary themes began to reflect the digital condition. Authors like Don DeLillo, Jennifer Egan, and Dave Eggers explored how the internet, surveillance, and data culture reshape identity, memory, and relationships. Egan's *A Visit from the Goon Squad* (2010) famously incorporated a PowerPoint chapter, blending form and content to reflect a world in flux. While not all of these writers were "digital authors" in the technical sense, their work responded to the anxieties and potentials of the digital era.

The blurring of genre and platform became more common as literature collided with visual art, gaming, film, and online culture. Web serials, digital poetry, fan fiction communities, and literary video games all emerged as spaces where narrative experimentation could flourish. Authors began collaborating with programmers and visual artists, while readers increasingly became participants—reshaping stories, contributing endings, or remixing texts in creative ways.

Despite concerns that digital media might "kill the novel" or undermine deep reading, the digital turn instead prompted literature to adapt and evolve. Just as the printing press once revolutionized access to the written word, the internet reshaped how literature could circulate and what it could look like. It also raised new questions: What counts as literature? Who is a reader? What role does attention play in the age of distraction?

The digital turn also encouraged a renewed focus on archiving, preservation, and ephemerality. Digital texts can be altered, deleted, or lost far more easily than printed works. This transience has prompted both innovative storytelling and a new awareness of the fragility of cultural memory in the information age.

As we transition into the 21st century, the legacy of the 20th century is visible not only in the themes and forms of literature, but in its adaptability and resilience. American literature, having passed through realism, modernism, postmodernism, and now the digital frontier, continues to respond to its cultural moment with creativity, critique, and complexity. The voices of the past century—diverse, experimental, and often disruptive—laid the foundation for a literary future that remains as restless and responsive as the society it seeks to understand.

Summary: The 20th Century—A Landscape of Change

The 20th century was a period of profound transformation in American literature, mirroring the broader social, political, and technological changes that shaped the nation. From the remnants of 19th-century realism to the innovative experiments of digital narratives, literature evolved in response to shifting understandings of truth, identity, power, and expression.

Section 1.1 introduced the century as a crucible of change, noting how major events such as two World Wars, the Great Depression, and the rise of civil rights movements reshaped not just society but also the literary imagination. Literature became a vital space for negotiating these upheavals, reflecting both fragmentation and resilience.

In Section 1.2, we explored the transition from Realism to Modernism. Early 20th-century authors rejected conventional storytelling in favor of fragmented structures, interior consciousness, and formal innovation. Writers like T.S. Eliot and William Faulkner broke with tradition to explore disillusionment and complexity in the wake of global crisis.

Section 1.3 highlighted the deep connection between literature and social context. From the Harlem Renaissance to Cold War paranoia, authors responded to historical moments with urgency and critique. Literature chronicled class struggles, war trauma, censorship, and movements for civil and human rights, offering both testimony and resistance.

Section 1.4 focused on the rise of marginalized voices. The inclusion of African American, feminist, Latinx, Native American, Asian American, and LGBTQ+ perspectives redefined the American literary canon. These writers reshaped the themes, forms, and scope of literature, challenging dominant narratives and expanding what counted as American experience.

In Section 1.5, the postmodern turn brought a radical questioning of truth, authorship, and narrative structure. Writers such as Pynchon and Vonnegut used irony, metafiction, and intertextuality to critique modern life, emphasize cultural relativism, and highlight the instability of meaning in a media-saturated world.

Finally, Section 1.6 examined the impact of the digital revolution on literature. With the rise of hypertext, multimedia storytelling, and online publication, literature entered new forms and formats. The digital turn reshaped the role of the reader, the nature of authorship, and the definition of what constitutes a literary text.

Together, these sections trace the evolution of 20th-century American literature as an ongoing dialogue between form and history, self and society, tradition and innovation. The chapter sets the foundation for deeper explorations of individual authors, movements, and themes in the chapters.

2

Modernism: The Early 20th Century

Shattering Tradition, Seeking Truth in Fragmentation

As the 20th century dawned, a profound disillusionment with traditional forms of authority—political, religious, artistic—swept across Europe and the United States. This mood found potent expression in a new literary movement: Modernism, a radical break from the past that sought not to comfort, but to confront. American modernist writers, shaped by the trauma of war, the dislocation of industrialization, and the disintegration of inherited values, rejected conventional storytelling in favor of experimentation, fragmentation, and introspection.

Modernism did not merely adjust older literary forms; it dismantled them. In place of coherent plots and omniscient narrators, modernist texts offered shifting perspectives, interior monologues, and non-linear time. The result was a literature that mirrored the fractured, unstable nature of modern life. Where 19th-century writers sought to reflect reality, modernists questioned whether reality itself could ever be truly known.

Inspired in part by European innovators such as James Joyce, Marcel Proust, and Virginia Woolf, American authors developed a distinctly national voice—one that grappled with uniquely American anxieties around identity, race, technology, and democracy. Writers like T.S. Eliot, Ezra Pound, Gertrude Stein, and William Faulkner became key figures in this transformation. Through their work, they upended conventional language, structure, and meaning, demanding that readers become active participants in the act of interpretation.

Modernism also marked a shift in thematic focus: from external realities to internal consciousness. The stream-of-consciousness technique allowed for a deeper exploration of memory, perception, and psychological conflict. Time was no longer chronological but subjective. Events were not always presented clearly, but layered and elusive—echoing the fragmented perception of modern existence.

This chapter delves into the origins, major characteristics, and cultural context of American Modernism. It examines the contributions of major authors, the literary techniques they pioneered, and the broader intellectual currents—such as existentialism, psychoanalysis, and symbolism—that informed their work. As we explore key texts, we will see how Modernist literature reframed the purpose of storytelling, not as a means of resolution, but as a way of exploring ambiguity, doubt, and the multiplicity of human experience.

The Roots of Modernism: Disillusionment and Discovery

The seeds of American Modernism were sown in a period of rapid transformation and growing uncertainty. At the heart of the movement lay a deep sense of disillusionment with the established world order—an order that had promised progress, stability, and meaning, but instead delivered war, alienation, and cultural fragmentation. Modernism arose not from a desire to reform the past, but to reject and reimagine it entirely.

The Industrial Revolution, which had gained momentum in the late 19th century, transformed American society with unprecedented speed. Cities expanded, machines replaced manual labor, and the pace of life accelerated. While this ushered in economic growth and technological advancement, it also led to a sense of anonymity, dehumanization, and estrangement. Traditional rural life and communal values were replaced by the impersonal forces of capitalism and urban sprawl. For many writers, these changes rendered old literary forms—centered on linear plots, fixed morality, and objective narration—hopelessly outdated.

The First World War (1914–1918) was the defining catalyst for the Modernist break. With over 16 million dead and the psychological scars of trench warfare, chemical weapons, and mechanized killing, the war shattered the Enlightenment ideal of rational progress. The sheer brutality and senselessness of the conflict made many question not only politics and religion, but language and art itself. How could literature continue to speak in the measured tones of 19th-century realism in a world where meaning itself seemed to have collapsed?

This cultural crisis prompted a search for new modes of expression. Writers turned inward, toward subjective perception and interior life. Theories of Sigmund Freud and Carl Jung—with their focus on the unconscious mind, dreams, and repressed desires—influenced the narrative techniques of modernist literature. Stream-of-consciousness writing, nonlinear timelines, and unreliable narrators all emerged from this focus on inner psychological reality.

Simultaneously, the early 20th century saw an intellectual and artistic migration from America to Europe, particularly to cities like Paris and London. Disillusioned with American materialism and conservatism, writers such as Gertrude Stein, Ezra Pound, Ernest Hemingway, and T.S. Eliot became part of a transatlantic modernist network. Stein's Paris salon brought together artists and writers experimenting with Cubism, abstraction, and literary minimalism. Pound's rallying cry to "Make it new" captured the modernist ethos: the past was a burden, and art needed to be remade for the modern age.

Back in the United States, racial tensions, gender inequality, and immigrant marginalization further destabilized cultural certainties. These realities prompted some modernists—particularly later in the movement—to begin questioning who got to define "truth" and whose stories were being told. While early Modernism was often centered on white, male, upper-class voices, it also opened doors for alternative perspectives to emerge in later decades.

In sum, Modernism's roots lie in a world deeply shaken by historical rupture and existential doubt. But this disillusionment also led to discovery—a search for new aesthetics, new truths, and new ways of knowing. Modernist literature does not attempt to repair the broken world; instead, it seeks to portray that brokenness honestly, and in doing so, to find beauty and meaning amid chaos.

Key Characteristics of Modernist Literature

Innovating the Art of the Possible: Language, Form, and Modern Consciousness

Modernist literature represents one of the most radical shifts in literary history, marking a profound departure from the conventions and confidence of 19th-century realism. Emerging from the rubble of world wars, industrialization, and shifting social mores, Modernist writers rejected linear narratives, stable identities, and objective truths. Instead, they sought to mirror the complexities, dislocations, and ambiguities of a rapidly changing world.

What defined this new literature was not merely its subjects—alienation, chaos, subjectivity—but its formal daring. Writers reshaped how language functioned, how stories could be told, and what literature could represent. Below are the key hallmarks that distinguish Modernist literature and continue to influence storytelling today.

Fragmentation: Form as Fracture

Fragmentation is perhaps the most defining trait of Modernist writing. Rather than presenting a smooth, continuous narrative, Modernist texts fracture plot, chronology, and character perspective, reflecting a world no longer governed by coherence or certainty.

- T.S. Eliot's *The Waste Land* (1922) is structured like a mosaic—jumping across centuries, cultures, and speakers to portray a disjointed civilization.
- Jean Toomer's *Cane* (1923) blends poetry, drama, and prose in fragmented vignettes of Black life in America, resisting any singular narrative arc.
- Virginia Woolf's *The Waves* (1931) breaks narrative into soliloquies from six characters, eliminating plot entirely in favor of poetic rhythm and interiority.

In Modernist hands, fragmentation becomes both technique and theme—emphasizing the psychological, cultural, and moral breakdowns of the modern condition.

Stream of Consciousness and Interior Monologue: The Mind Unfiltered

To explore the subjective depths of human experience, Modernist writers turned inward. Stream of consciousness and interior monologue allowed them to capture thought as it happens, unmediated by conventional structure or logic.

- James Joyce's *Ulysses* (1922) follows Leopold Bloom's meandering thoughts in real time, often without punctuation or explanation.
- William Faulkner's *The Sound and the Fury* (1929) begins with a non-verbal, cognitively impaired narrator, forcing the reader into raw perception and confusion.
- Virginia Woolf's *Mrs. Dalloway* (1925) drifts seamlessly between characters' inner thoughts, memories, and sensory impressions over a single day.

These techniques blur the line between thought and world, emphasizing how reality is filtered through individual consciousness—often in nonlinear, associative ways.

Alienation and Isolation: The Modern Condition

Modernist protagonists are often lonely, disoriented, and spiritually adrift. They live in societies that no longer offer moral clarity, religious assurance, or communal belonging.

- In Franz Kafka's *The Metamorphosis* (1915), Gregor Samsa wakes up as a bug, his humanity ignored even by his own family—an allegory of existential estrangement.
- Eliot's J. Alfred Prufrock asks, "Do I dare disturb the universe?"—but never finds the courage or the clarity to act. He is emblematic of the hesitant, self-conscious modern man.

- In Jean Rhys's *Good Morning, Midnight* (1939), the protagonist wanders Paris in a haze of grief and regret, disconnected from her own past and surroundings.

Rather than offer clear resolutions, Modernist literature dwells in the inner turmoil of characters for whom alienation is both a symptom and a stance against a bewildering world.

Experimentation with Form and Language: Breaking the Mold

Modernist authors distrusted traditional narrative conventions and believed language could no longer reliably represent reality. As a result, they embraced radical experimentation.

- Gertrude Stein's prose in *Tender Buttons* (1914) is intentionally disorienting, collapsing syntax and logic to focus on the sound and rhythm of language.
- E.E. Cummings's poetry breaks all grammatical rules, using spacing, typography, and capitalization as expressive tools.
- Joyce's *Finnegans Wake* (1939) invents words, combines languages, and erases the line between dreaming and waking in a literary experiment like no other.

These innovations weren't just aesthetic flourishes—they were acts of resistance, asserting that new times demanded new forms of expression.

Allusions and Intertextuality: The Weight of the Past

Modernist texts are densely allusive, drawing from classical mythology, religious scripture, philosophy, and literary history. These references often serve two purposes:

1. To connect the present to a grand cultural tradition, suggesting that despite the chaos, meaning might still be excavated.
2. To ironically highlight the distance between past grandeur and modern decay, emphasizing the failure of inherited wisdom.
    - In *The Waste Land*, Eliot invokes Dante, the Bible, Buddha, and Shakespeare—only to show that their harmonies can no longer unify modern life.
    - Ezra Pound's *The Cantos* mix Homer, Confucius, and Renaissance finance in a deliberately overwhelming and fragmented epic.
    - Faulkner's *Absalom, Absalom!* alludes to the Biblical story of King David's rebellious son, reframing the American South's legacy of pride and downfall.

This layering of intertexts challenges readers to read historically, critically, and creatively—never passively.

Ambiguity and Open-Endedness: Literature as Puzzle

Unlike Victorian novels, which often concluded with moral resolution or character transformation, Modernist works tend to end without closure or clarity.

- Kafka's *The Trial* ends in death and mystery, offering no resolution to its critique of bureaucracy and guilt.
- Woolf's *To the Lighthouse* spans decades, but its central events—death, war, reconciliation—are depicted elliptically, off-stage, or symbolically.
- Hemingway's minimalist stories, like "Hills Like White Elephants," leave crucial events implied rather than stated.

This deliberate ambiguity forces readers to become co-creators of meaning, mirroring the fragmented understanding of modern life itself.

Rejection of Traditional Morality and Narrative Authority

Modernist literature is skeptical of social norms, religious doctrines, and narrative omniscience. Morality is not fixed but subjective; truth is not absolute but constructed.

- Unreliable narrators like Nick Carraway in *The Great Gatsby* (1925) challenge the reader to question what they're being told.
- In *A Portrait of the Artist as a Young Man*, Joyce's Stephen Dedalus rejects Catholicism, nationalism, and family to become an "artist" detached from convention.
- D.H. Lawrence's characters challenge Victorian sexual and emotional repression, pushing toward a more visceral, embodied form of truth.

This shift reflects a broader crisis of belief—in institutions, in reason, and in the coherence of the self.

Urban Settings and the Modern City: The New Landscape

For Modernist writers, the city was both muse and metaphor—a site of alienation, fragmentation, and hyper-stimulation.

- In *The Waste Land*, Eliot's "Unreal City" represents spiritual decay beneath modern glamour.
- John Dos Passos's *Manhattan Transfer* captures New York as a place of intersecting lives and meaningless motion.
- James Joyce's *Dubliners* presents a city stuck in paralysis, where every life feels both ordinary and doomed.

The modern city is not just a backdrop—it becomes a symbolic character, embodying the contradictions of modern life: connection and isolation, opportunity and emptiness, speed and stasis.

Conclusion: A New Aesthetic for a New Age

Modernist literature redefined the function and form of literary art in the 20th century. It responded to a world in crisis—not with answers, but with new ways of asking questions. Through fragmentation, experimentation, ambiguity, and psychological intensity, Modernism reflected the fractured self and the fractured world in which that self had to survive.

Though difficult, even opaque, these works challenge us to read more deeply, to confront discomfort, and to accept that meaning may be uncertain, partial, and evolving. Their influence echoes in every literary innovation that followed—from Postmodernism to contemporary fiction—and their legacy lies in a simple, radical proposition:

To make literature reflect the fractured truths of human experience—not what life ought to be, but what it is.

In sum, Modernist literature is a bold and restless genre, rooted in the trauma and transformation of the early 20th century. Its formal innovations and thematic depth continue to influence contemporary writing. Modernist texts do not aim to comfort or entertain in conventional ways—they challenge, provoke, and demand engagement. They are literature for an uncertain world.

Major Figures of American Modernism

Rewriting the Literary Imagination in a Time of Upheaval

The Modernist movement in American literature was powered by a diverse and dynamic constellation of writers—each one reacting to the cultural dislocation and philosophical crises of the 20th century with their own bold experiments in form, voice, and meaning. Though their backgrounds, ideologies, and styles varied widely, they shared a common mission: to redefine literature for a world that no longer made sense in traditional terms.

These figures were not bound by a manifesto, but by a restless energy to break with the past. Their contributions helped shape not only American letters but also the global literary imagination for decades to come.

T.S. Eliot (1888–1965): The Architect of Literary Disillusionment

Often considered the intellectual cornerstone of Anglo-American Modernism, T.S. Eliot crafted poetry that blended rigorous classical learning with contemporary cultural despair. His seminal work, The Waste Land (1922), epitomizes the fragmented, allusive, and spiritually barren world of post–World War I Europe.

In poems like *The Love Song of J. Alfred Prufrock* and *The Hollow Men*, Eliot presented alienated individuals trapped in stasis and spiritual exhaustion. He was also a major theorist: his essay *Tradition and the Individual Talent* (1919) argued that literary innovation must be grounded in a deep historical consciousness. This notion of impersonal artistry, where the poet becomes a medium for cultural memory, became central to Modernist aesthetics.

Eliot's religious conversion later influenced works like *Four Quartets*, which sought spiritual order within cultural chaos—a journey emblematic of the Modernist search for meaning amid disintegration.

Ezra Pound (1885–1972): The Provocateur of Precision

The charismatic and controversial Ezra Pound was a driving force behind the early Modernist movement. His motto—"Make it new"—served as a clarion call for literary innovation. Through his leadership of the Imagist movement, Pound emphasized economy of language, vivid imagery, and musicality.

He championed fellow writers like Eliot, H.D., and Hemingway, often editing and reshaping their works with visionary intensity. Pound's epic project, *The Cantos*, remains a towering but difficult achievement: a sprawling mosaic of historical, mythological, and economic references that reflects both the promise and incoherence of modern life.

Although his political views—especially his support for fascism during World War II—tainted his legacy, his stylistic influence remains foundational in the development of 20th-century poetry.

Gertrude Stein (1874–1946): The Matriarch of Experimentalism

Few writers challenged linguistic norms more radically than Gertrude Stein. Operating outside the mainstream literary establishment, Stein made language itself the subject of her writing. In *Tender Buttons* (1914), she dismantled conventional syntax, punctuation, and narrative in favor of associative soundplay, repetition, and abstraction.

Living in Paris, Stein's salon became a hub for avant-garde artists and writers, including Picasso, Hemingway, and F. Scott Fitzgerald. Her emphasis on "the continuous present" and her belief in the fluidity of meaning laid the groundwork for later experimental, feminist, and queer literatures.

Stein's refusal to conform made her a polarizing figure—but also a pioneer who expanded the boundaries of what literature could be.

William Faulkner (1897–1962): The Southern Mythmaker

A Nobel laureate and one of America's most technically daring novelists, William Faulkner brought Modernism into the American South with an unmatched combination of psychological depth and narrative complexity.

His novels—especially *The Sound and the Fury* (1929), *As I Lay Dying* (1930), and *Absalom, Absalom!* (1936)—are marked by multiple narrators, non-linear timelines, and stream-of-consciousness narration. Faulkner explored themes of racial tension, decay, memory, and historical guilt, situating them within the fictional Yoknapatawpha County—a richly imagined world that served as a microcosm of the South's troubled legacy.

Faulkner's work often resists immediate comprehension, but his dense, lyrical prose and moral intensity have made him one of the most enduring voices of American Modernism.

F. Scott Fitzgerald (1896–1940): The Poet of Illusion and Loss

Though less experimental in form than some of his contemporaries, F. Scott Fitzgerald captured the ethos of Modernism with emotional depth and lyrical precision. His most famous novel, *The Great Gatsby* (1925), critiques the American Dream through the lens of wealth, identity, and romantic disillusionment.

While Gatsby's glittering world seduces, Fitzgerald's narrative voice—particularly through the morally ambivalent Nick Carraway—reveals the emptiness beneath the surface. Fitzgerald's exploration of postwar disillusionment and moral decay makes him a central figure in literary Modernism, even if his style was more accessible than avant-garde.

Works like *Tender Is the Night* (1934) further delve into themes of psychological collapse and personal failure, reflecting the fragility of identity in an era of instability.

Ernest Hemingway (1899–1961): The Master of Minimalism

Ernest Hemingway revolutionized prose style with his short, declarative sentences and iceberg theory of meaning, which held that the most important elements of a story lie beneath the surface.

A veteran of World War I, Hemingway brought themes of trauma, masculinity, dislocation, and stoicism to the forefront of Modernist literature. Novels like *The Sun Also Rises* (1926) and *A Farewell to Arms* (1929) reflect the emotional numbness of the "Lost Generation", while *In Our Time* (1925) showcases his spare yet resonant short fiction.

Though his style contrasts sharply with the density of Faulkner or the abstraction of Stein, Hemingway's moral gravity and formal restraint reflect the core tensions of Modernism—expressing emotional truths through stripped-down language.

Jean Toomer (1894–1967): The Lyric Voice of Hybrid Identity

Jean Toomer was a pioneering figure who blended Modernist technique with African American spiritual, cultural, and historical themes. His landmark work, *Cane* (1923), is a hybrid text combining poetry, prose, drama, and song. It paints a poignant, elliptical portrait of Black life in both the rural South and the industrial North.

Toomer rejected binary racial categorizations and instead explored mixed identity, dislocation, and spiritual yearning. His Modernist sensibility is evident in his use of fragmentation, lyrical ambiguity, and shifting perspective—placing *Cane* at the intersection of Modernism and the Harlem Renaissance.

Though his literary output was limited, Toomer's influence on later Black and experimental writers remains profound.

Djuna Barnes (1892–1982): The Poet of Obsession and Exile

Djuna Barnes is a singular figure in Modernist literature—her work is dense, emotionally turbulent, and stylistically bold. Her novel *Nightwood* (1936), praised and edited by T.S. Eliot, is a masterpiece of queer Modernism and a haunting meditation on love, religion, gender, and exile.

Set in a dreamlike, decadent Europe, *Nightwood* abandons linear plot for rich, surreal imagery and psychological intensity. Barnes's prose is poetic and symbolic, reflecting the inner fractures of her characters as they navigate identity, desire, and madness.

Long marginalized, Barnes has since been reclaimed as a major figure in both LGBTQ+ literature and the broader Modernist canon.

Conclusion: A Constellation of Innovation

These writers—from Eliot's despairing fragments to Faulkner's Southern mythologies, from Stein's radical syntax to Hemingway's bare prose—each carved out a unique space within Modernism. Collectively, they transformed literature from a mirror of society into a prism of human consciousness—fractured, unstable, but powerfully expressive.

While they shared a modernist impulse to break with tradition, their legacies are as distinct as they are interconnected. Each helped to remap the literary landscape, challenging readers to reimagine narrative, question identity, and embrace the unresolved questions of modern life.

Their influence endures, not as a single school, but as an open field of innovation—inviting every generation to ask anew: *What can literature be?*

Close Reading: T.S. Eliot's *The Waste Land*

Published in 1922, T.S. Eliot's *The Waste Land* stands as one of the most complex and defining texts of literary Modernism. Composed in the immediate aftermath of World War I, the poem reflects a world marked by disillusionment, spiritual aridity, and cultural decay. Eliot's work resists narrative clarity and emotional consolation, instead offering a fragmented tapestry of voices, references, and broken images. It is a poem of crisis—cultural, spiritual, psychological—and one that calls for the reader's active participation in navigating meaning amid chaos.

Structure and Fragmentation: A Mosaic of Ruins

The poem is famously divided into five sections, each contributing to a larger atmosphere of collapse and fragmentation:

1. **The Burial of the Dead** – Introduces the contrast between past fertility myths and the present sterility of modern life.
2. **A Game of Chess** – A scene of domestic disconnection, filled with anxiety, decay, and a failure of communication.
3. **The Fire Sermon** – Describes the degradation of sensuality and the spiritual emptiness of modern desire.
4. **Death by Water** – A brief, lyrical passage confronting mortality and the futility of material pursuits.
5. **What the Thunder Said** – A climactic blending of prophetic vision, apocalyptic imagery, and a cryptic spiritual epilogue.

Each section moves erratically across time, space, and speaker. There is no central plot or protagonist. Instead, Eliot constructs a literary landscape of ruin: fragments of culture, tradition, and voice that mirror a shattered civilization.

This dislocation is not accidental but essential. Eliot uses fragmentation as both a thematic expression of postwar cultural collapse and a formal technique. The reader is not comforted or guided; they are placed amid the wreckage and asked to assemble meaning from the fragments:

"These fragments I have shored against my ruins" (V)

This famous line encapsulates the essence of Modernist poetics: the salvage operation of meaning in a broken world, with no guarantee of coherence or redemption.

Allusion and Intertextuality: A Poetic Palimpsest

Few works in the English language are as saturated with intertextual reference as *The Waste Land*. Eliot draws upon a vast and eclectic range of sources—classical literature, religious scripture, myth, popular culture, opera, and modern conversation—layering his poem with echoes of lost civilizations and fading truths.

Examples of Intertextuality

- **Opening Lines ("April is the cruellest month…")** – A stark reversal of Chaucer's *Canterbury Tales*, where spring symbolizes renewal. Here, spring brings unwanted awakening in a spiritually dead landscape.
- **The Fisher King Myth** – A wounded king whose infertility blights the land, symbolizing the modern world's spiritual desolation. Eliot uses this archetype to suggest that the cultural body, like the mythical kingdom, can be healed only through a difficult journey of understanding.
- **Madame Sosostris** – A comic parody of clairvoyants and spiritualists, reflecting society's desperate search for guidance in an age of disbelief.
- **Dante, Shakespeare, and Ovid** – Voices from the Western canon recur throughout the poem, both anchoring the poem in tradition and underscoring its alienation from that very tradition.
- **Buddhist and Hindu Texts** – Especially the *Brihadaranyaka Upanishad*, which ends the poem with a cryptic message of potential renewal through giving (Datta), compassion (Dayadhvam), and self-restraint (Damyata).

These allusions do more than ornament the poem—they construct a modern literary consciousness haunted by its cultural inheritance. The past is present, but in fragments, and the act of remembering becomes a way of confronting contemporary emptiness.

Voice and Perspective: A Chorus of Disconnection

The Waste Land is polyphonic: it does not speak with a single voice, but rather a cacophony of perspectives. Eliot dissolves the traditional narrative persona, replacing it with shifting, often contradictory speakers:

- A traumatized war veteran.
- A jaded upper-class woman drowning in luxury and boredom (*A Game of Chess*).
- A typist and a clerk locked in a banal, mechanistic sexual encounter (*The Fire Sermon*).
- Eastern sages, biblical prophets, mythical figures, and anonymous urban wanderers.

This multitude of voices reflects the disintegration of identity in the modern world. The self is not a unified subject but a collage of roles, memories, and impressions. The effect is both alienating and deeply resonant, forcing the reader to navigate a modern world where coherence is elusive and subjectivity is fragmented.

Themes: Despair, Cultural Decay, and the Search for Redemption

At its core, *The Waste Land* is a meditation on spiritual barrenness and existential despair. Postwar Europe, Eliot suggests, is not just physically ruined but morally and metaphysically exhausted. Themes of sterility, disconnection, and cultural loss recur throughout:

- **Sterility and Infertility** – Symbolized in the barren land, the loveless relationships, and the dismembered myths. The poem laments the loss of fertile meaning—sexual, spiritual, and cultural.
- **Alienation and Communication Breakdown** – Characters speak past each other, unable to connect. Language itself seems insufficient to express genuine emotion or truth.
- **The Collapse of Tradition** – Myths, religions, and literary references appear not as unifying forces but as broken relics of a once-coherent worldview.

Yet, amid this despair, *The Waste Land* also gestures toward renewal—tentative, ambiguous, but present. The Upanishadic ending and the closing "Shantih shantih shantih" hint at a peace beyond understanding, suggesting that while meaning may be broken, the act of seeking it remains profoundly human.

Modernist Innovation and Literary Influence

T.S. Eliot's The Waste Land exemplifies the aesthetic and intellectual daring of Modernism. It broke decisively from traditional poetic form and redefined what poetry could be and do:

- **Formal innovation** – Free verse, disrupted meter, and erratic shifts in tone.
- **Cultural polyphony** – A layering of diverse cultural, historical, and mythological registers.
- **Psychological depth** – Interior monologue, symbolic imagery, and emotional dislocation.
- **Self-conscious artistry** – The poem is about poetry itself, its limitations and possibilities in a fragmented world.

Its publication marked a watershed moment. Critics were divided—some saw it as the death knell of meaningful art, others as the dawn of a new artistic epoch. Over time, however, it became clear that *The Waste Land* had transformed the landscape of 20th-century literature. It inspired generations of poets and novelists to experiment with form, embrace ambiguity, and write from within the fractures of modern life.

Conclusion: A Mirror to Modern Consciousness

The Waste Land does not offer answers—it embodies the modern condition of spiritual yearning in a world stripped of certainties. In its dense allusiveness, fragmented voices, and haunting beauty, it calls the reader to confront a reality where coherence must be actively constructed, not passively received.

The poem remains a literary landmark because it does not flinch from cultural despair, yet it refuses to surrender to nihilism. In confronting the wasteland, Eliot affirms the necessity of art—not as salvation, but as witness, testimony, and gesture toward meaning in a broken world.

William Faulkner and the American South

While T.S. Eliot's *The Waste Land* explored spiritual desolation in a disintegrating Europe, William Faulkner brought the disintegration home—to the American South. Where Eliot turned to myth and fragmentation to express modernity's collapse, Faulkner immersed readers in the haunted legacies of race, memory, decay, and identity that defined the Southern United States. In doing so, he became one of Modernism's boldest innovators—both in form and theme.

Reinventing the Southern Gothic

Faulkner's fiction is deeply rooted in the landscape and history of the post-Civil War South, particularly in the fictional Yoknapatawpha County—a stand-in for Lafayette County, Mississippi, where he spent most of his life. But rather than sentimentalize the South or romanticize its past, Faulkner revealed its moral rot, racial violence, and psychological decay. His work is steeped in Southern Gothic tradition, marked by decaying mansions, grotesque characters, and repressed family secrets.

Yet Faulkner's version of Southern Gothic is filtered through modernist innovation. He collapses chronology, blurs narrative voices, and plunges into the interiority of characters wracked by trauma and guilt. His South is not just a physical setting but a psychological landscape, one that mirrors the fractured consciousness of the modern individual.

Narrative Experimentation

Faulkner's stylistic boldness places him at the forefront of American Modernism. His novels are known for:

- Stream of consciousness narration
- Multiple narrators offering conflicting perspectives
- Nonlinear timelines

- Long, syntactically complex sentences
- Ambiguity and unreliability

These techniques immerse readers in the confusion, fragmentation, and moral ambiguity that define his characters' inner lives. Like Eliot, Faulkner demands that the reader assemble meaning from chaos—there are no easy answers, no clear moral judgments.

Key Work: The Sound and the Fury *(1929)*

Faulkner's masterpiece, *The Sound and the Fury*, exemplifies his formal daring and thematic depth. The novel is divided into four sections, each told from a different point of view. The first is narrated by Benjy, a cognitively disabled man whose stream-of-consciousness narrative shifts fluidly across time with no warning. The second is by Quentin, whose tortured interior monologue captures a mind unraveling. The third section presents Jason's, a cynical, racist, and bitter voice. Finally, the fourth offers a limited omniscient perspective.

The novel tells the story of the Compson family, once-proud Southern aristocrats now mired in decay, dishonor, and disintegration. Themes of time, memory, incest, race, gender, and identity intertwine in a haunting meditation on loss and legacy. The title, drawn from Macbeth—*"a tale told by an idiot, full of sound and fury, signifying nothing"*—underscores Faulkner's view of life as chaotic, tragic, and often meaningless, unless meaning is actively created by the reader.

Race and Southern History

Faulkner's work grapples unflinchingly with the legacy of slavery and racial injustice. In novels like *Absalom, Absalom!* (1936), he delves into the destructive consequences of white supremacy and miscegenation in the antebellum and postbellum South. The stories of enslaved people and their descendants are often mediated through white narrators, adding further layers of distortion and silencing. This narrative choice reflects Faulkner's awareness of the unspoken and unresolved traumas embedded in Southern memory.

Yet Faulkner's racial politics remain a point of debate. While he was one of the first white Southern writers to seriously confront the sins of slavery, he sometimes reproduced the very hierarchies he sought to expose. His African American characters are often symbolic or peripheral, and his position during the Civil Rights Movement was cautious and inconsistent. Nevertheless, his influence on later writers—particularly Toni Morrison, Jesmyn Ward, and Edward P. Jones—is profound.

Faulkner's Legacy

Faulkner was awarded the Nobel Prize in Literature in 1949, with the Swedish Academy praising his "powerful and artistically unique contribution to the modern American novel." His influence extends far beyond the South or even the United States. Writers as diverse as Gabriel García Márquez, Albert Camus, and Toni Morrison have cited him as a major inspiration.

What distinguishes Faulkner in the modernist pantheon is his ability to merge regional specificity with universal themes—to make the fallen South a mirror for the moral and spiritual struggles of the modern world. His novels are difficult, demanding, and deeply rewarding, offering a literary experience that is at once harrowing and beautiful.

Gender, Identity, and Experimental Form: The Role of Women in Modernist Literature

While the early narrative of Modernism was often dominated by male voices—Eliot, Faulkner, Hemingway, and Pound—women writers were no less central to the movement's innovations and insights. In fact, many of the most radical experiments in language, form, and identity came from women who used Modernist techniques to challenge not only aesthetic norms, but also social and gender hierarchies. Their work expanded the reach of Modernism, linking its formal innovations to deeper questions of subjectivity, marginality, and resistance.

Challenging Patriarchal Structures Through Form

Women modernists frequently rejected traditional narrative forms—not merely as a stylistic choice, but as an act of cultural subversion. Conventional literary structures often mirrored the patriarchal ideologies of control, authority, and linearity. By embracing fragmentation, non-linearity, and disjointed voice, women writers questioned the assumptions embedded in both literature and society.

Gertrude Stein is a primary example. Her prose works, such as *Tender Buttons* (1914), dismantle grammar, sentence structure, and sense-making itself. In doing so, Stein resists the idea that language must "mean" in the ways male-dominated literary traditions had prescribed. Her style is repetitive, associative, and rhythmically experimental—designed not to convey a message, but to evoke presence and perception.

The Interior Lives of Women: Subjectivity and Selfhood

Where male modernists often portrayed fragmented male psyches in crisis, female modernists turned inward to explore the richness, constraints, and contradictions of women's interior lives. In doing so, they broke from the stereotype of the passive female character and created active, thinking, desiring subjects.

Djuna Barnes, for example, crafted one of the most psychologically and formally complex novels of the era with *Nightwood* (1936). The novel's poetic, hallucinatory prose explores lesbian desire, spiritual despair, and gender fluidity in a modernist Paris marked by exile and alienation. Barnes's language is richly symbolic and densely lyrical—at once beautiful and bewildering, much like the world her characters inhabit.

Another powerful voice is Zora Neale Hurston, whose *Their Eyes Were Watching God* (1937) blends modernist form with African American vernacular. Though often associated with the Harlem Renaissance, Hurston's work bridges cultural and aesthetic traditions. Her protagonist, Janie Crawford, seeks personal freedom and voice within a world shaped by both racial and gender oppression. The novel's nonlinear structure and inner monologue reflect modernist concerns with memory and self-invention, while rooting those concerns in the Black Southern experience.

Intersectionality in Early Modernist Writing

Many women writers of color used modernist tools to explore the intersection of race, gender, and class, creating a space for voices long marginalized in American literature. In Nella Larsen's *Passing* (1929), for instance, modernist ambiguity and psychological subtlety are harnessed to examine the complexities of racial identity and female friendship. The novel's restrained prose and ironic tone reflect both the limitations and dangers faced by women negotiating dual identities in a racist, patriarchal society.

Larsen's work illustrates how modernist experimentation was not an end in itself, but a way to explore subjective instability and the pressures of societal expectation. Her protagonist's identity is fragmented not just psychologically, but socially and historically—underscoring how deeply personal and political questions are intertwined.

The Emergence of Queer and Feminist Aesthetics

Modernist women writers also played a crucial role in shaping early expressions of queer desire and proto-feminist consciousness. In texts like *Nightwood* or Virginia Woolf's *Orlando* (though British, Woolf's influence on American modernists was immense), gender and sexuality are no longer stable categories but fluid, performative, and constructed. These works anticipate later theories of gender and queer identity, showing that

Modernism was not merely an artistic revolution but also a reimagining of human identity itself.

Woolf's essays—particularly *A Room of One's Own* (1929)—advocated for the material and intellectual freedom necessary for women to write. Her argument—that women's voices had been systematically excluded from literary history—resonated deeply with American women writers who were pushing against similar boundaries.

Reception and Recovery

Many women modernists were overlooked or marginalized in their own time—dismissed as too experimental, too obscure, or simply ignored by a literary establishment shaped by male critics and publishers. Only in the latter half of the 20th century, through the efforts of feminist scholars and literary historians, were many of these authors recovered and canonized.

Today, figures like Stein, Barnes, Hurston, Larsen, H.D. (Hilda Doolittle), and Katherine Anne Porter are recognized not only as modernists, but as architects of a more inclusive, more dynamic literary modernism.

Conclusion: Women at the Center of Literary Modernism

Women writers helped define Modernism—not as a homogenous movement, but as a contested space of struggle, revision, and innovation. Their works exposed the limitations of patriarchal culture and expanded the boundaries of literary form. By exploring identity as fragmented, constructed, and fluid, they anticipated many of the concerns that would dominate literature in the postmodern and contemporary eras.

Far from being peripheral, women were at the center of modernist experimentation. Their voices continue to challenge, disturb, and inspire—demanding that readers rethink not only how stories are told, but who gets to tell them.

Legacy and Transition: From Modernism to Postmodernism

From Fragmentation to Irony: The Literary Landscape Evolves

As the mid-20th century unfolded, the once-radical innovations of Modernism no longer seemed quite so new. Though its aesthetic energy had transformed literary form and consciousness, a new generation of writers—shaped by global trauma, political unrest, and rapid technological change—began to interrogate the very possibility of meaning. If Modernism responded to a world that had lost coherence by searching for new forms of structure, Postmodernism emerged to doubt the existence of coherence itself.

This was not a total rejection, but an evolution. Postmodernism inherited much from its predecessor—its obsession with language, identity, fragmentation, and the inner life—but reframed these concerns with a spirit of playfulness, skepticism, and cultural critique. The transition from Modernism to Postmodernism was a shift in tone, perspective, and philosophical orientation, one that reflected a changing world and a growing distrust in master narratives.

Continuities: What Postmodernism Inherited from Modernism

Despite their differences, Postmodernism remains deeply indebted to Modernist breakthroughs. Many literary devices that seemed revolutionary in the early 20th century became foundational tools for later writers:

- Stream of consciousness, pioneered by Woolf and Faulkner, evolved into internal monologue and self-referential narration.
- Nonlinear storytelling, once shocking in works like The Sound and the Fury or Ulysses, became almost expected in postwar fiction.
- Fragmentation and collage, key Modernist modes, continued in postmodern works—but with added layers of irony and self-awareness.
- Multiplicity of voices and perspectives expanded further, challenging the idea of a single, authoritative point of view.

Importantly, Modernist literature often displayed a yearning for order and meaning, even amid disintegration. Writers like Eliot and Joyce built literary forms that grappled with loss but also tried to restore connection through myth, history, or spiritual insight. In contrast, Postmodernists frequently questioned whether any such restoration was possible—or even desirable.

The Postmodern Turn: Irony, Metafiction, and Cultural Critique

Where Modernism mourned the collapse of cultural authority, Postmodernism embraced it. If the Modernist writer was a tragic visionary attempting to rebuild meaning, the Postmodernist was a trickster—unmasking the absurdity of language, genre, and even authorship itself.

Key Characteristics of Postmodern Literature

- **Metafiction:** Fiction that draws attention to its own artifice, highlighting the constructed nature of storytelling. *John Barth's Lost in the Funhouse* and *Italo Calvino's If on a winter's night a traveler* exemplify this approach.
- **Pastiche:** The eclectic borrowing and recombination of styles, genres, and cultural references. Postmodern texts often juxtapose high and low culture, blending detective fiction with philosophy, or comic books with classical myth.

- **Playful Irony:** Satire and parody became tools not just of critique, but of resistance to ideological seriousness. *Thomas Pynchon's Gravity's Rainbow*, for instance, mocks everything from war to science to the novel form itself.
- **Simulacra and Hyperreality:** Influenced by theorists like Jean Baudrillard, postmodern texts often blur the line between the real and the represented. In novels like *Don DeLillo's White Noise*, media and consumer culture become more real than reality.
- **Intertextuality:** Postmodern authors frequently build on, revise, or parody prior works—turning literature into a vast conversation across time.

These strategies reflect a broader cultural condition of uncertainty. Postmodernism does not seek to unify contradictions, but rather to expose and perform them, suggesting that truth itself is layered, contingent, and always under construction.

Historical and Cultural Context of the Transition

The emergence of Postmodernism was not merely a stylistic shift—it was rooted in the profound disillusionments and disruptions of mid-20th century history.

1. **The Holocaust and Atomic Age:** World War II shattered the Enlightenment belief in rational progress. The mechanized slaughter of the Holocaust and the devastation of Hiroshima and Nagasaki revealed the dark underside of technological and bureaucratic modernity. Writers responded by questioning whether traditional humanist values could still hold.
2. **The Cold War and Surveillance Culture:** The postwar years brought paranoia, propaganda, and ideological polarization. McCarthyism, censorship, and nuclear brinkmanship fostered a culture of fear and simulation—reflected in the conspiratorial, fractured worlds of writers like Pynchon and DeLillo.
3. **Social Movements and Identity Politics:** The Civil Rights Movement, second-wave feminism, LGBTQ+ activism, and postcolonial struggles challenged dominant historical narratives and demanded space for marginalized voices. Postmodern literature mirrored this by destabilizing the notion of a single "truth" or unified national identity.
4. **Mass Media and Consumer Culture:** Television, advertising, film, and the rise of the internet transformed how people consumed information and related to the world. Postmodern writers often engaged with this mediated reality, exploring how spectacle and commodification replaced direct experience.

5. **Intellectual Developments:** The rise of poststructuralist theory—exemplified by Derrida, Foucault, and Barthes—offered a new vocabulary for analyzing language, power, and subjectivity. Postmodern literature absorbed these ideas, embracing ambiguity, contradiction, and the instability of meaning.

Bridging Figures: Writers at the Cusp

Some authors did not fit neatly into either Modernism or Postmodernism but instead straddled both traditions, embodying elements of each:

- Ralph Ellison, in *Invisible Man* (1952), used Modernist techniques—such as symbolic layering, fragmented narrative, and psychological realism—while also confronting race, invisibility, and narrative irony in ways that anticipated Postmodern themes.
- Vladimir Nabokov's *Lolita* (1955) combines intricate language, unreliable narration, and metafictional play to challenge moral and aesthetic conventions. Though deeply rooted in European modernism, it reads like a proto-postmodern parable about obsession and manipulation.
- Samuel Beckett, best known for *Waiting for Godot* (1953), exemplifies absurdist minimalism and the Modernist tradition of existential despair—yet his characters' empty repetitions, circular dialogues, and anti-narratives also prefigure the postmodern condition.
- Flannery O'Connor, whose Southern Gothic stories are steeped in grotesque violence, theological irony, and psychological tension, merges Modernist intensity with Postmodern ambiguity about grace, evil, and identity.

These writers remind us that literary movements are fluid. They evolve in overlapping waves, each one haunted by the unresolved questions of the last.

Conclusion: Modernism's Enduring Influence

Modernism did not vanish with the arrival of Postmodernism. Its concerns—with alienation, loss, language, and consciousness—remained central to American literature, even as its tone and tools shifted. Where Modernists sought wholeness in fragmentation, Postmodernists accepted fragmentation as the only reality left.

Yet the Modernist legacy endures in every postmodern writer who:

- Deconstructs the novel form,
- Explores interiority with skepticism,
- Seeks new ways to speak in a world saturated with old meanings.

From Eliot's lament to Pynchon's parody, from Faulkner's psychological spirals to Morrison's palimpsests of memory, the modernist impulse lives on—not as a fixed style, but as a challenge to every generation of writers: to reimagine the act of storytelling in a broken, beautiful, ever-changing world.

3

The Harlem Renaissance and the Black Literary Imagination

Voicing Black Identity, Creativity, and Resistance

The Harlem Renaissance stands as a foundational moment in American literature—a cultural explosion of Black creativity, political thought, and intellectual energy that reshaped the nation's literary landscape. More than a literary movement, it was a revolution in representation, one that challenged the erasure of African American experience and reclaimed Black identity on Black terms.

Emerging in the 1920s in Harlem, New York—a neighborhood transformed by the Great Migration—the Renaissance brought together poets, novelists, musicians, visual artists, and thinkers who sought to express the full complexity of Black life in America. This was a time of jazz and blues, nightclubs and salons, resistance and celebration. It was also a moment of tension—between art and politics, between assimilation and cultural nationalism, between modernism and tradition.

Historical Context: The Great Migration and Urban Black Consciousness

The Harlem Renaissance was not born in isolation—it was the culmination of a profound social transformation driven by one of the most significant internal migrations in American history. The Great Migration, spanning from approximately 1916 to 1970, saw over six million African Americans move from the rural South to urban centers in the North, Midwest, and West. Motivated by a complex combination of push and pull factors, this exodus redefined the contours of Black American life and seeded the cultural and intellectual conditions that would give rise to the Harlem Renaissance.

The Great Migration: A Movement of Liberation and Survival

In the Jim Crow South, African Americans faced not only economic hardship but also institutionalized racial terror, including disenfranchisement, lynchings, sharecropping debt cycles, and rigid segregation. The North, while far from a racial utopia, offered the promise of factory jobs, better education, voting rights, and relative safety. Cities like Chicago, Detroit, Pittsburgh, Philadelphia, and especially New York's Harlem became magnets for Black Southerners seeking both economic opportunity and personal autonomy.

This shift created new urban Black communities, dense with cultural energy and political ambition. Harlem—originally developed as an upper-class white neighborhood—quickly transformed into the epicenter of Black artistic, musical, and literary innovation in the United States. It became more than a geographical space: it was a symbolic capital of Black modernity, representing a break from rural pasts and a leap into modern, cosmopolitan identities.

Urban Consciousness and Intellectual Awakening

The concentration of Black professionals, writers, educators, musicians, and laborers in Harlem catalyzed a collective reimagining of Black identity. No longer defined solely by white narratives or Southern plantation legacies, African Americans in the urban North began crafting their own voices, informed by both their heritage and the modern world.

This new urban Black consciousness was shaped by a vibrant intersection of cultural pride, political activism, and artistic experimentation. The influence of Pan-Africanism, particularly through the work of Marcus Garvey and his Universal Negro Improvement Association (UNIA), provided a vision of global Black unity and self-reliance. Garvey's call to "return to Africa" was not merely literal but also metaphorical: a call to reclaim African heritage and pride in the face of systemic dehumanization.

At the same time, W.E.B. Du Bois's concept of the "Talented Tenth"—the belief that a cultivated Black elite could lead the race toward equality—galvanized intellectuals, educators, and artists to take their work seriously as a tool of uplift and resistance. Du Bois, editor of The Crisis, provided a critical platform for emerging voices, publishing poetry, essays, and fiction by Harlem Renaissance writers.

The Cultural Infrastructure: Journals, Patrons, and Debate

The Harlem Renaissance was made possible not only by the artists themselves but by the cultural infrastructure that supported them. Journals like *The Crisis* and *Opportunity* (edited by Charles S. Johnson of the National Urban League) provided crucial publishing space and recognition. These publications often sponsored contests and offered cash prizes, fostering a sense of legitimacy and visibility for Black writers who had historically been excluded from mainstream literary circles.

Additionally, white patrons such as Carl Van Vechten, Charlotte Mason, and others played a complex role. On one hand, their financial support opened doors to publication and broader readership. On the other, it introduced tensions about creative autonomy, with some artists feeling pressured to conform to white expectations or portray Blackness in exotic or primitive terms. This led to heated debates within the movement about authenticity, audience, and the role of art in political struggle.

Figures like Langston Hughes insisted that Black art should reflect the fullness of Black life—not just its respectable or palatable aspects. He famously wrote in his 1926 essay *The Negro Artist and the Racial Mountain* that Black artists must not be afraid to embrace their identity:

> "*We younger Negro artists who create now intend to express our individual dark-skinned selves without fear or shame.*"

This declaration became a rallying cry for a new generation of Black writers, determined to speak in their own voices, in their own rhythms, and for their own communities.

Conclusion: The Urban Black Renaissance

Thus, the Harlem Renaissance must be understood as both a product of migration and transformation. It emerged from the upheaval of millions seeking freedom and opportunity, and it was nurtured in the crucible of Harlem—a space of encounter between rural memory and urban possibility, African legacy and American struggle, private pain and public performance.

The movement did not only produce art; it reimagined Black citizenship, modernity, and cultural power. In Harlem's streets, salons, nightclubs, and classrooms, African Americans claimed their place not just in American letters, but in the global conversation about race, identity, and the future of culture.

Redefining the Black Self through Literature

At the heart of the Harlem Renaissance was a powerful, collective act of self-definition—a turning of the lens inward to represent the complexity, richness, and diversity of African American life. In a country that had long caricatured or silenced Black voices, the writers of this era strove to articulate the Black experience on their own terms, in their own styles, and with full creative authority. Their literature became a transformative force—a site where identity, resistance, and cultural pride converged.

Moving Beyond Stereotypes: The Literary Revolution

Historically, African American characters in American literature had been depicted through dehumanizing and reductive stereotypes—either as docile, comic caricatures or tragic symbols of racial victimhood. The Harlem Renaissance challenged these portrayals by creating multidimensional characters, asserting emotional and intellectual depth, and depicting a wide spectrum of Black experiences.

Authors like Langston Hughes, Zora Neale Hurston, Claude McKay, and Jean Toomer sought to reclaim the image of the Black individual—not as a symbol, but as a living, breathing human being. Their protagonists were lovers, dreamers, rebels, mothers, wanderers, thinkers—figures shaped not only by racism and oppression but also by joy, humor, faith, desire, and creative resilience.

Themes of Racial Pride and Double Consciousness

One of the defining features of Harlem Renaissance literature was its celebration of racial pride. Writers embraced African heritage, Southern folklore, urban jazz culture, and Black vernacular speech as sources of beauty and identity. They rejected the notion that "success" meant assimilation into white culture, and instead centered Blackness as a source of strength and creativity.

At the same time, many works explored the complexities of "double consciousness," a concept famously articulated by W.E.B. Du Bois—the sense of having one's identity split between how one sees oneself and how one is seen by a dominant white society. This psychological conflict plays out in literature through characters who struggle with internalized racism, cultural alienation, or the pressure to "pass" as white.

Jean Toomer's Cane (1923), for example, portrays the fragmentation of Black identity through a nonlinear collage of poems, stories, and lyrical sketches. Its characters are torn between rural Southern roots and the modern urban North, navigating colorism, memory, and sexual desire. Toomer's structure—hybrid, fractured, and ambiguous—mirrors the complexity of Black subjectivity itself.

Folklore, Dialect, and the Celebration of Everyday Life

A key aspect of Harlem Renaissance literature was its embrace of folk traditions and Black vernacular culture—long dismissed by mainstream America as crude or unsophisticated. Writers like Zora Neale Hurston elevated these cultural expressions into high art.

Hurston, a trained anthropologist as well as a novelist, used her fiction to document and dramatize the rich oral traditions of the African American South. In *Their Eyes Were Watching God* (1937), she wrote in the cadence of Black Southern speech, portraying a woman's journey toward selfhood against a backdrop of love, community, and loss. Hurston's work celebrates not just survival but Black joy, wit, and storytelling as acts of cultural preservation.

This emphasis on the beauty of ordinary Black life stood in contrast to more assimilationist voices who preferred to highlight exceptionalism or respectability. The tension between these approaches—between folk culture and elite culture, between political protest and aesthetic exploration—defined many of the literary debates within the Harlem Renaissance.

Sexuality, Gender, and the Politics of the Personal

Harlem Renaissance literature also opened space for exploring gender and sexuality in new ways. While overt discussions of queerness and female desire were often suppressed by publishers or constrained by social norms, many writers found subtle or symbolic means of addressing these themes.

Claude McKay's poems, for instance, express erotic longing and emotional vulnerability that challenge heteronormative ideals of masculinity. Meanwhile, novels like *Passing* (1929) by Nella Larsen confront issues of sexual and racial identity through stories of women navigating ambiguous social roles. Larsen's portrayal of two light-skinned Black women—one who "passes" for white and one who doesn't—raises questions about authenticity, betrayal, and the costs of assimilation.

Through such works, Harlem Renaissance literature became a space for contesting restrictive gender norms and exploring the intersections of race, gender, and power.

Modernism Reimagined Through a Black Lens

Harlem Renaissance authors were not merely borrowing from the literary innovations of Modernism—they were transforming them. The fragmented narrative, stream-of-consciousness technique, and lyrical intensity of the modernist form found new life when adapted to the Black experience.

Writers integrated African American speech patterns, jazz rhythms, and spiritual motifs into their work, creating a uniquely Black aesthetic that challenged the whiteness of the literary canon. Langston Hughes famously described jazz as "a heartbeat for the race," and his poetry reflects this musicality, spontaneity, and improvisational spirit.

This blending of form and content allowed Black writers to engage with modernist themes—alienation, identity crisis, the search for meaning—while rooting their art in Black life and community.

Conclusion: Claiming the Right to Be Complex

The literature of the Harlem Renaissance was ultimately an assertion of humanity—the right to be complex, contradictory, beautiful, flawed, proud, and unafraid. It opened up new literary and psychological terrains, redefining what it meant to be Black, American, and modern. By doing so, it laid the groundwork for later generations of writers—from James Baldwin and Toni Morrison to Ta-Nehisi Coates and Jesmyn Ward—who would continue to expand and reimagine the Black literary tradition.

Key Writers and Their Contributions

The Harlem Renaissance was not a monolith, but a vibrant mosaic of voices—each distinct in style, vision, and thematic focus. While united by a shared commitment to Black cultural expression, the writers of this era brought diverse perspectives to questions of race, art, politics, and identity. Their work helped redefine the American literary canon, challenging inherited assumptions and expanding the boundaries of artistic freedom.

Here, we focus on four of the most influential figures: Langston Hughes, Zora Neale Hurston, Claude McKay, and Jean Toomer—each of whom made unique and lasting contributions to the Renaissance and to American literature as a whole.

Langston Hughes: The Voice of the People

Langston Hughes (1902–1967) was arguably the most recognizable literary figure of the Harlem Renaissance. A poet, playwright, novelist, and essayist, Hughes championed an accessible, musical, and emotionally direct style that captured the rhythms of African American life. He was a people's poet, writing not for elites but for the everyday Black man and woman—for barbers, preachers, musicians, maids, and dreamers.

His 1926 essay *The Negro Artist and the Racial Mountain* became a manifesto for the Renaissance. In it, Hughes argued that Black artists should not aspire to whiteness or middle-class values, but instead find beauty in their own culture:

> "*We build our temples for tomorrow, strong as we know how, and we stand on top of the mountain, free within ourselves.*"

His poetry collections—*The Weary Blues* (1926), *Fine Clothes to the Jew* (1927), and *Montage of a Dream Deferred* (1951)—combine modernist experimentation with jazz and blues rhythms. Poems like "Mother to Son,"

"I, Too," and "Harlem (A Dream Deferred)" gave voice to both the suffering and the enduring hope of Black America.

Beyond poetry, Hughes wrote plays (*Mulatto*), short stories (the Jesse B. Semple series), and children's books. His wide-ranging output and commitment to social justice made him a cultural icon far beyond the Renaissance.

Zora Neale Hurston: The Storyteller of the Folk

Zora Neale Hurston (1891–1960) was a novelist, folklorist, and anthropologist whose work celebrated the vernacular speech, folklore, and cultural richness of rural Southern Black life. While often marginalized in her time—partly because of her gender and her refusal to conform to political expectations—Hurston's work has since been reclaimed as foundational to both African American literature and feminist thought.

Her most famous novel, *Their Eyes Were Watching God* (1937), follows the journey of Janie Crawford, a Black woman searching for love, freedom, and a voice of her own. Written in rich dialect and full of poetic imagery, the novel explores themes of female autonomy, community, and emotional self-realization.

Hurston's earlier work, such as *Jonah's Gourd Vine* (1934) and her folklore collection *Mules and Men* (1935), preserves oral stories, songs, and rituals from the Black South. Trained under Franz Boas, she was one of the first to blend ethnography and fiction, insisting that Black culture was not only worthy of academic study but of literary celebration.

While contemporaries like Richard Wright criticized her for not writing more politically charged material, Hurston defended her focus on the everyday lives of Black people as a radical affirmation of their beauty and complexity.

Claude McKay: The Poet of Resistance and Rage

Claude McKay (1889–1948), born in Jamaica, brought a Caribbean and international perspective to the Harlem Renaissance. A fierce critic of racism and colonialism, McKay's work combined political urgency with lyrical elegance. His poetry often expressed anger at racial injustice while affirming the strength and dignity of Black people.

His landmark poem "If We Must Die" (1919), written in response to the Red Summer of white supremacist violence, remains one of the most powerful calls for resistance in American literature:

> *"If we must die—let it not be like hogs / Hunted and penned in an inglorious spot."*

His poetry collections—*Harlem Shadows* (1922) and later works like *Constab Ballads*—tackled themes of exile, oppression, and the longing for liberation. McKay's novel *Home to Harlem* (1928), the first by a Black writer to become a bestseller in America, depicted the vibrant, chaotic life of Harlem's working-class community. Though criticized by some (notably Du Bois) for its gritty realism, the novel broke new ground by portraying Black life without apology or sanitization.

McKay's political journey—flirting with communism, exploring religion, and eventually retreating from public activism—reflected the complexity of the Renaissance's relationship with ideology. Nonetheless, his fierce poetic voice left a lasting legacy of protest and pride.

Jean Toomer: The Visionary of Black Modernism

Jean Toomer (1894–1967) was a writer of mixed racial heritage whose seminal work *Cane* (1923) stands as one of the most enigmatic and innovative texts of the Harlem Renaissance. A hybrid of poetry, prose, and drama, Cane defied conventional genre and narrative, reflecting both modernist influence and deep engagement with Black Southern culture.

Toomer's work is characterized by its lyrical, fragmented structure, haunting imagery, and spiritual undertones. *Cane* moves from rural Georgia to urban Washington, D.C., capturing the alienation and longing experienced by African Americans caught between two worlds—North and South, past and future, self and society.

Though Toomer later distanced himself from racial identification and the Renaissance itself, his influence was profound. Cane anticipated later developments in African American literature, particularly the nonlinear storytelling and poetic sensibility seen in the works of Toni Morrison, Alice Walker, and others.

Themes, Conflicts, and Legacy of the Harlem Renaissance

Struggle and Celebration in the Making of a Literary Revolution

While the Harlem Renaissance was a flowering of creativity, pride, and cultural affirmation, it was also a period marked by significant tensions and contradictions. Artists and intellectuals negotiated competing ideals: between art and politics, elite and folk culture, racial uplift and honest expression, integration and separatism. These tensions did not diminish the movement—they defined it, giving the Harlem Renaissance its rich dialectical energy and enduring relevance.

Themes: The Soul of the Renaissance

Racial Identity and Pride

The Renaissance was rooted in an effort to reclaim Black identity from centuries of caricature and erasure. Writers explored the beauty of African heritage, the dignity of Black labor, and the power of ancestral memory. Art became a form of resistance—an assertion of humanity against a society that had long denied it.

This affirmation found expression in a range of styles: Hughes's jazz-inflected odes to Harlem, Hurston's folk-rooted celebration of Black womanhood, and McKay's militant cries against racial violence. These texts did not present a single view of Blackness, but rather a mosaic of experiences that reflected the diversity of the Black diaspora.

Double Consciousness and Psychological Conflict

W.E.B. Du Bois's notion of double consciousness—the internal struggle of African Americans to reconcile their Black identity with their American nationality—haunted much of Harlem Renaissance literature. Characters in novels and poems wrestled with feelings of dislocation, self-doubt, and the desire to be accepted without assimilation.

Nella Larsen's *Passing* and Jean Toomer's *Cane* dramatized this inner tension, exploring the psychological fragmentation brought on by a racially divided society. The Renaissance thus became a forum not just for celebrating identity, but for interrogating its complexity.

The City as Stage and Symbol

Urban life—especially in Harlem—became a central motif. Cities symbolized freedom, modernity, and cultural mixing, but also anonymity, exploitation, and spiritual loss. Writers captured both the vibrancy and the alienation of Black urban existence, often contrasting it with the memory of rural life in the South.

This duality—the city as both liberator and oppressor—gave Harlem Renaissance literature a uniquely modern tension, mirroring the broader experience of 20th-century migration and modernization.

Gender, Sexuality, and Desire

Though often constrained by social norms, many Harlem Renaissance writers explored themes of gender and sexuality—sometimes boldly, sometimes elliptically. Women authors like Zora Neale Hurston and Jessie Fauset depicted female characters in search of autonomy, voice, and emotional fulfillment, while male writers like Claude McKay and Richard

Bruce Nugent addressed queer desire and masculinity in groundbreaking, if coded, ways.

These narratives complicated simplistic notions of identity, showing that Black life, like all human life, was shaped by desire, contradiction, and self-invention.

Conflicts: Debating the Purpose of Black Art

While united by a broad cultural awakening, the Harlem Renaissance was riven by intellectual and aesthetic debates. Chief among them:

Art for Art's Sake vs. Art as Political Tool

Should Black literature serve the cause of racial uplift, or should it be free to explore any subject, including the mundane, the taboo, or the unflattering? W.E.B. Du Bois believed art should be a weapon in the struggle for equality, whereas Langston Hughes and Zora Neale Hurston argued for creative independence and the right to depict Black life in all its complexity.
This debate reflected a larger tension between **respectability politics and radical authenticity**, a dilemma that would echo through later movements like the Civil Rights era and Black Arts Movement.

2. Folk Culture vs. Elite Culture

Some Renaissance figures, like Hurston, celebrated **folk traditions, dialects, and oral storytelling**. Others sought to align Black literature with **European high culture**, using classical forms and formal language to demonstrate refinement and capability.
This conflict mirrored class divisions within Black communities, and raised questions about **who Black art was for**: white audiences, the Black bourgeoisie, or working-class African Americans?

Patronage and Power

Many Harlem Renaissance artists relied on white patrons for financial and institutional support. This relationship—while sometimes fruitful—was fraught with issues of control and expectation. Some patrons encouraged exotic or primitivist portrayals of Blackness, reinforcing stereotypes under the guise of admiration.

Writers often had to navigate these dynamics carefully, balancing gratitude with resistance to exploitation and misrepresentation.

Legacy: Echoes Beyond Harlem

Although the Harlem Renaissance began to wane in the 1930s—due to the Great Depression, political disillusionment, and shifting cultural priorities—its impact was profound and lasting.

1. **Expanding the Literary Canon:** The Renaissance legitimized African American literature as a serious and valuable tradition within American letters. Writers like Hughes, Hurston, and McKay became touchstones for future generations, opening the door for voices like James Baldwin, Ralph Ellison, Maya Angelou, Alice Walker, and Toni Morrison.
2. **Reclaiming Black Cultural Power:** By asserting Black creativity as central to American culture, the Harlem Renaissance helped reshape national identity. Jazz, blues, spirituals, and slang all influenced mainstream art, film, and literature, forever altering American aesthetics.
3. **Laying the Foundation for Future Movements:** The Harlem Renaissance laid the intellectual and artistic groundwork for later social and political movements, including the Civil Rights Movement, Black Power Movement, and the Black Arts Movement of the 1960s–70s. Its insistence on Black visibility, dignity, and voice would become rallying cries for generations to come.

Conclusion: The Renaissance as a Cultural Revolution

The Harlem Renaissance was not just a moment—it was a **movement of the mind and soul**, a declaration of creative sovereignty. It taught the world that Black experience was not peripheral, but central; not marginal, but profound. Through its vibrant voices and visionary literature, the Renaissance redefined what it meant to be both Black and American.

It asked enduring questions about freedom, belonging, beauty, and justice—and it answered them in a chorus of songs, stories, and stanzas that continue to shape the nation's conscience.

4

The Beat Generation and Literary Dissent

Rebellion, Rhythm, and the Road to a New Consciousness

Introduction: The Rise of the Beats

In the aftermath of World War II, the United States found itself in the throes of a dual transformation. Economically, the country experienced a historic boom: suburban homes mushroomed across the landscape, consumer goods filled stores and households, and the American Dream seemed, to many, finally attainable. Yet beneath this glossy exterior lay an undercurrent of tension and anxiety. The Cold War cast a nuclear shadow over daily life, McCarthyism stifled political dissent, and rigid gender norms and racial segregation reinforced a stifling social order. In this cultural crucible, a new literary movement emerged—disruptive, defiant, and deeply dissatisfied.

The Beat Generation rose not as a cohesive political group, but as a loosely connected circle of poets, novelists, and thinkers bound together by shared sensibilities. Reacting against the conformity of 1950s America, they sought authenticity in a world they deemed artificial and spiritually bankrupt. They yearned for experiences that transcended material wealth—seeking truth in the rhythms of jazz, the teachings of Zen Buddhism, the raw energy of the street, and the primal drive of sexual and artistic freedom.

The Beats—most notably Allen Ginsberg, Jack Kerouac, William S. Burroughs, Neal Cassady, and Gregory Corso—rejected the literary formalism and polite decorum of the establishment. Their writing was spontaneous, often improvised, and deeply personal. They challenged the taboos of their time, addressing topics like homosexuality, drug use, interracial relationships, and existential despair with unapologetic candor. Their work was not crafted for the academy; it was written for fellow travelers, for those who, like them, were searching for meaning beyond the shopping malls and suburban lawns.

Though initially marginalized by critics and institutions—often labeled as obscene, incoherent, or anarchic—the Beats sparked a cultural and literary revolution. Their style, characterized by free verse, breath-length lines, and a jazz-inspired cadence, opened new possibilities for poetic form. Their prose, often unstructured and stream-of-consciousness, anticipated the stylistic innovations of later postmodern literature. But beyond form, the Beats gave voice to those America preferred to ignore: the drifters, addicts, mystics, outcasts, and visionaries. They democratized literature by insisting that the stories of society's "outsiders" were just as vital as those of its heroes.

The emergence of the Beat Generation also marked a profound shift in the purpose of literature itself. For the Beats, writing was not a purely intellectual exercise—it was a spiritual quest, a political act, a cry for liberation. Literature became a means of survival and transformation, both personal and collective. Through their works, the Beats paved the way for the 1960s counterculture, influencing movements for civil rights, anti-war resistance, and sexual freedom. Their legacy echoed in the protests, music, and lifestyle revolutions of the decades that followed.

In essence, the Beat Generation represented a literary insurgency against the dominant narratives of postwar America. They rejected not only the content of the American mainstream but its entire mode of expression. In doing so, they carved out a new space for dissent—one rooted in rhythm, rebellion, and the radical reimagining of consciousness. As we delve into the lives, works, and impact of these maverick writers, we come to understand how a handful of rebels with typewriters ignited one of the most transformative cultural fires in American history.

Cultural and Political Backdrop of the Beat Generation

To understand the emergence of the Beat Generation, it is essential to situate their work within the broader historical and cultural landscape of post-World War II America. The 1950s were a paradoxical decade—defined by outward prosperity and inward turmoil. The war had transformed the U.S. into a global superpower, and with that came widespread economic growth, a burgeoning middle class, and the proliferation of consumer culture. Television sets, suburban homes, and automobiles became symbols of success. However, this new American ideal was built upon a foundation of exclusion and repression.

Politically, the Cold War dominated public life. The fear of communism permeated the air, leading to McCarthyist purges, loyalty oaths, and the blacklisting of artists, intellectuals, and government employees. The House Un-American Activities Committee (HUAC) created a climate in which dissent—intellectual or otherwise—was equated with treason. This culture of surveillance and suppression profoundly shaped the Beats, who responded with a literature of resistance—where truth-telling became an act of rebellion.

Socially, the period was characterized by rigid norms. Patriarchal family structures, racial segregation, and the marginalization of LGBTQ+ individuals were upheld as part of the "natural order." Gender roles were sharply defined, and deviation from the norm was pathologized. The Beats rejected this enforced normalcy, embracing fluidity in identity, lifestyle, and artistic expression. Their defiance of gender binaries, traditional sexual mores, and racial boundaries stood in stark contrast to the dominant vision of a homogenized, white, middle-class America.

Culturally, the Beats found themselves at odds with both the literary establishment and the broader values of American society. The prevailing literary scene favored formalism and social realism—measured, controlled, and focused on middle-class life. The Beats, by contrast, favored spontaneity over structure, jazz-like improvisation over revision, and existential questioning over resolution. Drawing inspiration from African American culture, Eastern religion, and the avant-garde, they sought to expand consciousness and connect with the deeper, often darker truths of human existence.

In many ways, the Beat Generation was a response to a world perceived as emotionally sterile and spiritually vacuous. Their literature became a means of challenging not only literary conventions but the moral, political, and spiritual status quo. In celebrating imperfection, disorder, and raw experience, the Beats refused to be tamed by conformity. Their rebellion was not just cultural—it was deeply personal, reflecting a broader crisis of identity in a world where mass culture threatened to erase individuality.

Timeline: Major Events and Publications of the Beat Generation

Year	Event / Publication	Significance
1944	Lucien Carr stabs David Kammerer	Incident that bonded the early Beat circle and inspired works like Kerouac's Vanity of Duluoz
1947	Kerouac meets Neal Cassady	Cassady becomes the inspiration for Dean Moriarty in On the Road
1948	Ginsberg experiences a vision of William Blake	Spiritual awakening that influences his poetic philosophy
1951	Kerouac writes On the Road in a three-week burst	Marks the stylistic shift to "spontaneous prose"
1955	First public reading of Howl at Six Gallery, San Francisco	Considered the moment the Beat Generation "arrived"

Year	Event / Publication	Significance
1956	Publication of Howl and Other Poems by Allen Ginsberg	Sparks obscenity trial; landmark case for freedom of expression
1957	On the Road published by Viking Press	Becomes a bestseller, bringing Beat ideas into mainstream awareness
1959	Naked Lunch by William S. Burroughs published in Paris	Challenges narrative form and is later banned in the U.S.
1962	The Yage Letters by Burroughs and Ginsberg published	Explores psychedelic experiences and Amazonian shamanism
1965	Ginsberg co-founds Poet's March on the Pentagon	Links Beat literature to the antiwar movement
1966	U.S. Supreme Court rules Naked Lunch is not obscene	Marks victory for literary freedom and artistic experimentation
1969	Death of Jack Kerouac	Signals the symbolic end of the original Beat movement
1970s–present	Beat influence spreads to music, visual art, and spoken-word poetry	Legacy lives on through counterculture, punk, hip-hop, and performance poetry

Key Figures and Works of the Beat Generation

The Beat Generation was not a formal school or unified movement but rather a constellation of like-minded individuals who found common cause in their rejection of postwar American values. Their friendships, collaborations, and mutual influence gave rise to some of the most radical and enduring works of 20th-century American literature. Below are the major figures whose writings and philosophies defined the Beat ethos.

Allen Ginsberg and *Howl*: The Poet as Prophet

Allen Ginsberg (1926–1997) emerged as the spiritual and political voice of the Beat Generation. A Columbia University graduate steeped in literature and mysticism, Ginsberg sought to challenge both poetic form and social norms. His breakthrough came with the poem *Howl* (1956), a work that fused ecstatic emotion, political critique, and sexual candor.

Howl begins with the now-famous line, "I saw the best minds of my generation destroyed by madness," and continues with a breathless outpouring of images—drugs, madness, cities, angels, machines—that capture the psychic breakdown of modern life. The poem's structure mimics the rhythm of jazz improvisation and draws inspiration from Walt Whitman's long lines and prophetic tone. Ginsberg's unflinching openness about his homosexuality, spiritual longing, and disdain for capitalist values led to an obscenity trial in 1957. The court ultimately ruled in favor of *Howl*, defending its "redeeming social importance" and setting a precedent for free expression in literature.

Ginsberg continued to write prolifically and remained politically active, aligning himself with antiwar protests, gay rights, and Buddhist practice. His later works such as *Kaddish* and *Wichita Vortex Sutra* reveal a complex blend of personal grief, political rage, and transcendental insight.

Jack Kerouac and *On the Road*: Spontaneity, Jazz, and the Search for Meaning

Jack Kerouac (1922–1969), often hailed as the chronicler of the Beat Generation, was a novelist whose most influential work, *On the Road* (1957), became a cultural landmark. Born to French-Canadian parents in Lowell, Massachusetts, Kerouac initially envisioned himself as a traditional novelist. However, his encounter with fellow Beats led him toward a radical rethinking of prose form and purpose.

On the Road is a thinly veiled autobiographical account of Kerouac's travels across the United States with Neal Cassady (the inspiration for the novel's Dean Moriarty). Written in a burst of inspiration on a continuous scroll of paper, the book exemplifies what Kerouac called "spontaneous prose"—a style intended to bypass the censoring intellect and capture the immediacy of thought and experience.

The novel's celebration of jazz, drugs, sex, and spiritual hunger struck a chord with disaffected youth and ushered in a new era of literary rebellion. While critics debated its artistic merit, *On the Road* became a generational text—symbolizing a quest for freedom and authenticity beyond the confines of American normalcy.

Kerouac's later works, including *The Dharma Bums* and *Big Sur*, delve into themes of Buddhism, guilt, and psychological unraveling, reflecting the toll that fame and inner turmoil took on him.

William S. Burroughs and *Naked Lunch*: The Avant-Garde Visionary

William S. Burroughs (1914–1997) stood at the darker edge of the Beat movement. A Harvard-educated writer with a background in medicine and anthropology, Burroughs brought a sardonic intelligence to his exploration of addiction, control, and human consciousness. His most controversial and groundbreaking work, *Naked Lunch* (1959), is an avant-garde novel that defies linear narrative and conventional realism.

Naked Lunch was written during Burroughs' heroin addiction and is structured as a series of loosely connected "routines" or vignettes that feature grotesque humor, hallucinatory images, and a relentless critique of institutional power. The book's fragmented form and graphic content provoked widespread outrage, culminating in an obscenity trial that was eventually resolved in Burroughs's favor.

Burroughs developed the "cut-up technique" with artist Brion Gysin—an approach in which texts are literally cut and rearranged to produce new meanings, anticipating postmodern and cyberpunk aesthetics. Later works like *The Soft Machine* and *The Ticket That Exploded* continued to experiment with narrative form and interrogate themes of addiction, language, and state surveillance.

Burroughs became a cult figure and influenced generations of writers and musicians, from J.G. Ballard and Kathy Acker to Patti Smith and Kurt Cobain.

Neal Cassady: The Catalyst of Motion

Though not a traditional writer, **Neal Cassady** (1926–1968) played an instrumental role in the Beat mythology. He was the real-life inspiration for Kerouac's Dean Moriarty and Ginsberg's muse. A drifter, car thief, and natural storyteller, Cassady embodied the spontaneous, restless spirit that the Beats admired. His stream-of-consciousness letters—particularly those to Kerouac—helped shape the style and philosophy of spontaneous prose. Cassady later became the driver of Ken Kesey's psychedelic bus and a central figure in the transition from Beat to hippie counterculture. Though his own literary output was limited, Cassady's personality and kinetic energy helped define the Beat ideal of unfiltered, ecstatic living.

Diane di Prima and the Female Beat Voice

Often overlooked in male-dominated narratives, **Diane di Prima** (1934–2020) emerged as a powerful poetic voice who challenged both patriarchal norms and Beat masculinity. Her poetry, as seen in *Memoirs of a Beatnik* and *Revolutionary Letters*, blended sensuality, political radicalism, and spiritual reflection. Di Prima co-founded the New York Poets Theatre and played an integral role in the San Francisco Renaissance.

Her presence among the Beats emphasized the role of women not just as muses or lovers but as creators and disruptors in their own right. Later feminist scholarship has highlighted di Prima's work as crucial to understanding the intersection of gender, politics, and poetry within the Beat movement.

Gregory Corso: The Trickster Poet

Gregory Corso (1930–2001), often described as the enfant terrible of the Beats, combined a wild wit with lyrical intensity. Born in poverty and raised in orphanages, Corso brought a rebellious voice steeped in classical knowledge and street wisdom. His collections, including *Gasoline* (1958) and *The Happy Birthday of Death* (1960), explore themes of war, love, time, and mortality with both humor and rage.

Corso's poems often mirrored the musicality of jazz and the surrealism of dream logic. He brought a playfulness and ironic detachment that counterbalanced the intensity of Ginsberg and the mysticism of Kerouac.

Thematic Concerns: Dissent, Identity, and the Spiritual Quest

The Beat Generation was far more than a loose collective of writers—it was a cultural current that grappled with the most pressing questions of identity, freedom, and meaning in postwar America. While stylistically diverse, Beat literature is unified by a constellation of recurring themes that reflect the movement's resistance to conventional morality and its yearning for transcendence.

Rebellion Against Conformity

At the heart of Beat writing lies a profound and unyielding resistance to social conformity. The Beats viewed mainstream America—its suburban dreams, consumer goods, and corporate ladders—as a spiritual dead zone. Their writing is filled with critiques of "Moloch," the industrial-capitalist monster that Allen Ginsberg so famously attacked in *Howl*. This metaphor captured the dehumanizing force of modern institutions: government, religion, education, and capitalism.

Beat writers rejected the sanitized norms of 1950s life, including the expectation to marry, produce children, hold stable jobs, and participate in Cold War patriotism. They embraced the outcast, the wanderer, the addict, the queer, and the seeker—not as cautionary figures, but as spiritual pioneers. Their heroes were not the successful businessman or soldier, but the ecstatic poet, the mad prophet, the wayward traveler.

Exploration of Identity and Sexual Liberation

In a society rigidly bound by binary norms of gender and sexuality, the Beats were radically transgressive. Ginsberg's openness about his homosexuality was both courageous and groundbreaking at a time when same-sex love was criminalized and pathologized. Similarly, Diane di Prima's work gave voice to female sexual agency and challenged patriarchal assumptions within and beyond the Beat circle.

Identity in Beat literature is fluid, fragmented, and evolving. The writers often portrayed themselves as spiritual refugees, drifting through cities and relationships in search of authenticity. This quest for identity involved breaking down ego, transcending labels, and writing from the rawness of lived experience. The result was literature that often blurred the line between autobiography and fiction, confession and performance.

The Road and the Journey

Movement is a central motif in Beat writing. Whether it is Dean Moriarty and Sal Paradise crisscrossing America in *On the Road*, or Ginsberg's travels through India in search of Buddhist teachers, the road becomes both a literal and metaphorical space of liberation. It is a rejection of stasis and domesticity, and an embrace of the unpredictable, the open, and the sublime.

For the Beats, travel was not escapism but an existential imperative. The journey was a means of breaking from routine, confronting the self, and encountering the unknown. In this way, they revived the archetype of the wanderer or pilgrim, reimagined in the neon-lit landscapes of modern America.

Eastern Spirituality and Mysticism

Perhaps one of the most enduring legacies of the Beat Generation is its introduction of Eastern philosophy—particularly Zen Buddhism—into American consciousness. Disillusioned with Western religion and the Judeo-Christian moral framework, the Beats turned eastward for spiritual nourishment.

Jack Kerouac's *The Dharma Bums* reflects his engagement with Buddhism, celebrating meditation, simplicity, and the sacredness of nature. Ginsberg's travels to India and his immersion in Tibetan Buddhism later informed both his poetry and activism. The concept of "satori" (sudden enlightenment) informed their aesthetic of spontaneity and presence. Instead of seeking salvation in institutions, the Beats sought awakening in poetry, music, and lived experience.

Their embrace of Eastern mysticism wasn't without critique—some saw it as appropriation—but it marked a genuine spiritual hunger that contrasted sharply with the moralistic religiosity of the era.

Drugs, Consciousness, and Reality

The Beat Generation's use of drugs was not merely recreational; it was philosophical. Substances like marijuana, peyote, and Benzedrine were seen as tools for consciousness expansion and artistic experimentation.

William S. Burroughs's heroin-fueled visions in *Naked Lunch* and Ginsberg's psychedelic insights were attempts to bypass the rational mind and tap into the primal or mystical.

For the Beats, altered states of consciousness allowed access to suppressed truths—emotional, spiritual, political. Their exploration of the subconscious, dreams, hallucinations, and madness anticipated later developments in psychedelic literature and the countercultural fascination with LSD and mescaline.

Language, Form, and Artistic Experimentation

Form was as much a site of rebellion as content. The Beats rejected academic formalism and sought instead to develop a language that mimicked life itself—raw, unfiltered, rhythmic, and improvisational. Kerouac's "spontaneous prose" sought to write thought as it occurred, without censorship or revision. Ginsberg's lines in *Howl* were designed to be read aloud in a single breath, echoing the phrasing of jazz musicians like Charlie Parker and Lester Young.

Burroughs's "cut-up technique," which involved slicing up texts and rearranging them at random, anticipated later developments in postmodern literature and multimedia art. The Beats saw writing as a living act—fluid, expressive, and often chaotic. Their works blurred boundaries: between poetry and prose, fiction and memoir, sanity and madness.

Social and Political Dissent

While not all Beats were overtly political, their very lives and writing were forms of protest. They opposed racial segregation, embraced interracial relationships, spoke out against war, and rejected economic materialism. Ginsberg's poetry would later be central to the antiwar movement, while Burroughs's writings critiqued the control mechanisms of law, psychiatry, and government.

By aligning themselves with the marginalized—drug users, queer individuals, spiritual seekers—the Beats engaged in a politics of visibility and resistance. They gave voice to those silenced by Cold War conformity and laid the groundwork for future liberation movements.

Literary Style and Techniques

The Beat Generation not only redefined what could be said in literature but also how it could be said. Their radical departure from conventional literary forms reflected a deeper philosophical aim: to collapse the distance between life and art, thought and expression, inner experience and outer form. Their writing styles were dynamic, disruptive, and often improvised—meant not to impress critics, but to express raw human reality. Below are some of the most significant techniques that characterized Beat literature.

Spontaneous Prose: Jack Kerouac's Experiment in Authenticity

At the core of Jack Kerouac's literary project was the idea of "spontaneous prose"—a writing method designed to capture the immediacy of thought, feeling, and sensory experience without the interference of revision or rational control. Kerouac compared his technique to jazz improvisation: the writer, like the jazz musician, should surrender to the flow of inspiration and ride its rhythms without hesitation.

Kerouac first employed this technique in *On the Road*, which he famously typed on a 120-foot scroll of taped-together paper over the course of three frenzied weeks. The resulting prose is breathless, kinetic, and associative—full of digressions, repetitions, and sudden shifts in focus. For Kerouac, editing was a betrayal of the moment; his writing aimed to convey the purity of lived experience as it unfolded in real time.

Spontaneous prose defied the literary norms of structure, punctuation, and narrative order. While critics often derided it as undisciplined, it became a defining feature of Beat aesthetics, reflecting their rejection of control and conformity.

Oral Tradition and Performance: The Jazz of Beat Poetry

The Beats were not just writers on the page—they were performers of the spoken word. Beat poetry developed in a time when literary culture was increasingly moving out of academic institutions and into nightclubs, cafes, and public readings. These informal spaces allowed for greater experimentation and audience engagement.

Figures like Allen Ginsberg, Gregory Corso, and Diane di Prima brought their poetry to life through live performance, often accompanied by jazz musicians. The cadences of jazz—improvisational, syncopated, and emotionally expressive—profoundly influenced the rhythm and delivery of Beat poetry. Poems like *Howl* were composed with performance in mind: long lines intended to be read in a single breath, filled with repetitions, incantations, and crescendos that mimicked musical phrasing.

This performative aspect connected the Beats to oral traditions that predated written literature. In this way, they not only revived poetry as a living, communal act but also challenged the elitism of literary institutions. Their performances were democratic, inclusive, and visceral—breaking down the wall between poet and audience.

Cut-Up Technique: Burroughs and the Fragmentation of Meaning

William S. Burroughs, in collaboration with painter and writer Brion Gysin, developed one of the most radical literary innovations of the Beat era: the cut-up technique. This experimental method involved physically cutting up written texts—newspapers, manuscripts, letters—and rearranging the fragments to create new juxtapositions and associations. The resulting texts often bore a surreal, hallucinatory quality that disrupted linear storytelling and challenged conventional meaning.

Burroughs employed this technique in works like *The Soft Machine* and *The Ticket That Exploded*, where narrative logic gives way to a mosaic of fragmented images, voices, and symbols. The goal was not simply aesthetic but philosophical. Burroughs believed language itself was a form of social control, and that by breaking it apart, one could expose and subvert its power.

The cut-up technique also aligned with contemporary developments in visual art (e.g., collage and assemblage) and would later influence postmodern literature, punk aesthetics, and experimental film. By treating language as a material object—subject to manipulation and reconfiguration—Burroughs and Gysin opened new frontiers in literary form.

Breath, Rhythm, and Improvisation: The Beat Sound

Beat writing, especially poetry, often followed a principle that Allen Ginsberg described as "writing in the breath." This concept, inspired by both Walt Whitman's long lines and the breath control of Buddhist meditation, suggested that each line should correspond to a single exhalation. This technique freed poetry from strict meter and allowed for a more organic, bodily rhythm.

Improvisation, borrowed from jazz and oral storytelling, was also central. The Beats valued unpredictability, spontaneity, and the interplay between language and intuition. Their texts frequently shifted in tone, perspective, and pace—mirroring the chaotic flow of thought and the improvisational freedom of the artist in the moment.

This rhythmic, breath-based, and improvisational style marked a break with formalism and prefigured the spoken word and slam poetry movements that would emerge decades later.

Stream of Consciousness and Subjectivity

While stream-of-consciousness was not invented by the Beats, they brought it into a new cultural register. Influenced by modernists like James Joyce and Virginia Woolf, Beat writers infused stream-of-consciousness with a visceral intensity that emphasized the body, the senses, and emotional extremes.

Kerouac's interior monologues, Ginsberg's ecstatic visions, and Burroughs's surreal hallucinations all reflected an interest in capturing the unfiltered flow of consciousness. These works often lacked traditional plot structures or moral resolutions, focusing instead on the raw interiority of the narrator's experience. The boundary between self and world was porous; perception and reality were constantly in flux.

This style reflected the Beat commitment to personal authenticity. By revealing the inner chaos, the writers challenged the cultural demand for order, logic, and restraint.

Visual and Textual Hybridity

Some Beat texts also incorporated visual elements—layout, typography, and even drawings. Lawrence Ferlinghetti's *A Coney Island of the Mind* used typography to emphasize sound and silence, while Ginsberg's *Reality Sandwiches* played with spatial dynamics on the page. The emphasis on form as meaning foreshadowed the emergence of concrete poetry and multimodal literary expression.

This willingness to experiment with the *look* of literature aligned with the movement's overall ethos: to break boundaries, defy expectations, and reimagine the relationship between writer, reader, and text.

The Beats and Modernism/Postmodernism

The Beat Generation occupies a fascinating and transitional space in the landscape of 20th-century literature—poised between the high experimentation of Modernism and the radical playfulness of Postmodernism. While the Beats rejected many of the academic and elitist tendencies of literary Modernism, their aesthetic impulses and philosophical concerns reflected significant continuity with it. At the same time, their innovations in form, tone, and subject matter laid crucial groundwork for the emergence of Postmodern literature.

Continuity with Modernism: Shared Aesthetics and Philosophical Inquiry

The Beats inherited much from the Modernist revolution that reshaped Western literature in the early 20th century. Like the Modernists—T.S. Eliot, Ezra Pound, James Joyce, and Virginia Woolf—the Beats challenged linear narrative, objective realism, and the decorum of traditional prose. Both movements were concerned with representing the fragmented nature of modern consciousness and expressing the alienation of the individual in a rapidly changing world.

Allen Ginsberg, for example, modeled his long lines and sweeping invocations in *Howl* on Walt Whitman's democratic verse, but also drew deeply from the prophetic voice of Modernist poetry. William S. Burroughs's textual experiments, including his adoption of the "cut-up" technique, echoed the collage aesthetics and narrative disjunctions found in Eliot's *The Waste Land* or Joyce's *Ulysses*.

The Beats also shared the Modernists' cosmopolitan sensibilities. They looked beyond American borders for intellectual and spiritual inspiration. Like Eliot and Pound, they absorbed European philosophy, psychoanalysis, Eastern mysticism, and avant-garde art. They were steeped in existentialism, Buddhism, Surrealism, and Dada—all legacies of the early 20th-century cultural ferment.

Yet the Beats diverged from Modernism in crucial ways. While Modernism often maintained an ironic distance or an intellectual austerity, Beat writing was more visceral, emotive, and autobiographical. Where Modernists strove for formal elegance and literary authority, the Beats celebrated spontaneity, messiness, and improvisation. Their work was often less concerned with aesthetic perfection and more with authenticity, immediacy, and liberation.

Precursor to Postmodernism: The Beats as Bridge Figures

In many ways, the Beat Generation can be seen as a bridge between Modernism and Postmodernism. They carried forward the experimental spirit of the former while pioneering the themes and techniques that would come to define the latter.

Postmodern literature is characterized by fragmentation, pastiche, metafiction, irony, and a distrust of grand narratives and absolute truths. These qualities are evident in much of Beat writing—particularly in the works of William S. Burroughs. His nonlinear narratives, absurdist logic, and cut-up collages dismantled narrative coherence and challenged the notion of a stable authorial voice. Burroughs's novels like *Naked Lunch* and *The Soft Machine* are full of disjointed episodes, overlapping identities, and dark humor—all hallmarks of postmodern fiction.

The Beats also engaged in metafictional practices, often blurring the line between the author and the character. Kerouac's alter ego Sal Paradise in *On the Road*, or Ginsberg's autobiographical persona in *Kaddish*, reflect a self-referential impulse that anticipates postmodern play with identity and narrative.

Moreover, the Beats' anti-establishment ethos and skepticism toward mainstream culture parallel the postmodern critique of authority, ideology, and institutional control. Their embrace of multiplicity—of voice, form, identity, and experience—anticipated the pluralism of postmodern thought.

Philosophical Resonances and Shifts

The Beats and Modernists were both preoccupied with the crisis of meaning in modern life. However, while Modernists often responded with a sense of despair or formal complexity, the Beats sought transcendence—through mysticism, art, drugs, and love. Their work is often infused with spiritual longing, ecstatic revelation, and a quest for unity, setting them apart from the ironic detachment and skepticism that would come to dominate postmodern literature.

Postmodern writers like Thomas Pynchon, Don DeLillo, and Kathy Acker would later take inspiration from the Beats' formal daring and cultural critique, but often infused it with more irony and nihilism. Where the Beats believed in the redemptive power of experience, later postmodernists questioned even the possibility of redemption.

Influence and Legacy

The influence of the Beat Generation on both literary and cultural Postmodernism is undeniable. Their innovations in form, style, and content helped loosen the boundaries of what literature could be. They made room for the absurd, the obscene, the sacred, and the experimental—making the literary world more inclusive of outsider voices and unconventional narratives.

From the metafiction of *Gravity's Rainbow* to the countercultural ethos of *Fear and Loathing in Las Vegas*, the Beat imprint is everywhere. They democratized literature, paving the way for the punk zines of the 1980s, the spoken-word poets of the 1990s, and the hybrid memoirs and autofiction of the 21st century.

Criticism and Controversy

Though the Beat Generation profoundly shaped the course of American literature and countercultural thought, their legacy has not gone uncontested. From their earliest publications, Beat writers were met with skepticism, censorship, and backlash—much of it centered not just on what they wrote, but how they lived. Over time, a deeper and more nuanced body of critical engagement has emerged, highlighting key limitations, contradictions, and problematic aspects of their work and worldview.

Accusations of Self-Indulgence and Narcissism

One of the most persistent critiques of the Beat writers—especially Jack Kerouac and Allen Ginsberg—is that their work is overly self-absorbed, undisciplined, and narcissistic. Critics in the 1950s and '60s often dismissed Beat literature as lacking form, purpose, and intellectual rigor. The emphasis on spontaneous prose and raw emotion was viewed by many literary traditionalists as a rejection of craftsmanship.

Writers such as Kerouac were accused of glorifying personal excess, romanticizing drug use, and treating the act of writing as an exercise in catharsis rather than structured communication. To some, the Beat project appeared more like an indulgent diary than serious literature.

However, defenders of the Beats argue that this rawness was intentional—part of a broader rebellion against sterile academic norms and an effort to infuse literature with immediacy and truth. Their style may have broken from conventional aesthetics, but it resonated with readers precisely because it felt alive, vulnerable, and unfiltered.

Gender Critiques and the Marginalization of Women

Feminist scholars and writers have drawn attention to the deeply patriarchal dynamics within the Beat movement. While Beat literature promoted liberation in many forms—sexual, spiritual, artistic—it often did so within frameworks that excluded or objectified women. Female characters in works like *On the Road* frequently serve as muses, lovers, or spiritual waypoints rather than as complex individuals in their own right.

Additionally, the male-dominated culture of the Beat circle was often hostile or indifferent to women's voices. Diane di Prima, one of the few prominent female Beats, later recounted the ways in which her gender limited her participation in the movement's inner circles. Other women associated with the Beats, such as Carolyn Cassady and Joan Vollmer, were too often remembered for their relationships with male writers rather than for their own intellect and creativity.

In recent decades, feminist scholarship has recovered and celebrated the contributions of female Beat writers, highlighting works that had been overlooked or dismissed. This reassessment has led to a broader and more inclusive understanding of what the Beat movement was—and what it could have been.

Cultural Appropriation and the Exoticizing of the East

Another major criticism concerns the Beats' engagement with Eastern spirituality. Writers like Ginsberg and Kerouac turned to Buddhism, Hinduism, and other non-Western belief systems in their search for spiritual depth and alternatives to Judeo-Christian values. However, some scholars and cultural critics have argued that their interpretations were often superficial or selectively appropriated.

Rather than engaging deeply with the traditions they admired, the Beats are sometimes seen as having cherry-picked ideas that aligned with their own philosophies—especially concepts like detachment, transcendence, and non-duality—without fully grasping the cultural and religious contexts from which those ideas emerged.

This critique is part of a larger conversation about the dangers of Orientalism and spiritual commodification. While many Beats approached Eastern traditions with genuine reverence and curiosity, their outsider status and lack of sustained study often led to simplifications or distortions of complex philosophies.

Issues of Race and Privilege

Although the Beats frequently identified with the oppressed and marginalized, they were not immune to the blind spots of their time. Many of them romanticized African American culture, particularly jazz and blues, without sufficiently acknowledging the systemic racism from which those cultural forms emerged.

Moreover, the freedom the Beats celebrated—wandering the country, experimenting with drugs, rejecting societal norms—was in many ways a freedom afforded by their position as predominantly white, male, and educated. The risks they took were real, but the social consequences they faced were often less severe than those faced by people of color or working-class individuals engaging in similar behaviors.

These critiques have led to important conversations about the intersection of race, class, and countercultural expression—forcing a reassessment of who gets to rebel and what kinds of rebellion are celebrated in American literary history.

Enduring Importance Despite Criticism

Despite these valid critiques, the significance of the Beat Generation in reshaping American literature and culture is undeniable. They dismantled the boundaries of literary form, gave voice to experiences previously excluded from polite society, and inspired generations of writers, artists, and activists to explore their own margins. Their rawness, their urgency, and their willingness to live and write on the edge remain powerful reminders of literature's capacity for personal and collective transformation.

In grappling with the Beats' limitations, we deepen our understanding of their work and legacy. Criticism does not erase their achievements;

rather, it enriches our engagement with them and allows for a more nuanced appreciation of their role in literary dissent.

Conclusion: Legacy and Contemporary Resonance

The Beat Generation was never a unified literary school or ideology—it was a movement born of discontent, urgency, and a hunger for authenticity. In a postwar America marked by consumerism, conformity, and Cold War paranoia, the Beats reimagined what it meant to live and write freely. Their revolution was not political in the conventional sense, but literary, spiritual, and cultural—a rebellion of the soul against the machine.

Over the decades, the legacy of the Beat Generation has only grown more complex and more vital. In terms of literary innovation, their stylistic experiments opened up new possibilities for prose and poetry. Kerouac's spontaneous prose, Ginsberg's oral and breath-based verse, and Burroughs's radical cut-up narratives broke open the formal constraints of traditional literature and encouraged a generation of writers to prioritize voice, rhythm, and intuition over polish and precision. Their bold formalism laid the groundwork for everything from slam poetry and performance art to postmodern metafiction and autofiction.

Equally important was their challenge to social taboos. The Beats gave voice to homosexuality, drug use, mental illness, and spiritual seeking at a time when such subjects were censored, stigmatized, or silenced. They championed personal freedom, bodily autonomy, and inner exploration long before these became central to mainstream discourse. Through their literature and lives, they modeled ways of resisting cultural repression and exploring non-conformist identities.

Despite justified criticisms—ranging from gender marginalization and cultural appropriation to romanticized self-indulgence—the Beats remain essential figures in American literary history. Feminist and postcolonial revisions of the Beat canon have not erased their influence, but rather complicated and enriched our understanding of it. The reclamation of writers like Diane di Prima and Joyce Johnson has also shown that Beat literature was more diverse and layered than its original, male-dominated mythos suggested.

Today, echoes of the Beat spirit can be found in spoken-word poets, political activists, experimental writers, and artists of all genres. Their questions—about freedom, alienation, consciousness, and truth—are no less urgent now than they were in the 1950s. As contemporary writers continue to grapple with global crises, identity politics, and the role of the artist in society, the Beat Generation stands as both a model and a cautionary tale: a reminder of literature's power to disrupt, illuminate, and liberate.

In the end, the Beats did not just write differently—they lived differently. They demanded that literature be an act of presence, a rebellion of feeling, and a tool for awakening. And in doing so, they helped redefine what it means to be a writer in the modern world.

5

Postmodernism and Literary Experimentation

Deconstructing Meaning in a Fragmented World

Introduction: From Modern to Postmodern

The evolution from modernism to postmodernism marks one of the most significant shifts in the history of Western literature and thought. As the world moved beyond the early 20th century's promise of technological progress—and reeled from the twin devastations of two world wars—faith in linear narratives, stable identities, and absolute truths began to erode. By the mid-20th century, a new literary consciousness emerged: skeptical, playful, and radically experimental. This consciousness was postmodernism.

Modernism, the dominant literary and cultural movement of the early 1900s, had already broken from traditional narratives and forms. Writers such as T.S. Eliot, James Joyce, Virginia Woolf, and Franz Kafka had introduced fragmentation, stream of consciousness, and alienation into their texts as a way to reflect the disintegration of modern life. Yet, beneath the experimentation of modernism lay a tragic longing for coherence and order. Even when they depicted chaos, modernists often did so in search of redemption or deeper understanding—a desperate attempt to salvage meaning from the ruins.

Postmodernism, by contrast, questioned the very premise that such meaning could—or should—exist. Emerging fully after World War II, and gaining momentum in the 1960s and beyond, postmodern literature rejected the modernist impulse toward depth, authenticity, and unity. Instead, it embraced multiplicity, surface, fragmentation, intertextuality, and contradiction. In a world now shaped by television, advertising, nuclear deterrence, corporate bureaucracy, and late capitalism, postmodern writers saw traditional forms of narrative and knowledge as inadequate—or even complicit in systems of power.

As Jean-François Lyotard would famously argue, postmodernism is marked by an "incredulity toward metanarratives"—a skepticism toward grand, totalizing explanations of history, identity, or progress. Where modernism often sought to reassemble broken cultural fragments into new structures, postmodernism deconstructed those very structures, exposing their artificiality and ideological underpinnings.

In literature, this shift manifested in several defining characteristics. Postmodern texts blurred the lines between fiction and reality, author and character, high art and popular culture. They questioned authorship and originality, often through techniques like pastiche, parody, metafiction, and bricolage. They employed irony not merely as a rhetorical device but as a worldview. And they foregrounded the constructedness of language, suggesting that meaning itself is slippery, contingent, and endlessly deferred.

Postmodernism was not merely a reaction to modernist literature—it was a philosophical and aesthetic response to the world that produced it. The postwar rise of mass media, the Cold War's paranoid dualisms, the rise of global capitalism, the explosion of identity politics, and the emergence of post-structuralist theory all contributed to a cultural environment in which certainty gave way to doubt, and structure gave way to play.

Yet, despite—or perhaps because of—its ambivalence, postmodernism also opened new creative possibilities. It expanded literature's boundaries, challenging traditional hierarchies of genre, medium, and message. It made room for marginalized voices, hybrid forms, and radical reimaginings of identity, history, and reality itself.

As we move through this chapter, we will explore how postmodern literature transformed storytelling and literary technique. We will examine the works of major postmodern writers, including Thomas Pynchon, Don DeLillo, Kathy Acker, Angela Carter, and Salman Rushdie. We will also consider the broader cultural, philosophical, and political contexts that gave rise to this movement—and the critiques it continues to provoke.

Where modernism mourned the collapse of tradition, postmodernism danced in its ruins. It asked: What happens when the center no longer holds? What can literature be in a world of simulacra, spectacle, and uncertainty? And how do writers respond when meaning itself is suspect?

Defining Features of Postmodern Literature

Postmodern literature defies neat classification. It resists definitive labels, rejects singular interpretation, and often mocks the very idea of literary stability or authority. Nevertheless, several distinctive features recur across the works of postmodern writers, revealing a shared set of aesthetic strategies and thematic concerns. These features reflect not only a literary style but a broader philosophical orientation—one shaped by skepticism toward truth, grand narratives, and the stability of identity, language, and meaning.

Metafiction: Literature About Literature

One of the hallmark features of postmodern literature is metafiction—narratives that consciously reflect on their own fictionality. In contrast to traditional realist fiction, which seeks to immerse the reader in a believable world, metafiction draws attention to the constructedness of the story itself. It often breaks the fourth wall, calls out narrative conventions, and plays with the reader's expectations.

In John Fowles's *The French Lieutenant's Woman*, the narrator inserts himself into the story, commenting on the plot, offering alternative endings, and disrupting the illusion of narrative omniscience. Similarly, Italo Calvino's *If on a Winter's Night a Traveler* explicitly centers the reader as a character, creating a labyrinthine structure that satirizes the act of reading itself.

By turning fiction into a self-referential game, metafiction challenges the authority of the author, the coherence of narrative, and the boundaries between reality and representation. It embodies the postmodern claim that all texts are constructs—and that truth is mediated through language.

Pastiche: A Mosaic of Styles

Pastiche refers to the postmodern tendency to combine, imitate, or juxtapose multiple genres and styles within a single work, often without privileging any one mode of expression. This differs from parody in that it may be less critical or mocking; instead, pastiche often reflects a world in which originality is viewed as impossible, and all cultural production is derivative or recombinant.

A classic example is Thomas Pynchon's *Gravity's Rainbow*, which fuses science fiction, war narrative, detective fiction, slapstick comedy, and surrealist prose in a sprawling, chaotic tapestry. Pastiche allows postmodern writers to borrow from both high and low culture—combining Shakespeare with soap operas, or myth with pop music—blurring the distinctions between cultural hierarchies.

This aesthetic reflects a postmodern world saturated by media, where meaning is made through collage, remix, and reinterpretation rather than innovation or purity of form.

Irony and Parody: The Play of Meaning

Irony, in postmodern literature, is not simply a rhetorical flourish but a worldview—a deep-seated skepticism about sincerity, originality, and authority. Postmodern texts often adopt a playful, mocking tone, parodying literary forms, cultural values, or political ideologies.

Kathy Acker's *Blood and Guts in High School*, for example, parodies the Bildungsroman by inserting pornography, fragmented drawings, and surrealist digressions into the narrative of a young girl's "education." Don DeLillo's *White Noise* employs irony to satirize the absurdity of media culture and consumer anxiety, presenting existential dread in the language of advertising and infotainment.

Irony and parody in postmodern literature often serve to destabilize traditional meaning, inviting multiple interpretations and exposing the absurdity of dominant narratives. In this sense, postmodernism is deeply self-aware: it mocks the tropes it uses, even as it revels in them.

Temporal Dislocation: Nonlinear and Fragmented Time

Unlike the linear progression typical of classical and realist narratives, postmodern literature often fractures time, presenting events out of sequence, looping through memory, or omitting causality altogether. This temporal dislocation reflects a broader mistrust of narrative coherence and a belief that history and identity are not linear but layered, recursive, and unstable.

For instance, Kurt Vonnegut's *Slaughterhouse-Five* famously moves back and forth through time, mirroring the trauma of war and the fragmented nature of memory. Similarly, Jeanette Winterson's *The Passion* fluidly shifts between different times and locations, blurring historical periods and mythic resonance.

Temporal experimentation in postmodern literature emphasizes that stories—and time itself—are narrative constructs, shaped by the storyteller's perspective, memory, and agenda.

Unreliable Narrators: The Collapse of Certainty

Postmodernism frequently employs unreliable narrators—characters whose versions of reality are suspect, contradictory, or deliberately misleading. This technique reflects a central postmodern concern: the instability of knowledge and the constructed nature of truth.

In Vladimir Nabokov's *Pale Fire*, the novel is structured as a poem with a wildly digressive commentary by a potentially delusional editor, Charles Kinbote, whose narrative undermines the reader's trust. Similarly, Bret

Easton Ellis's *American Psycho* presents the murderous fantasies of a wealthy corporate sociopath, blurring the line between real and imagined violence.

Through unreliable narration, postmodern literature interrogates the very foundations of epistemology: How do we know what we know? Whose voice do we trust? And what happens when narrative coherence gives way to ambiguity?

Intertextuality: Literature as a Web of Texts

Postmodern literature is deeply intertextual—constantly referencing, quoting, and echoing other texts, genres, and media. This concept, introduced by theorists such as Julia Kristeva and Roland Barthes, suggests that all texts exist in relation to others. Meaning, therefore, is never original but always relational and derivative.

Salman Rushdie's *The Satanic Verses*, for example, weaves together Islamic myth, Western literature, Bollywood films, and postcolonial history. Angela Carter's *The Bloody Chamber* retells classic fairy tales through a feminist lens, rewriting the familiar in unfamiliar ways.

Intertextuality not only celebrates cultural hybridity but also disrupts the idea of textual authority. Postmodernism embraces the echo, the remix, the citation—making literature a space of endless dialogue and deconstruction.

Key Figures and Major Works

While postmodernism resists the notion of a canon or hierarchy, certain writers have come to represent the movement's most influential and enduring voices. These authors not only exemplify the stylistic innovations of postmodern literature—metafiction, irony, fragmentation, intertextuality—but also explore the psychological, cultural, and political uncertainties of the late 20th century. Among these, Thomas Pynchon, Kurt Vonnegut, and Don DeLillo stand out for their visionary works that probe the very nature of reality, truth, and human agency in a world overwhelmed by technology, information, and spectacle.

Thomas Pynchon (b. 1937)

The High Priest of Postmodern Complexity

Thomas Pynchon is often regarded as the quintessential postmodern novelist—an author whose intricate, labyrinthine works epitomize the genre's intellectual ambition and aesthetic playfulness. Known for his reclusiveness and densely allusive prose, Pynchon's writing blends historical fiction, scientific theory, philosophy, popular culture, and conspiracy.

Gravity's Rainbow (1973)

Widely considered Pynchon's magnum opus, *Gravity's Rainbow* is a sprawling, 760-page novel that defies conventional narrative form. Set during the final months of World War II, the novel orbits around the V-2 rocket program and a mysterious character named Tyrone Slothrop, whose sexual experiences bizarrely predict rocket strikes.

The novel refuses to adhere to a single storyline, instead weaving together hundreds of characters, tangential digressions, songs, and historical documents. Themes of paranoia, entropy, colonial violence, and technological determinism permeate the text. Pynchon's style—at once erudite and absurdist—forces readers to question the nature of meaning itself.

As a postmodern artifact, *Gravity's Rainbow* embodies:

- Metafiction (with direct narrative intrusions),
- Pastiche (borrowing from pulp fiction, cartoons, science manuals),
- Temporal dislocation (non-linear chronology), and
- Epistemological doubt (truth is destabilized at every turn).

Pynchon's other key works, such as *The Crying of Lot 49* and *Against the Day*, continue these explorations, offering critiques of late capitalism, information overload, and political power.

Kurt Vonnegut (1922–2007)

Satirist of Science, War, and Human Folly

Kurt Vonnegut occupies a unique position in postmodern literature as a writer who employed accessible language and dark humor to expose the contradictions and absurdities of modern existence. Though often associated with science fiction, Vonnegut's works transcend genre through philosophical depth and formal innovation.

Slaughterhouse-Five (1969)

This semi-autobiographical novel centers on Billy Pilgrim, a World War II veteran who becomes "unstuck in time," experiencing moments of his life out of sequence. The novel's nonlinear structure mirrors the fractured psyche of a man grappling with trauma, particularly the firebombing of Dresden, which Vonnegut himself survived.

The alien Tralfamadorians, who view all moments as eternally present, symbolize postmodern relativism and fatalism. The recurring phrase "So it goes" after each death punctuates the novel with a resigned acknowledgment of life's randomness and inevitable end.

Vonnegut's use of:

- Irony and parody,
- Temporal fragmentation, and
- self-referentiality (Vonnegut appears as a character in the book)

positions *Slaughterhouse-Five* as a masterful postmodern work. Despite its humor and simplicity, the novel offers a profound critique of war, mechanized violence, and the illusion of progress.

In other works like *Breakfast of Champions* and *Cat's Cradle*, Vonnegut expands on themes of free will, meaninglessness, and human delusion, often using metafictional strategies and cartoonish illustrations to undercut narrative authority.

Don DeLillo (b. 1936)

Chronicler of Postmodern Anxiety and Hyperreality

Don DeLillo's fiction explores the psychological and sociopolitical effects of mass media, consumerism, and technology on the individual and society. His works are often haunted by death, catastrophe, and the simulation of reality—a direct reflection of postmodern concerns about authenticity, identity, and truth.

White Noise (1985)

Set in a fictional American college town, the novel follows Jack Gladney, a professor of "Hitler Studies," and his family as they navigate an increasingly surreal and mediated world. When a mysterious chemical spill—referred to as "the Airborne Toxic Event"—disrupts their lives, the novel shifts into a meditation on mortality, fear, and simulation.

DeLillo's satirical depiction of academic jargon, television commercials, supermarket scenes, and pharmaceutical culture illustrates a world where hyperreality (a term drawn from theorist Jean Baudrillard) replaces genuine experience. The novel's postmodern features include:

- Unreliable narration,
- Media saturation,
- Intertextual cultural critique, and
- parody of suburban life and academia.

Libra (1988)

This fictionalized account of Lee Harvey Oswald's life and the JFK assassination explores the construction of history, conspiracy, and narrative multiplicity. By presenting multiple versions of events and perspectives, DeLillo undermines any single "truth," echoing postmodern skepticism about historical objectivity.

In both novels, DeLillo masterfully captures the sense of dislocation, uncertainty, and anxiety that defines the postmodern condition. His prose—at once coolly detached and hauntingly lyrical—exposes the alienation of individuals in a world ruled by data, signs, and simulations.

Thematic Concerns

Postmodern literature is not merely a stylistic evolution of modernism—it represents a deep philosophical and cultural response to a world transformed by technological advancement, ideological collapse, mass media, and global capitalism. At the heart of postmodern fiction lies a series of interrelated themes that question long-held assumptions about reality, identity, authorship, and originality. These thematic concerns reflect a broader cultural condition of disorientation, ambivalence, and critical interrogation of systems once considered stable.

Reality vs. Representation

A defining anxiety of postmodernism is the blurring of boundaries between the real and its representations. Postmodern literature frequently suggests that what we understand as "reality" is not directly accessible, but mediated—constructed by language, cultural codes, and technologies of representation.

In novels like *White Noise* by Don DeLillo, the characters experience the world through screens, advertisements, and academic theories. The novel questions whether individuals can still experience anything *directly* or if all perception is filtered through a system of signs. This theme is central to the postmodern understanding of simulacra, where representations no longer refer to any external reality but instead become self-referential.

This idea destabilizes the authority of narrative, suggesting that all storytelling is ideological—reflecting not the world as it is, but as it is mediated and interpreted.

Hyperreality: Simulation and Substitution

French theorist Jean Baudrillard's concept of **hyperreality**—the condition in which simulations of reality become more real than reality itself—is a cornerstone of postmodern theory and literature. Hyperreality describes a cultural environment in which representations, media, and signs precede and replace the real, leading to a collapse of the distinction between fact and fiction.

This is vividly portrayed in Thomas Pynchon's *The Crying of Lot 49*, where protagonist Oedipa Maas becomes entangled in a possibly imaginary postal conspiracy. The reader, like the protagonist, is unable to determine whether the system she uncovers is real, invented, or a symptom of paranoia.

In such narratives, reality is unstable, suspect, and overwritten by narrative codes. The media-saturated world of postmodern literature suggests that our experiences are shaped by simulations—whether through advertising, entertainment, or surveillance—rather than lived, physical realities.

Fragmentation of Identity

Whereas modernism often depicted the fractured self as a condition to be mourned or transcended, postmodernism embraces the fragmentation of identity as inevitable, even liberating. The postmodern subject is not a unified, autonomous individual but a collage of social roles, discourses, and desires shaped by cultural and technological systems.

In Kathy Acker's *Blood and Guts in High School*, the protagonist's identity is fragmented across various textual forms—drawings, letters, pornographic imagery—highlighting how gender, sexuality, and power shape selfhood. Likewise, in Salman Rushdie's *Midnight's Children*, the protagonist Saleem Sinai's identity is fused with national, historical, and mythic narratives, suggesting that the self is always culturally constructed and unstable.

This thematic concern reflects post-structuralist theories of subjectivity, particularly those of Jacques Lacan and Michel Foucault, who argued that identity is shaped by language and power relations rather than innate essence.

Surveillance and Control

Postmodern literature frequently expresses a paranoid awareness of surveillance, manipulation, and control, both by governments and by less visible systems—corporations, media, bureaucracies, or algorithms. This theme reflects postmodern distrust of authority and skepticism toward the apparent neutrality of information systems.

In Pynchon's *Gravity's Rainbow*, characters are constantly watched, categorized, and analyzed, often by impersonal technological forces that blur the boundary between state and corporate control. Similarly, in DeLillo's *Libra*, the life of Lee Harvey Oswald is depicted as a composite of surveillance, ideological scripting, and historical manipulation—questioning the possibility of autonomous agency.

This theme also resonates with Foucault's theory of panopticism, where internalized surveillance becomes a tool of discipline. Postmodern texts interrogate how narratives, institutions, and technologies function as invisible mechanisms of power, eroding privacy and individuality.

Cultural Exhaustion and the Death of Originality

Postmodern writers often operate under the assumption that everything has already been said or done—that originality is a myth and all that remains is to recombine, recycle, and recontextualize existing forms. This condition of cultural exhaustion leads to the aesthetic strategy of pastiche: the borrowing and blending of historical styles, literary genres, and cultural references.

For example, in *The Satanic Verses*, Salman Rushdie draws on Islamic mythology, magical realism, Western pop culture, and political allegory to construct a postcolonial, postmodern narrative. Yet the text is also conscious of its own borrowings and contradictions—challenging the idea of a pure origin or singular voice.

This sense of exhaustion does not necessarily signal despair; rather, it often results in playful experimentation, as seen in metafictional novels like *If on a Winter's Night a Traveler* by Italo Calvino, where narrative construction becomes a source of creative freedom.

Postmodernism thus redefines authorship as curation, interpretation, and disruption—not creation from nothing.

Narrative Techniques and Innovations

Postmodern literature is as much defined by its *how* as its *what*. While its themes interrogate identity, reality, and authority, its form actively enacts those concerns. Postmodern writers rejected traditional narrative conventions—not simply to be provocative, but to more accurately represent a world they saw as fragmented, paradoxical, and oversaturated with meaning.

These innovations reflect a radical rethinking of what narrative is and how it functions. Whether through collage, metafiction, or structural disruption, postmodern literature draws attention to its own artificiality, refusing to allow the reader a passive or comfortable reading experience.

Collage and Montage: Narrative as Patchwork

Borrowing from visual arts and cinema, many postmodern texts employ collage and montage to assemble stories from disparate fragments—letters, news articles, advertisements, scientific formulas, song lyrics, historical records, or even other literary texts. This patchwork approach mirrors a world in which unified perspectives are no longer tenable, and where media bombardment fragments individual consciousness.

In *Gravity's Rainbow*, Thomas Pynchon constructs his narrative like a collage of discourses: military reports, surreal dream sequences, musical interludes, and mythological pastiche all coexist in a disorienting textual landscape. Similarly, in Kathy Acker's *Empire of the Senseless*, narrative fragments are layered like graffiti, mixing sex, violence, autobiography, and political critique with no clear hierarchy.

By juxtaposing voices, genres, and styles, collage and montage expose the constructedness of narrative and the multiplicity of meanings possible within any given text. These techniques resist closure, instead producing an open-ended textual experience where meaning is not found but forged in the reader's interaction with the fragments.

Paranoia as Structure: The Feeling of Being Watched

Postmodern narratives often feature protagonists who experience intense paranoia—a feeling that unseen forces are watching, manipulating, or controlling them. This is not merely a psychological motif; it becomes a structural metaphor for the postmodern condition itself, where meaning is obscured, systems are vast and unknowable, and every pattern may be a trap.

In Don DeLillo's *Libra*, the narrative of Lee Harvey Oswald is told through layers of government plots, rogue intelligence agents, and historical fabrications—suggesting that the truth about the JFK assassination may be unknowable, lost in a web of competing realities. Pynchon's *The Crying of Lot 49* similarly presents a protagonist who cannot discern whether she has uncovered a vast conspiracy or is descending into madness.

Paranoia in postmodern literature often mirrors the reader's own confusion, as texts deny linear plot development or definitive resolution. This sense of entrapment within opaque systems of meaning is both a theme and a narrative experience.

Authorial Disappearance: The Death of the Author

One of the most radical innovations in postmodern literature is the displacement—or erasure—of the author's authority. Influenced by Roland Barthes's essay *The Death of the Author* (1967), postmodern writers challenge the idea that a text has a single, stable meaning dictated by its creator.

This "death" of the author manifests in various ways:

- **Narrative instability:** Multiple, conflicting voices with no central guiding perspective.
- **Metafiction:** Stories that expose their own fabrication, thereby undermining any illusion of authorial control.
- **Intertextuality:** Texts that are composed of other texts, leaving the author's "originality" in question.

In Italo Calvino's *If on a Winter's Night a Traveler*, the author becomes a trickster figure, playing with reader expectations and refusing to deliver a coherent narrative. In much of Borges's fiction, stories are structured like essays or fake historical documents, with invented sources and authors—suggesting that all storytelling is already a form of reinterpretation.

Postmodernism thus positions the reader—not the author—as the central producer of meaning, embracing ambiguity and multiplicity over fixed interpretation.

Disruption of Genre: Breaking Down Boundaries

Another key narrative innovation in postmodern literature is the dissolution of genre distinctions. Rather than adhering to the formal expectations of realism, autobiography, science fiction, or historical fiction, postmodern texts blend these genres to challenge the idea that any form of storytelling is ideologically neutral or pure.

In *Slaughterhouse-Five*, Kurt Vonnegut fuses historical memoir, science fiction, and absurdist comedy to explore trauma and the unreliability of memory. Salman Rushdie's *Midnight's Children* merges magical realism, political satire, myth, and postcolonial allegory, creating a hybrid form that resists categorization.

This genre-blending reflects the postmodern suspicion of boundaries—whether those of nation, identity, or discourse. It also opens space for marginalized voices and non-Western narrative traditions, breaking the hegemony of the realist novel and expanding the possibilities of literary expression.

Other Significant Voices

While the postmodern literary canon is often dominated by figures like Pynchon, DeLillo, and Vonnegut, a broader and more inclusive understanding of the movement must also consider other significant voices. These authors demonstrate how postmodern techniques—such as metafiction, pastiche, irony, and fragmentation—have been employed across genres, cultures, and political contexts to challenge dominant narratives and interrogate the relationship between language, identity, and power.

Some of these writers work firmly within the postmodern aesthetic, while others intersect with it from more peripheral or critical positions. Together, they reveal the diversity and global reach of postmodern literary experimentation.

John Barth: Metafiction and the Limits of Storytelling

John Barth is one of the most influential American practitioners of metafiction, a form that explicitly foregrounds the artifice of storytelling. His works are highly self-referential, philosophical, and intertextual, often commenting on the exhaustion of narrative forms and the impossibility of originality in the postmodern age.

Lost in the Funhouse (1968)

This groundbreaking collection of short stories exemplifies Barth's concept of the "literature of exhaustion." In stories such as the titular *"Lost in the Funhouse"*, Barth dramatizes the collapse of traditional narrative by embedding commentary about fiction within the fiction itself. The stories question authorship, reader engagement, and the stability of form—sometimes even incorporating typographic play and alternative textual structures.

Barth's work is central to postmodernism's turn toward reflexivity and narrative play. He offers a sustained meditation on storytelling in a world where meaning is fragmented and endlessly deferred.

Paul Auster: Identity, Language, and Urban Labyrinths

Paul Auster's fiction combines elements of detective fiction, existential philosophy, and poststructuralist thought. His writing often explores the instability of language and identity, placing his characters in urban landscapes where meaning is elusive and subjectivity is fractured.

The New York Trilogy (1985–1986)

This trio of metafictional detective novels—*City of Glass*, *Ghosts*, and *The Locked Room*—dismantles the conventions of the noir genre while probing questions of authorship, surveillance, and the limits of language. In *City of Glass*, for example, the protagonist is a writer named Daniel Quinn who receives a mysterious phone call asking for a detective named Paul Auster—a confusion that spirals into an existential investigation of identity and authorship.

Auster's minimalist prose and recursive plots echo postmodern concerns about the collapse of narrative coherence and the unreliability of signifiers. His work invites readers to question the relationship between words, self, and reality.

Toni Morrison: Memory, History, and Narrative Reconstruction

Though Toni Morrison is not typically categorized as a postmodern writer, her narrative techniques—particularly her use of nonlinear storytelling, polyphony, and intertextuality—align her with many postmodern strategies. Morrison uses these tools not to indulge in abstraction, but to reclaim and reconfigure African American histories and subjectivities that have been silenced or distorted by dominant cultural narratives.

Beloved (1987)

This Pulitzer Prize-winning novel is structured around memory and trauma, using fragmented chronology and shifting perspectives to narrate the legacy of slavery. The novel disrupts linear time, blurs the boundary between the living and the dead, and challenges the reader to reconstruct meaning from a nontraditional narrative structure.

Morrison's work aligns with postmodern historiographic metafiction, yet it does so from a politically charged, ethically grounded perspective, interrogating the gaps and silences in American history. Her fusion of postmodern form with historical urgency demonstrates the adaptability of literary experimentation to serve culturally specific goals.

Ishmael Reed: Satire, Myth, and Cultural Reclamation

Ishmael Reed is a pioneering African American author whose fiction blends satire, magical realism, historical revisionism, and pastiche to critique Western cultural hegemony and celebrate African diasporic traditions.

Mumbo Jumbo (1972)

This genre-defying novel tells the story of an epidemic called "Jes Grew"—a metaphor for Black cultural expression—spreading through 1920s America. The novel is an irreverent, politically charged collage of newspaper clippings, mythic references, detective tropes, and Afrofuturist visions. Reed rewrites history through a postmodern lens, exposing how dominant narratives suppress alternative worldviews.

Mumbo Jumbo exemplifies cultural pastiche as resistance, combining postmodern technique with Afrocentric historiography. Reed's fusion of forms challenges both the Western literary canon and the assumption that postmodernism is a Euro-American phenomenon.

Critiques of Postmodernism

Despite its widespread influence across literature, theory, architecture, art, and cultural studies, postmodernism has not escaped criticism. Detractors from across the political and intellectual spectrum have expressed concerns about its ethical implications, political disengagement, and alienating aesthetics. While some see postmodernism as an incisive reflection of contemporary complexity, others view it as a symptom of cultural decline—a retreat from meaning, truth, and moral responsibility.

This section examines the major critiques leveled against postmodern literature and the theoretical movement more broadly, as well as responses from those who defend its methods and insights.

Relativism and Nihilism: The Collapse of Meaning

One of the most persistent critiques of postmodernism is that its **rejection of universal truths** leads to **epistemological relativism** and, ultimately, **nihilism**. By refusing to affirm any single narrative, moral framework, or truth claim, postmodernism is accused of fostering a worldview where all positions are equally valid—or equally meaningless.

This philosophical anything-goes attitude is seen by critics as dangerous, particularly in times of social or political crisis. Without shared values or truth standards, the worry is that postmodernism may paralyze moral judgment and lead to ethical apathy. Thinkers such as Jürgen Habermas have critiqued postmodern thought for what he calls "performative contradiction"—questioning truth claims while continuing to rely on them.

In literature, this can manifest as ironic detachment, where authors highlight absurdity without offering solutions or even expressing sincere emotional investment. Detractors argue that such approaches may promote cynicism rather than critique, reducing serious issues to games of language and form.

Counterpoint: Defenders of postmodernism argue that it does not erase truth but exposes its constructed and contingent nature. Rather than retreating into nihilism, postmodernism demands greater critical awareness of the ways truth and morality are shaped by power, ideology, and language.

Elitism and Obscurity: The Problem of Accessibility

Another frequent critique of postmodern literature is its **intellectual elitism**. With its dense intertextuality, fragmented structures, metafictional devices, and theoretical jargon, much postmodern writing can be **inaccessible** to general readers. Critics argue that instead of democratizing literature, postmodernism often creates texts that cater to academic or avant-garde audiences, reinforcing cultural hierarchies.

Thomas Pynchon's *Gravity's Rainbow* or John Barth's *Giles Goat-Boy*, for example, are lauded for their complexity but often criticized for their impenetrability. The expectation that readers recognize obscure references—from physics and mythology to 18th-century satire and poststructuralist theory—can make engagement with such texts feel exclusionary.

This critique is particularly resonant in the context of mass media and popular culture, where literature must compete with more accessible forms of storytelling. Some argue that postmodern literature's emphasis on form over content leads to an aesthetic of excess, privileging cleverness over clarity or emotional resonance.

Counterpoint: Proponents of postmodern literature argue that these complexities reflect a media-saturated, fragmented reality that cannot be captured by traditional linear narratives. They see the demand for active, critical reading not as elitist but as empowering—encouraging readers to interrogate assumptions rather than passively absorb meaning.

Political Inaction and Irony Fatigue

Postmodernism's ironic stance and rejection of grand narratives have led some critics to accuse it of political quietism—a disengagement from real-world struggles in favor of aesthetic or philosophical play. In an era of climate crisis, racial injustice, and rising authoritarianism, the concern is that postmodernism lacks the moral clarity and activist energy needed to confront such challenges.

For example, Fredric Jameson, a Marxist theorist, has argued that postmodernism is the "cultural logic of late capitalism"—a form of commodified expression that offers stylized simulations of resistance while leaving dominant power structures untouched. Under this view, postmodern literature is not subversive but complicit, mirroring the surface-level spectacle of consumer society rather than challenging it.

Moreover, the pervasive use of irony in postmodern texts—once a tool for critique—has been accused of devolving into irony fatigue, where genuine political and emotional expression becomes difficult or suspect. This has led some scholars and writers to call for a return to sincerity, engagement, and affect, as seen in movements like post-postmodernism or New Sincerity.

Counterpoint: Others argue that postmodernism's irony is not apolitical but deeply strategic—designed to unmask ideological manipulation and reveal the contradictions of political discourse. Authors like Ishmael Reed or Don DeLillo use irony and parody not to avoid political engagement but to critique the spectacle of power, media, and historical amnesia.

Beyond the Critique: Postmodernism as Cultural Mirror

While these critiques raise valid concerns, many scholars assert that postmodernism is less a cause of cultural disorientation than a mirror of it. In an age shaped by globalization, media saturation, surveillance capitalism, and epistemic instability, postmodernism reflects the conditions of contemporary life. Its fragmentation, intertextuality, and ironic tone are responses to a world already fragmented, recycled, and ironic.

In this sense, postmodernism can be read as a diagnostic tool rather than a moral or political solution. It provides frameworks for understanding how meaning is produced and manipulated, how identity is constructed, and how power is exercised through language and representation.

Postmodernism and the American Dream

One of the central cultural narratives interrogated by postmodern literature is the American Dream—the enduring ideal that hard work, moral virtue, and individual initiative lead to success, prosperity, and personal fulfillment. Rooted in Enlightenment rationality and postwar optimism, this mythos has long served as a foundational pillar of American identity. However, postmodern writers systematically deconstruct these assumptions, portraying a nation where such ideals are increasingly unattainable, illusory, or absurd.

In postmodern fiction, the American Dream is not merely challenged—it is rendered hollow, revealed as a cultural construct shaped by media, capitalism, and systemic inequity. The narratives of self-made success and national greatness dissolve into a kaleidoscope of fragmented identities, corporate manipulation, and existential dread. Through irony, satire, and narrative disruption, postmodern authors present a deeply skeptical—and often darkly humorous—portrait of American life in the late 20th century.

Pynchon: Systems of Control and the Disintegration of Agency

In the works of Thomas Pynchon, characters are often caught in the webs of unfathomable systems—military-industrial complexes, intelligence networks, corporate conglomerates, or metaphysical conspiracies. In novels like *Gravity's Rainbow* and *The Crying of Lot 49*, the individual is no longer the architect of their destiny, but a pawn in games they cannot understand.

This loss of personal agency stands in stark contrast to the traditional American Dream's faith in self-determination and upward mobility. Pynchon's America is a landscape of entropy, paranoia, and symbolic overload, where progress is an illusion and freedom a carefully engineered spectacle. In this world, dreams are subverted not by personal failure, but by the very structure of society.

Vonnegut: Bureaucratic Absurdity and Cosmic Indifference

Kurt Vonnegut offers a more satirical but equally devastating critique of American ideals. In *Slaughterhouse-Five*, protagonist Billy Pilgrim becomes "unstuck in time," reliving the firebombing of Dresden and his alien abduction by the Tralfamadorians. Vonnegut juxtaposes cosmic absurdity with bureaucratic dysfunction, portraying a universe—and a nation—governed by systems that defy logic and compassion.

Vonnegut's protagonists are often helpless and disillusioned, rendered passive by a world that mocks the American Dream's promises of progress and purpose. His recurring phrase, "*So it goes,*" signals a resigned acknowledgment of life's randomness and tragedy—a sharp departure from the idealism traditionally associated with American success narratives.

DeLillo: Simulacra, Spectacle, and Consumer Anxiety

In the novels of Don DeLillo, the American Dream is subsumed by media simulation, consumerism, and technological abstraction. In *White Noise*, for example, the fear of death is mediated through pharmaceutical advertisements, shopping malls, and television broadcasts. The novel's central "airborne toxic event" is less important than how it is reported, consumed, and commodified.

DeLillo presents a version of America in which appearance replaces substance—where the simulation of meaning overtakes meaning itself. This reflects Jean Baudrillard's concept of *hyperreality*, in which reality is no longer distinguishable from its representation. The American Dream, in DeLillo's vision, has been reduced to a corporate slogan, a marketing device severed from the lived realities of inequality, anxiety, and alienation.

Postmodern Irony and the Collapse of Idealism

Across postmodern literature, there is a shared suspicion toward grand narratives—including the myth of American exceptionalism. The postmodern critique does not necessarily replace the American Dream with a dystopian alternative; rather, it exposes the gaps between ideology and lived experience. It asks: Who benefits from this dream? Whose stories are excluded? What forces shape and distort our aspirations?

Through ironic detachment, narrative fragmentation, and metafictional self-awareness, postmodern writers dismantle the traditional tropes of meritocracy, frontier heroism, and national virtue. Their America is not a land of opportunity, but a textual and cultural labyrinth, where meaning is fluid and truth is suspect.

Conclusion: Disillusionment and Cultural Reckoning

In questioning the American Dream, postmodern literature performs a vital cultural function—it reflects a growing disillusionment with national myths, especially in the wake of Vietnam, Watergate, consumerism, and the rise of the surveillance state. The resulting literature is not merely pessimistic; it is analytical, resistant, and radically self-aware.

By holding a mirror to late 20th-century American society, postmodernism challenges readers to confront the contradictions at the heart of the nation's identity. It reveals that behind the promises of prosperity and liberty lies a far more complex—and often troubling—reality shaped by control, illusion, and fragmentation.

Conclusion: Deconstruction as Invention

Postmodernism did not merely continue the literary revolution initiated by modernism; it radically redefined the very foundations of storytelling. Where modernism sought to reconstruct meaning from the ruins of war, disillusionment, and fractured subjectivity, postmodernism embraced the impossibility of narrative coherence. It did not mourn the loss of certainty but celebrated the plurality, instability, and playfulness that emerged in its wake.

By dismantling the assumptions of realism, linearity, and authorial authority, postmodernism shattered the mirror that literature once held up to the world. In its place, it offered funhouse reflections, simulacra, and intertextual echoes—forms that foregrounded the artificiality of representation and the constructed nature of knowledge. Parody, pastiche, irony, metafiction, and fragmentation became tools not of evasion, but of exploration—means to expose the limitations of traditional forms and to imagine new possibilities for literary expression.

Rather than asserting a singular truth, postmodern literature multiplied perspectives, inviting the reader to question, interpret, and participate in the creation of meaning. It insisted that stories are never neutral containers of truth but are shaped by language, ideology, and historical context. Thus, storytelling became not a transparent window into reality, but a process of invention, a mode of resistance, and a reflection of post-industrial, media-saturated, and politically ambiguous modern life.

If modernism was a lament for the trauma of lost meaning, then postmodernism represents the freedom discovered in that loss. It resists closure, embraces contradiction, and insists on ambiguity—not out of nihilism, but from a conviction that literature must respond to the complexity, absurdity, and fragmentation of the contemporary world.

In doing so, postmodernism reshaped the reader's role. No longer a passive recipient of a coherent narrative, the reader is repositioned as a co-creator, called upon to navigate intertextual webs, decode cultural signs, and confront the uncertainties embedded in every word. The postmodern text is not a stable monument but an event of interpretation, constantly shifting according to context, perspective, and performance.

Ultimately, postmodernism is both critique and creativity—a literature of dismantling that simultaneously constructs new ways of thinking about fiction, identity, and truth. In asking whether stories are even possible, it affirms that stories, however fragmented, are essential tools for making sense of an incoherent world. And in that tension between breakdown and invention lies the enduring power of the postmodern imagination.

6

African American Literature after the Harlem Renaissance

Continuing the Struggle, Expanding the Voice

Introduction: Beyond the Renaissance

The Harlem Renaissance of the 1920s stands as a landmark in African American literary and cultural history—a period in which Black writers, artists, and intellectuals boldly asserted their voices in defiance of racist exclusion and cultural marginalization. Figures like Langston Hughes, Zora Neale Hurston, Claude McKay, and Countee Cullen laid the groundwork for a vibrant, autonomous Black literary tradition rooted in racial pride, folk heritage, and aesthetic innovation. Yet, the literary journey of African Americans did not culminate with this cultural flourishing; it merely set the stage for a far more complex and urgent literary evolution.

In the decades that followed—particularly from the 1940s through the post–Civil Rights era—African American literature expanded its thematic and stylistic range. The triumphs of the Harlem Renaissance gave way to new literary imperatives shaped by the realities of Jim Crow segregation, urban displacement, police brutality, economic disenfranchisement, and political resistance. Writers during this period moved beyond the Romantic idealism and celebratory tone of their Harlem predecessors, embracing a literature that was more confrontational, introspective, and diverse in its representation of Black life in America.

This next phase of African American literature was deeply intertwined with sociopolitical movements—from the fight for civil rights and the rise of Black Power to the feminist and postcolonial awakenings of the 1970s and 1980s. Authors no longer wrote only to affirm Black humanity but to interrogate the structures that threatened it, to expose internal and external fractures within Black identity, and to assert a multiplicity of experiences shaped by gender, class, sexuality, and geography.

Moreover, this era witnessed formal experimentation and a rich diversification of genres. Writers turned to autobiography, poetry, drama, speculative fiction, and historical novels as vehicles for representing Black existence in all its contradictions. Some, like James Baldwin and Ralph Ellison, grappled with alienation, cultural duality, and the burdens of representation in a white-dominated literary world. Others, such as Toni Morrison, Alice Walker, Amiri Baraka, and Maya Angelou, reclaimed ancestral narratives, elevated Black vernacular traditions, and foregrounded the role of Black women's voices in shaping both literature and resistance.

Crucially, post-Renaissance African American literature became a powerful force within American letters more broadly. It challenged the racial, aesthetic, and canonical boundaries of the U.S. literary tradition, demanding new critical frameworks and affirming literature's role as a site of cultural survival, historical memory, and visionary justice.

Thus, the period after the Harlem Renaissance is not merely a continuation—it is an expansion and deepening of the African American literary project. It reflects a community's enduring struggle for liberation and dignity, but also its capacity for linguistic innovation, spiritual resilience, and narrative brilliance in the face of continued oppression. As this chapter will explore, the Black writers of the mid- to late-20th century were not only heirs to the Renaissance; they were architects of a new, expansive American literature.

Historical and Cultural Context

The evolution of African American literature in the decades following the Harlem Renaissance cannot be fully understood without reference to the historical, social, and political forces that shaped Black life in 20th-century America. From continued geographic shifts to transformative political movements, the literary output of this era emerged not in isolation, but as a response to lived realities, collective struggles, and aspirations for justice and self-determination. This section outlines five key historical forces that influenced African American literature after the Harlem Renaissance.

The Great Migration: Urbanization and New Black Realities

The Great Migration, which began in the early 20th century and continued well into the 1970s, saw millions of African Americans leave the oppressive conditions of the rural South in search of better opportunities in Northern and Western cities. This demographic shift had a profound impact on Black literary production. As African Americans entered increasingly urban environments like Chicago, Detroit, Los Angeles, and New York, writers began to focus on urban alienation, industrial labor, gang violence, housing discrimination, and the psychological impact of dislocation.

Works such as Richard Wright's *Native Son* (1940) or Gwendolyn Brooks' poetry reflect this urban transformation—capturing both the hope and the harshness of Black life in America's growing metropolises. The migration narrative itself became a literary motif, symbolizing both physical movement and a complex journey toward cultural and personal identity.

Jim Crow Laws and the Legacy of Segregation

Although the Harlem Renaissance offered a sense of artistic liberation, most African Americans remained subject to racial segregation, systemic violence, and second-class citizenship under Jim Crow laws. Writers of the mid-20th century responded to this reality with unflinching critiques of institutionalized racism and its psychological toll.

James Baldwin, for instance, used both fiction and essays to expose the emotional trauma and moral contradictions of a society that preached equality while practicing exclusion. Similarly, Lorraine Hansberry's *A Raisin in the Sun* (1959) dramatized the persistent economic and social barriers faced by Black families, especially in housing. The literature of this period often emphasized the endurance and dignity of Black communities while highlighting the urgent need for social transformation.

The Civil Rights Movement: Literature as Protest and Witness

The rise of the Civil Rights Movement in the 1950s and 1960s inspired a powerful wave of socially conscious and politically engaged literature. Writers assumed the roles of witnesses, chroniclers, and agitators, using literature to document racial injustice and galvanize resistance.

Poets such as Margaret Walker, Robert Hayden, and Maya Angelou wove personal and historical narratives into works that spoke to both the pain and the pride of Black America. The movement's influence extended into novels, essays, and plays that explored not only collective struggle but also the psychic and existential dimensions of being Black in a racially divided nation. Literature became both a tool of advocacy and a form of moral testimony, amplifying the voices of those long silenced.

Black Power and the Black Arts Movement: Radical Aesthetics and Identity

Emerging in the late 1960s as a cultural counterpart to the Black Power movement, the Black Arts Movement (BAM) called for a redefinition of Black aesthetics. Spearheaded by figures like Amiri Baraka, Nikki Giovanni, and Sonia Sanchez, BAM encouraged African American writers to craft works that were politically radical, culturally specific, and unapologetically Black.

Rejecting assimilationist ideals, Black Arts literature embraced Afrocentrism, street vernacular, oral traditions, and revolutionary themes. The emphasis was on producing art that served the community, challenged white literary norms, and affirmed Black identity in all its complexity. This period also witnessed the rise of performance poetry, community theater, and independent Black publishing houses—ushering in a more grassroots, activist-oriented literary culture.

Post-Civil Rights America: Memory, Intersectionality, and the Internal Landscape

By the 1970s and 1980s, African American literature began to reflect the ambiguous aftermath of legal desegregation and the unfinished business of racial justice. While legislative victories had been achieved, economic inequality, police violence, and cultural marginalization persisted. Writers of this period turned inward, exploring psychological fragmentation, intergenerational trauma, cultural memory, and the intersection of race with gender, class, and sexuality.

This introspective turn is exemplified in the works of Toni Morrison, Alice Walker, and Gloria Naylor, who centered Black women's experiences and questioned the patriarchal assumptions of earlier movements. The rise of intersectionality—a term later theorized by Kimberlé Crenshaw—shaped literary narratives that examined how overlapping identities shaped access to power, representation, and dignity.

African American literature in the post-Civil Rights era became increasingly global, experimental, and genre-defying, reflecting both personal introspection and collective struggle. It affirmed that the Black literary voice was not monolithic, but diverse, evolving, and profoundly engaged with the moral complexities of modern life.

Dominant Themes

The development of African American literature in the post-Harlem Renaissance era is marked not only by aesthetic experimentation and a widening of voices, but by a deep engagement with recurring themes that reflect the lived realities of Black Americans. These themes—rooted in both historical experience and evolving cultural consciousness—reveal how literature has served as a form of witness, resistance, healing, and identity-making. This section outlines several of the most prominent thematic concerns that shaped mid- to late-20th century African American writing.

Racial Injustice: Exposing Systemic Oppression

One of the most pervasive themes in African American literature has been the exposure of racial injustice—both its systemic foundations and its intimate effects on daily life. From Jim Crow segregation to covert institutional racism in housing, education, and policing, Black writers used their work to interrogate America's racial hypocrisies and demand recognition of Black humanity.

James Baldwin, in works such as *The Fire Next Time* (1963), provided a searing moral and political analysis of American racism, combining personal testimony with philosophical rigor. Toni Morrison's novels, like *Beloved* (1987) and *The Bluest Eye* (1970), illuminated the psychological and generational scars left by slavery and racial trauma. The literature of this period often foregrounded marginalized voices, offering a counter-narrative to mainstream depictions of American society.

Identity and Double Consciousness: Negotiating Cultural Duality

Influenced by W.E.B. Du Bois' concept of "double consciousness"—the internal conflict of viewing oneself through both one's own cultural lens and the gaze of a racially prejudiced society—African American writers explored the complexities of Black identity in a nation that both denied and demanded their presence.

This tension appears in Ralph Ellison's *Invisible Man* (1952), where the narrator struggles to assert an authentic self in a world that refuses to see him. Similarly, Lorraine Hansberry's work grapples with characters negotiating personal dreams and societal limitations. Writers examined how race intersects with language, community, art, and national belonging, often portraying the Black self as fluid, multifaceted, and embattled.

Urban Experience: Cityscapes of Survival and Creativity

As the Great Migration continued to reshape the demographic map of America, African American literature increasingly turned to the urban landscape—both as a site of trauma and creativity. Cities like Chicago, New York, and Los Angeles became central settings for exploring themes of poverty, ghettoization, gang violence, economic exploitation, and cultural resilience.

Gwendolyn Brooks, in poems like "We Real Cool," and Amiri Baraka, through his Newark-based prose and poetry, portrayed the stark realities of urban life while also highlighting the strength and ingenuity of Black communities. These urban narratives often juxtaposed decay and hope, showing how cities could be both oppressive systems and incubators of radical expression.

Resistance and Liberation: Literature as Political and Cultural Struggle

Post-Renaissance African American literature is inherently political. Writers of this era frequently embraced literature as a tool of resistance, expressing anger, critique, and defiance in the face of dehumanization. This was particularly evident during the Civil Rights and Black Power movements, when literature took on the role of a mobilizing force.

Poets such as Nikki Giovanni and Sonia Sanchez used their verses to denounce oppression and celebrate Black pride, while playwrights like August Wilson chronicled the dignity and struggles of Black life across decades. The Black Arts Movement explicitly advocated for art that was "by, for, and about" Black people—positioning literature as a vehicle for liberation and cultural sovereignty.

Gender and Intersectionality: Centering Black Women's Voices

By the 1970s and 1980s, a critical shift occurred as African American women began to reshape the literary landscape, challenging both white feminism and Black male-dominated narratives. Writers like Toni Morrison, Alice Walker, Gloria Naylor, and Audre Lorde foregrounded the intersectional experience of being Black and female in a society structured by racism, patriarchy, and classism.

Their work expanded the thematic scope of African American literature to include sexuality, domestic labor, colorism, reproductive rights, intergenerational trauma, and queer identity. Audre Lorde, in particular, infused her poetry and prose with an exploration of Black lesbian identity, arguing for a politics that affirmed difference as a source of power.

This thematic turn not only deepened the psychological and emotional textures of Black literature but also insisted on a more inclusive, pluralistic understanding of African American experience.

Pioneering Authors and Major Works

The mid-20th century marked a decisive moment in African American literature, as a generation of writers emerged who not only built upon the achievements of the Harlem Renaissance but also radically expanded the thematic, aesthetic, and political horizons of Black writing. These pioneering authors confronted the moral contradictions of American democracy, chronicled the psychological toll of racism, and explored the complexities of identity, alienation, and resistance. Through both fiction and non-fiction, they redefined the role of literature as a vehicle for cultural critique and social transformation. Among the most influential voices were Richard Wright, Ralph Ellison, and James Baldwin, each of whom contributed indelibly to the canon of American letters.

Richard Wright (1908–1960): Protest Literature and Psychological Realism

Richard Wright stands as a foundational figure in 20th-century African American literature, widely credited with ushering in a new era of protest fiction that did not shy away from depicting the brutal realities of racism, poverty, and psychological trauma. His writing was instrumental in forcing American readers—especially white audiences—to confront the systemic structures that dehumanized Black lives.

- *Native Son* (1940): Wright's landmark novel centers on Bigger Thomas, a young Black man in Depression-era Chicago whose life spirals into violence and tragedy as a result of entrenched racial and economic injustice. The novel was a critical and commercial success, selling hundreds of thousands of copies, and remains a defining work of American naturalism. It boldly addressed themes of fear, alienation, rage, and social determinism, compelling readers to examine how racial hierarchies shape individual psychology and fate.
- Wright's literary style was marked by gritty realism, psychological depth, and a radical political consciousness informed by Marxist theory. His autobiography, *Black Boy* (1945), further solidified his reputation as a writer committed to truth-telling, unmasking the violence and humiliation of Southern Black life through the lens of personal experience.

Ralph Ellison (1914–1994): Identity, Invisibility, and the American Paradox

While Richard Wright focused on overt social critique, Ralph Ellison offered a more symbolic and philosophical exploration of Black identity, weaving elements of modernism, existentialism, and African American folk culture into his work. Ellison believed in the power of art to reveal the moral complexities of race and individuality, often resisting the didacticism associated with protest literature.

- *Invisible Man* (1952): Ellison's only completed novel remains one of the most celebrated works in American literature. The book follows a nameless Black narrator as he journeys through various social and ideological spaces—college, labor movements, street activism—only to discover that society renders him "invisible" because it refuses to see him outside of stereotypes. The novel's nonlinear structure, hallucinatory imagery, and narrative unreliability reflect the inner disorientation of its protagonist, making it not just a political statement but a meditation on being, recognition, and the construction of self.

- Ellison's writing combined lyrical prose, philosophical inquiry, and jazz-influenced rhythms, challenging the expectation that Black literature should be defined solely by social grievance. His essays, compiled in *Shadow and Act* (1964), further articulate his views on the role of the Black artist in American culture and critique reductive readings of African American identity.

James Baldwin (1924–1987): Moral Vision and Emotional Truth

Few writers have matched the eloquence, compassion, and prophetic urgency of James Baldwin. Equally accomplished in fiction, essay, and memoir, Baldwin became one of the most important public intellectuals of the 20th century—an unflinching critic of racism, sexual repression, religious hypocrisy, and the moral failures of both Black and white America.

- *Go Tell It on the Mountain* (1953): Baldwin's first novel is a semi-autobiographical exploration of family trauma, religious experience, and adolescent identity in Harlem. It is a deeply spiritual and psychologically nuanced work that draws upon Biblical symbolism and Black church traditions to examine themes of guilt, redemption, and self-knowledge.
- *The Fire Next Time* (1963): A seminal collection of two essays, this work cemented Baldwin's status as a leading voice in the struggle for racial justice. Addressed both to his nephew and the nation, the book is a searing indictment of American racism and a plea for moral reckoning. Baldwin argues that the future of the nation depends on its willingness to confront the reality of its racial past and present.
- Baldwin's writing is characterized by clarity, lyricism, and introspective honesty. He often blurred the boundaries between the personal and the political, revealing how love, fear, shame, and longing shape the way we live in a divided society. His essays—such as "Notes of a Native Son" and "Nobody Knows My Name"—remain central to discussions of race, democracy, and American identity.

The Rise of African American Women Writers

The 1970s and 1980s marked a watershed moment in African American literature with the powerful emergence of Black women writers who redefined the literary landscape. Building on the legacies of earlier voices such as Zora Neale Hurston and Ann Petry, this new generation of authors centered the experiences of Black women—not as marginal figures in a male-dominated racial discourse, but as complex protagonists of their own histories, desires, traumas, and triumphs.

Amid broader social movements—feminism, civil rights, Black nationalism, and queer liberation—these writers crafted narratives that explored intersectionality, historical recovery, intergenerational trauma, and the emotional interior lives of Black women. Their literary innovations challenged both the racism of white literary institutions and the patriarchal assumptions embedded within Black cultural traditions. They did not simply add to African American literature; they transformed its themes, form, and canon.

Toni Morrison (1931–2019): Cultural Memory and the Poetics of Pain

Toni Morrison is widely regarded as one of the most significant literary figures of the 20th century—not only in African American literature but in American letters as a whole. A Nobel Prize laureate and editor at Random House, Morrison was deeply committed to telling stories from within the Black cultural and historical framework, free from the need for white validation or explanation.

- *The Bluest Eye* (1970): Morrison's debut novel is a haunting tale of a young Black girl, Pecola Breedlove, who yearns for blue eyes—symbolizing the internalized racism and self-hatred cultivated by white beauty standards. The novel examines themes of sexual violence, familial dysfunction, and cultural erasure, using fragmented narrative and shifting perspectives to reflect the fractured psyche of its characters.
- *Beloved* (1987): A landmark novel that won the Pulitzer Prize, Beloved tells the story of a formerly enslaved woman, Sethe, who is haunted—both literally and metaphorically—by the memory of a child she killed to save from slavery. Morrison masterfully weaves historical fact, magical realism, oral storytelling, and psychological realism to explore the enduring trauma of slavery and the radical power of maternal love.

Morrison's prose is known for its lyrical intensity, structural experimentation, and deep psychological nuance. She redefined the American novel by placing Black women's lives and voices at the center of national memory, resisting the impulse to universalize or sanitize Black suffering.

Alice Walker (b. 1944): Womanism, Survival, and Sisterhood

Alice Walker, a novelist, poet, and activist, played a pivotal role in recovering the lost voices of Black women writers (most notably Zora Neale Hurston) and articulating what she called "womanism"—a Black feminist framework that affirms the complexity of Black women's lives beyond white or male-centric paradigms.

- *The Color Purple* (1982): Walker's Pulitzer Prize- and National Book Award-winning novel is an epistolary narrative that chronicles the life of Celie, a poor, uneducated Black woman in the early 20th-century American South. Through her letters—first to God and then to her sister—the novel tracks Celie's journey from abuse and silence to self-knowledge, independence, and solidarity with other women.

The Color Purple is notable for its use of Black vernacular, its candid exploration of sexuality and gender oppression, and its celebration of female empowerment through community and creativity. The novel was both lauded for its emotional depth and criticized—particularly by some Black male critics—for its depiction of gendered violence. Yet, it remains a foundational work of intersectional literature.

Maya Angelou (1928–2014): Memoir, Voice, and Empowerment

Maya Angelou made her mark not primarily through fiction but through her innovative autobiographical writing and poetry, which bridged the personal and the political. As a performer, educator, and activist, Angelou brought her lived experience of poverty, sexual trauma, racism, and global travel into a narrative arc of resilience and artistic rebirth.

- *I Know Why the Caged Bird Sings* (1969): The first in a series of autobiographical works, this memoir tells the story of Angelou's early life in the segregated South, her experience of sexual abuse, and her subsequent journey toward self-expression and healing through literature. The book's blend of lyrical prose, social critique, and emotional candor redefined the possibilities of life-writing for Black women.

Angelou's influence extends beyond the page. Her poetic work, including collections like *Phenomenal Woman* and *And Still I Rise*, became rallying cries for Black dignity, especially among women. She was celebrated not only for her words but for her public presence—reading at President Clinton's inauguration in 1993 and serving as a cultural ambassador and educator until her death.

Literary Style and Innovation

The post-Harlem Renaissance period witnessed not only a deepening of thematic complexity in African American literature but also a remarkable experimentation with form, structure, and voice. Writers sought innovative ways to express the nuances of Black life, memory, and resistance—often breaking from Eurocentric literary conventions and forging new aesthetic pathways grounded in African American cultural traditions. These formal innovations were not merely stylistic flourishes but political and cultural acts, asserting the legitimacy of Black modes of storytelling and challenging dominant literary norms.

Use of Oral Tradition: Reclaiming Ancestral Voice

A defining feature of African American literary innovation has been its deep engagement with the oral tradition, a cultural inheritance rooted in African storytelling, spirituals, gospel, blues, and sermonizing. Writers such as Toni Cade Bambara, Alice Walker, and James Baldwin infused their prose and dialogue with the rhythms, idioms, and cadences of spoken Black English. This stylistic choice evoked authenticity and immediacy, capturing the performative and communal aspects of African American expression.

Toni Morrison, in particular, emphasized the oral quality of her fiction, striving to replicate the call-and-response dynamics of the Black church and folktale. This approach aimed not just to tell a story but to engage the reader as a listener, echoing communal storytelling traditions where memory, identity, and morality are negotiated aloud.

Code-Switching and Vernacular Language: Linguistic Sovereignty

Another hallmark of African American literary innovation is the practice of code-switching—the strategic shifting between standard English and African American Vernacular English (AAVE). Far from being a mere linguistic device, this stylistic practice affirms the richness, versatility, and political power of Black speech.

Authors like Zora Neale Hurston (revived in the 1970s by Alice Walker) and August Wilson unapologetically foregrounded vernacular language, challenging literary elitism and validating Black linguistic identity. Contemporary writers continued this trend, blending registers and idioms to reflect the polyvocal realities of Black life in America—simultaneously asserting cultural pride and navigating spaces of marginalization.

Nonlinear Narratives: Fragmented Time and Memory

Time and memory occupy a unique place in African American literature, especially in the aftermath of slavery, diaspora, and historical erasure. Post-1960s writers increasingly turned to nonlinear structures to portray the disjointed and traumatic nature of Black historical experience. Nowhere is this more evident than in Toni Morrison's novels—such as *Beloved* and *Song of Solomon*—where time is cyclical, memory is unreliable, and history is experienced viscerally, not chronologically.

This stylistic fragmentation reflects both the psychic disruptions of oppression and the creative reconstitution of cultural memory. Through shifting perspectives, temporal leaps, and interwoven ancestral narratives, writers resist the linear logic of Western historiography, instead offering a more embodied and spiritual reckoning with the past.

Genre Blending: Fluid Boundaries Between Forms

African American writers in the late 20th century also blurred the boundaries between genres, refusing to be confined by rigid literary classifications. Fiction incorporated elements of memoir, essay, poetry, folklore, history, and political commentary, resulting in works that were hybrid in form and expansive in meaning.

Maya Angelou's autobiographical series reads like a blend of lyric memoir and social analysis. Gloria Naylor's *The Women of Brewster Place* interweaves short stories and collective biography. Audre Lorde's Zami: *A New Spelling of My Name* is subtitled a "biomythography," combining mythology, autobiography, and fiction to create a new literary category altogether.

This genre fluidity reflects the writers' refusal to separate personal experience from political critique, art from activism, or imagination from historical reality. The result is a body of literature that is formally bold, emotionally resonant, and politically potent.

The Black Arts Movement: Revolution in Word and Form

The Black Arts Movement (BAM) of the 1960s and 1970s represents one of the most radical and transformative periods in African American literary and cultural history. Often referred to as the "aesthetic and spiritual sister of the Black Power Movement," BAM was not merely a literary phenomenon but a cultural revolution that sought to realign art with Black political and communal consciousness. It emphasized self-determination, racial pride, militant resistance, and a commitment to Afrocentric aesthetics.

Emerging in the wake of Malcolm X's assassination and the height of the Civil Rights Movement's ideological shifts, the Black Arts Movement challenged both white aesthetic standards and the perceived complacency of integrationist liberalism. For BAM artists, literature and art were tools for empowerment, consciousness-raising, and liberation.

Historical and Political Context

The movement arose in a time of civil unrest, police violence, anti-colonial struggle abroad, and growing disillusionment with the slow pace of racial progress. Influenced by Malcolm X's vision of Black nationalism and cultural sovereignty, BAM artists rejected assimilationist narratives and instead called for a distinctly Black aesthetic—art created *by*, *for*, and *about* Black people.

This artistic reorientation was mirrored in the development of community-based theaters, publishing houses, journals, and cultural centers across the United States, most notably in urban centers like Harlem, Chicago, Detroit, and Oakland.

Key Figures and Contributions

Amiri Baraka (1934–2014)

Formerly known as LeRoi Jones, Baraka is widely regarded as the founder of the Black Arts Movement. After breaking with the predominantly white Beat literary scene, he established the Black Arts Repertory Theatre/School (BARTS) in Harlem in 1965. His work is known for its confrontational style, revolutionary tone, and Afrocentric ideology.

- Notable Works: *Dutchman* (1964), *Black Magic* (1969), *It's Nation Time* (1970)
- His poetry, plays, and essays argued that Black art must be functional, collective, and politically engaged—serving the needs of the Black community rather than the tastes of white literary institutions.

Nikki Giovanni (b. 1943)

One of the most celebrated poets of the movement, Giovanni infused her work with personal lyricism, political passion, and Black feminist insight. Her poems often spoke to the experiences of Black youth, women, and families.

- Notable Works: *Black Feeling, Black Talk* (1968), *Re:Creation* (1970)
- Giovanni's accessible style and public presence made her a beloved voice of empowerment, especially for young Black readers and activists.

Sonia Sanchez (b. 1934)

A poet, playwright, and educator, Sanchez was a major architect of Black feminist thought within BAM. Her work explored gender, race, spirituality, and liberation, and she was a pioneer in incorporating musical forms like blues and jazz into poetry.

- Notable Works: *Homecoming* (1969), *We a BaddDDD People* (1970)
- Her poetic experimentation and commitment to community engagement and education made her one of the most influential literary voices of the era.

Larry Neal (1937–1981)

A critic, essayist, and playwright, Neal was a principal theorist of the Black Arts Movement. He co-edited *Black Fire: An Anthology of Afro-American Writing* (1968) with Baraka and wrote extensively on the need for a distinct Black aesthetic that rejected European models of art and literature.

- Neal emphasized that Black culture must reclaim its African roots and that artists must serve as revolutionaries for their communities.

Principles and Aesthetic Vision

The Black Arts Movement advanced several core principles:

- **Afrocentrism:** A conscious turn toward African cultural traditions, mythologies, and spiritual systems as sources of artistic inspiration and identity formation.
- **Radical Aesthetics:** A rejection of Euro-American literary norms in favor of oral expression, rhythm, performance, vernacular language, and nonlinear forms rooted in Black experience.
- **Militancy and Political Urgency:** BAM art was unflinching in its critique of white supremacy, capitalism, and colonialism. It promoted themes of resistance, revolution, and solidarity.
- **Institution Building:** BAM fostered an infrastructure of independent Black publishing houses, theater collectives, art spaces, and workshops aimed at creating and distributing art within the Black community.

Examples include Third World Press, Broadside Press, and Black Theatre Alliance, which played key roles in cultivating new literary talent outside of mainstream (and often exclusionary) channels.

Critiques and Legacy

While the Black Arts Movement was revolutionary, it was not without criticism:

- **Gender Politics:** Early BAM discourse often marginalized women's voices, and some male-authored works reinforced patriarchal norms, prompting interventions from writers like Giovanni, Sanchez, and later Audre Lorde.
- **Ideological Rigidity:** Some critics argued that BAM's emphasis on didacticism and political utility narrowed aesthetic possibilities, occasionally sacrificing nuance for polemic.

Nevertheless, the legacy of the Black Arts Movement is enduring. It redefined the purpose of literature in America, inspired future generations of hip-hop artists, spoken word poets, Afro-futurists, and community-centered creators, and paved the way for institutional recognition of African American literature in academia.

Influence on Contemporary Literature: Inheriting the Struggle, Reimagining the Voice

The rich legacy of post-Harlem African American literature remains profoundly influential in shaping contemporary American literary discourse. Writers of the 21st century continue to engage with the thematic, aesthetic, and political concerns of their predecessors while responding to the complexities of a new historical moment—one shaped by ongoing racial injustice, economic inequality, police brutality, and evolving questions of gender, sexuality, and national identity.

Contemporary African American writers are not only heirs to the tradition established by figures such as Richard Wright, Toni Morrison, James Baldwin, and Alice Walker; they are also innovators, expanding the boundaries of genre, voice, and form. Through novels, memoirs, poetry, and hybrid texts, they examine the continuities and ruptures between the past and the present, often blending personal narrative with historical recovery and social critique.

Ta-Nehisi Coates (b. 1975): Rhetoric, Memory, and Black Consciousness

Ta-Nehisi Coates emerged as a prominent literary and cultural critic through his journalism and essays in *The Atlantic*, before achieving wide acclaim for his memoir:

- *Between the World and Me* (2015): Written as a letter to his teenage son, this National Book Award-winning work addresses the embodied experience of Blackness in America, the trauma of systemic racism, and the elusive nature of justice. Drawing on the legacy of Baldwin's *The Fire Next Time*, Coates combines lyrical prose with historical analysis, creating a meditative and urgent account of Black life in the 21st century.

His work is marked by a blend of personal vulnerability and intellectual rigor, echoing the moral clarity and emotional power of earlier African American nonfiction while speaking directly to a generation shaped by mass incarceration, Black Lives Matter, and digital media.

Jesmyn Ward (b. 1977): Southern Gothic, Grief, and Resilience

Jesmyn Ward has been hailed as one of the most important novelists of her generation, especially for her lyrical depictions of Black life in the rural American South:

- *Salvage the Bones* (2011): Set in the days leading up to Hurricane Katrina, the novel follows a poor Black family in Mississippi. It won the National Book Award for its visceral portrayal of poverty, family bonds, and survival in the face of environmental and social devastation.
- *Sing, Unburied, Sing* (2017): A haunting novel that combines magical realism, ghost narratives, and road-trip fiction to explore themes of incarceration, addiction, and ancestral trauma. The book channels the spiritual and historical dimensions of Morrison's work, particularly *Beloved*, while firmly grounding itself in contemporary crises.

Ward's fiction blends the realism of Zora Neale Hurston with the gothic intensity of William Faulkner, crafting narratives that are both timeless and urgently current.

Colson Whitehead (b. 1969): Rewriting History, Reinventing Form

Colson Whitehead stands at the forefront of historical and speculative fiction in contemporary African American literature. His novels creatively reimagine the American past to critique its myths and expose its hidden violence.

- *The Underground Railroad* (2016): Winner of the Pulitzer Prize and National Book Award, the novel transforms the historical underground railroad into a literal subterranean train system, blending realism with speculative allegory. It revisits slavery through surreal yet emotionally grounded storytelling, inviting comparison with Morrison, Ellison, and Gabriel García Márquez.
- *The Nickel Boys* (2019): Also a Pulitzer Prize winner, this novel is based on a real reform school in Jim Crow-era Florida. It explores the psychological and physical abuse of young Black men, raising questions about truth, justice, and the erasure of history.

Whitehead's work is distinguished by its structural innovation, moral clarity, and ability to bridge historical memory with contemporary resonance.

Other Notable Voices: Multiplicity and Intersectionality

A diverse array of contemporary African American writers continues to expand the tradition:

- **Jacqueline Woodson:** Known for her novels and poetry for both young adults and adults, Woodson explores memory, sexuality, race, and belonging in lyrical and accessible prose. Works like *Brown Girl Dreaming* and *Red at the Bone* showcase her talent for nonlinear storytelling and poetic introspection.

- **Terrance Hayes:** A leading poet whose work merges formal experimentation (such as the "golden shovel" form) with themes of Black masculinity, surveillance, violence, and artistic legacy. His collection *American Sonnets for My Past and Future Assassin* (2018) is a searing response to the Trump era and American racial politics.
- **Roxane Gay:** An essayist, novelist, and cultural commentator whose work examines feminism, body politics, trauma, and racial identity. Her best-selling memoir *Hunger* (2017) and essay collection *Bad Feminist* (2014) challenge conventional boundaries between personal narrative and political critique.

These writers exemplify a multivocal, intersectional, and genre-defying tradition that speaks to the plurality of Black experience in the 21st century.

Continuities and Departures

Contemporary African American literature reflects a dialogue between past and present:

- It retains the political urgency, moral conviction, and cultural affirmation that animated the work of Baldwin, Morrison, and Baraka.
- At the same time, it embraces genre hybridity, digital storytelling, queer identity, and global diasporic connections, responding to the expanded horizons of post-Civil Rights, post-9/11, and post-George Floyd America.

Through memoirs, novels, poetry, and new media, today's writers are not merely continuing the tradition—they are remaking it, proving that African American literature remains one of the most vital and transformative forces in American letters.

Conclusion: A Resilient and Expanding Voice

The trajectory of African American literature after the Harlem Renaissance represents one of the most dynamic and transformative arcs in American literary history. From the urban realism of Richard Wright to the spiritual introspection of James Baldwin, from the poetic intensity of Sonia Sanchez to the historical imagination of Toni Morrison, African American writers have persistently articulated the complexities of Black life—its pain, beauty, struggle, and triumph.

Building on the foundations laid during the Harlem Renaissance, the post-Renaissance period did not simply continue a legacy—it complicated, expanded, and redefined it. Writers moved beyond celebratory racial uplift to confront the brutal realities of institutional racism, gendered violence, economic injustice, cultural erasure, and psychological fragmentation. In doing so, they forged new literary forms, adopted radical aesthetics, and introduced Afrocentric, feminist, queer, and diasporic perspectives into the national narrative.

What unites these diverse voices is not a singular aesthetic or ideological stance but a shared commitment to truth-telling, cultural memory, and resistance through art. Whether through the biting satire of Ishmael Reed, the intergenerational trauma of Jesmyn Ward, or the metaphysical meditations of Terrance Hayes, African American literature has consistently challenged dominant paradigms and insisted on the full humanity of Black lives.

Moreover, African American literature has helped reshape the canon of American literature itself. No longer confined to the margins, these voices now occupy central positions in literary scholarship, curricula, and public discourse. The works of Morrison, Ellison, Walker, and Coates are not only celebrated within African American studies but also recognized as essential contributions to world literature.

Importantly, this literature does not rest on the accomplishments of the past. It continues to evolve—fluid, intersectional, and globally resonant. In an era marked by renewed struggles for racial justice, the legacy of post-Harlem African American writers remains urgently relevant. Their literary innovations and moral clarity remind us of literature's enduring capacity to heal wounds, recover silenced histories, and envision more just futures.

In the final analysis, African American literature after the Harlem Renaissance exemplifies what literature can and must be: a living force, capable of bearing witness, instigating change, and expanding the possibilities of expression for all people. Its voice—resilient, rebellious, poetic, and profound—continues not only to survive but to shape the soul of a nation still wrestling with its conscience.

7

Gender, Identity, and the American Literary Imagination

Voicing the Silenced, Rewriting the Self

Introduction: Literature as Liberation

The twentieth century was not only an era of stylistic innovation and narrative experimentation in American literature—it was also a century marked by a radical reimagining of who could speak, whose voices were heard, and how identity could be expressed through language. Against the backdrop of seismic social changes—women's suffrage, the sexual revolution, civil rights, second- and third-wave feminism, and LGBTQ+ liberation—literature became a vital site of resistance, reclamation, and reinvention.

As the century progressed, American writers began to interrogate the deeply entrenched cultural norms surrounding gender, sexuality, and the body. What emerged was a powerful current of writing that refused to accept traditional binaries or hegemonic identities. Through poetry, fiction, memoir, and experimental prose, these authors challenged patriarchal structures, exposed heteronormativity, and explored the fluidity of desire and identity. This body of work did not merely reflect social change—it catalyzed it, providing language for marginalized experiences and helping to forge new understandings of the self.

Early in the century, first-wave feminist writers fought for political representation and education. By mid-century, second-wave feminists expanded their critique to the personal sphere, tackling issues like domestic labor, reproductive rights, and the representation of women's bodies. Literary figures such as Sylvia Plath, Adrienne Rich, and Audre Lorde explored the psychological and social dimensions of womanhood in deeply introspective and often confrontational terms.

At the same time, LGBTQ+ authors were emerging as major forces in American letters, often writing against a culture of silence, criminalization, and erasure. From the coded queerness of early 20th-century modernists to the out-and-proud declarations of James Baldwin, Allen Ginsberg, and

Leslie Feinberg, queer writers used literature not only to document their realities but to imagine alternative ways of being. Their work engaged themes of alienation, secrecy, community, pride, and transformation—often articulating desires that mainstream narratives either ignored or condemned.

By the late twentieth century, literature had become a dynamic arena for the performance of gender and the politics of visibility. Writers increasingly explored intersectionality, a term coined by Kimberlé Crenshaw, to account for how race, class, gender, and sexuality intersect to shape lived experience. Feminist and queer literature expanded beyond the binary logic of male/female or gay/straight, incorporating nonbinary identities, trans embodiment, and post-structuralist critiques of the self. The rise of postmodernism further destabilized fixed notions of identity, enabling authors to experiment with fragmented narratives, unreliable narrators, and metafictional reflections on language and power.

In this evolving literary landscape, the personal was political, and the body became a site of struggle, revelation, and expression. Literature served not merely as art or entertainment but as a form of activism—a means of documenting oppression, resisting conformity, and envisioning liberation.

This chapter will trace the multi-dimensional evolution of gender and sexuality in American literature, examining how writers from diverse backgrounds have used the written word to resist marginalization, articulate complex identities, and expand the possibilities of literary form and cultural discourse. From the voices of feminist pioneers and queer trailblazers to the contemporary authors pushing the boundaries of gender and genre, we explore literature not just as a reflection of society, but as a tool for its transformation.

Feminist Literary Movement in America

The evolution of feminist literature in the United States mirrors the broader trajectories of feminist activism and theory. Spanning more than a century, this literary tradition has served as a site of resistance, exploration, and reimagination of gender roles and power structures. Feminist literature has not only voiced women's experiences but also disrupted patriarchal narratives, interrogated systems of oppression, and proposed alternative visions of identity and community. Broadly speaking, this movement can be mapped across three major waves, each with distinct thematic preoccupations, ideological emphases, and literary innovations.

First Wave (Late 19th Century to Early 20th Century): Foundations of Dissent

The first wave of feminism focused primarily on legal and civic rights, most notably the right to vote, to receive education, and to participate in public life. While its political goals were crystallized in the suffragist movement, its literary expressions often delved into the emotional, psychological, and existential consequences of women's confinement within patriarchal domesticity.

- Charlotte Perkins Gilman's "The Yellow Wallpaper" (1892) is a seminal short story that critiques the medical and cultural silencing of women, particularly in the context of mental illness. The story's unnamed female narrator, trapped in a room and forbidden from writing, slowly descends into madness—offering a chilling allegory of gendered oppression and the pathologization of female dissent.
- Kate Chopin's *The Awakening* (1899) explores the emotional and sexual self-discovery of Edna Pontellier, a married woman who ultimately rebels against the restrictive conventions of motherhood and marriage. Though condemned upon its publication, the novel later gained recognition as a foundational text of American feminist fiction.

While these authors wrote before the term "feminist literature" gained traction, their work anticipated central concerns of later feminist literary criticism: the institutional disciplining of women, the intersection of sexuality and power, and the search for female agency and voice.

Second Wave (1960s–1980s): Personal is Political

Emerging during a period of intense social upheaval, the second wave of feminism extended the fight from legal equality to issues of sexuality, reproductive rights, domestic labor, workplace discrimination, and cultural representation. Feminist literature of this era was more overtly political and often radical, aiming to dismantle patriarchal ideologies embedded in both society and literature.

- Betty Friedan's *The Feminine Mystique* (1963) marked a watershed moment. Her articulation of "the problem that has no name"—the dissatisfaction felt by many suburban housewives despite their material comfort—sparked a widespread feminist awakening. Though critiqued later for its lack of intersectionality, Friedan's work laid the foundation for feminist discourse in the mainstream.
- Adrienne Rich, in works such as *Of Woman Born* (1976) and *Compulsory Heterosexuality and Lesbian Existence* (1980), combined poetry and theory to examine motherhood, sexuality, and the erasure of lesbian

identity. Her formal innovation and moral urgency helped redefine poetry as a medium for feminist thought.

- Audre Lorde, a Black lesbian poet and theorist, challenged white, heteronormative feminism by emphasizing the need for intersectionality—a term not yet popularized but central to her thought. In Sister Outsider (1984), Lorde declared, "The master's tools will never dismantle the master's house," calling for new feminist paradigms that embraced difference as a source of strength.
- Gloria Anzaldúa's *Borderlands/La Frontera* (1987) broke barriers in both language and genre, combining autobiography, theory, and poetry. Writing from the perspective of a queer Chicana, Anzaldúa theorized "mestiza consciousness", a hybrid identity forged in resistance to dualisms of gender, race, and nation.

These voices helped bring intersectional concerns into feminist literature, expanding its scope to include race, sexuality, class, and ethnicity. The literary output of the second wave was not only a vehicle for political critique, but also a space for imagining new subjectivities and collective solidarities.

Third Wave and Beyond (1990s–Present): Multiplicity, Fluidity, and Globalism

The third wave of feminist literature responded to the perceived limitations of the second wave, especially its focus on the experiences of white, middle-class, cisgender women. Writers and thinkers of this period emphasized diversity, fluidity, and transnational perspectives, challenging essentialist definitions of womanhood and embracing gender nonconformity, queer identities, and global feminist solidarity.

- Third-wave writers explored gender as a spectrum, recognizing identities that fall outside traditional male/female binaries. Many embraced poststructuralist and postmodernist theories that questioned the stability of identity and truth itself.
- Rebecca Walker, credited with popularizing the term "third wave," advocated for a feminism that was more inclusive of Black women, LGBTQ+ individuals, and youth culture.
- Writers such as bell hooks and Chimamanda Ngozi Adichie blended theory with memoir to examine the entanglements of race, patriarchy, capitalism, and colonialism. hooks's *Feminism is for Everybody* (2000) and Adichie's *We Should All Be Feminists* (2014) made feminist thought accessible to broad audiences.

- Trans and nonbinary authors, such as Janet Mock, Alok Vaid-Menon, and Julia Serano, have further reshaped feminist literature by centering trans experiences, deconstructing cisnormativity, and emphasizing bodily autonomy as a fundamental feminist concern.

Moreover, contemporary feminist literature increasingly engages with digital culture, climate justice, disability rights, and anti-capitalist critiques. Writers work across genres—combining prose, poetry, zines, blogs, and performance—and challenge what counts as literature and who counts as a writer.

Notable Female and Feminist Authors

The feminist literary tradition in America has been shaped by an array of powerful voices who challenged dominant paradigms and offered nuanced representations of gender, identity, and agency. From confessional poets to intersectional storytellers, these writers redefined both content and form in American literature. Their contributions span across genres and movements, yet they are united in their commitment to exploring the complexities of womanhood, mental health, racial identity, sexual politics, and social resistance.

Sylvia Plath (1932–1963)

Sylvia Plath remains one of the most iconic figures in 20th-century American literature, known for her deeply personal, often harrowing explorations of mental illness, gender oppression, and artistic alienation. Her semi-autobiographical novel, *The Bell Jar* (1963), follows Esther Greenwood, a gifted young woman whose psychological descent mirrors the suffocating effects of societal expectations placed upon women. The novel critiques the postwar ideal of domestic femininity, revealing the emotional toll of enforced conformity.

Plath's confessional poetry, especially in the collection Ariel (published posthumously in 1965), broke literary taboos by addressing death, depression, motherhood, and rage with stark intensity. Her poems—such as "Lady Lazarus" and "Daddy"—use visceral metaphors and mythological references to confront patriarchal power and the fragmentation of self. Though her life ended tragically early, Plath's work has since become central to feminist literary studies, symbolizing the often-destructive intersection of gender, creativity, and mental health.

Adrienne Rich (1929–2012)

Adrienne Rich was not only one of America's most accomplished poets but also one of its most committed public intellectuals. Her work merged literary excellence with feminist and political activism. In collections like *Diving into the Wreck* (1973), Rich explored themes of patriarchy, language, survival, and the reclamation of women's histories. The titular poem is often read as an allegory for feminist excavation—plunging into the wreckage of a male-dominated culture to recover and rewrite lost narratives.

Her groundbreaking nonfiction work, *Of Woman Born: Motherhood as Experience and Institution* (1976), challenged the idealization of motherhood, analyzing how it has been socially constructed to serve patriarchal interests. Rich openly identified as a lesbian in her later life and used her platform to advocate for lesbian existence, intersectionality, and the political power of female relationships. Her contributions expanded the scope of feminist thought to include questions of identity, desire, and collective liberation.

Toni Cade Bambara (1939–1995)

Toni Cade Bambara's work bridges the literary and the political, grounded in a Black feminist sensibility that affirms community, cultural pride, and resistance to oppression. Her 1972 short story collection, *Gorilla, My Love*, showcases narratives centered on strong-willed African American girls and women navigating urban life, familial expectations, and systemic racism. Her characters are notable for their intelligence, wit, and agency, offering a counter-narrative to prevailing stereotypes of Black womanhood.

Bambara was deeply influenced by the Black Arts Movement, and her work reflects its emphasis on community-based art, vernacular voice, and cultural sovereignty. Through her fiction and activism, Bambara emphasized that storytelling is a collective, healing, and political act, particularly for marginalized communities. Her influence endures in contemporary Black feminist writing, which continues to balance political critique with rich, character-driven storytelling.

Sandra Cisneros (b. 1954)

A leading voice in contemporary Chicana literature, Sandra Cisneros brought the complexities of Mexican-American female identity into the American literary mainstream. Her breakthrough novel, *The House on Mango Street* (1984), is a series of lyrical vignettes told through the eyes of Esperanza Cordero, a young Latina girl coming of age in a Chicago barrio. The text explores themes of poverty, cultural hybridity, gender roles, sexual awakening, and the search for self-definition.

Cisneros's work is notable for its accessible yet poetic prose, use of bilingualism, and incorporation of oral storytelling traditions. Her narratives often center on girls and women attempting to escape limiting cultural scripts, particularly those related to marianismo, machismo, and familial expectations. In doing so, Cisneros has played a pivotal role in expanding the feminist literary canon to include Latinx and working-class voices, and she continues to be an advocate for literature that speaks across borders—cultural, linguistic, and generational.

LGBTQ+ Literature: Coming Out and Coming Alive

The trajectory of LGBTQ+ literature in the United States reflects a profound shift in visibility, voice, and political engagement. While queer themes can be traced back to earlier periods, it was not until the post-Stonewall era (after 1969)—marked by the 1969 Stonewall Riots in New York City, often cited as the birth of the modern LGBTQ+ rights movement—that a distinct and unapologetic queer literary culture emerged. This period saw a burgeoning of works that openly challenged heteronormativity, redefined identity, and claimed space for queer desire and experience.

LGBTQ+ writers of this era explored the complexities of sexual orientation, gender identity, societal marginalization, internalized shame, chosen families, and resistance to normative structures. Literature became a means of "coming out" both individually and collectively, functioning as both self-expression and cultural activism. These authors expanded the literary canon while also forging new forms of community, solidarity, and self-definition.

James Baldwin (1924–1987)

Though often associated with the civil rights movement and African American literature, James Baldwin is also a foundational figure in queer literature. His novel *Giovanni's Room* (1956)—decades ahead of its time—narrates the inner conflict of a young American man in Paris who falls in love with another man, Giovanni. The novel's raw emotional landscape probes themes of sexual identity, societal alienation, internalized homophobia, and exile, refusing to offer easy resolutions or moral judgments.

Baldwin's courage in writing about homosexuality in an era of deep repression marked him as a literary and moral trailblazer. His essays, particularly in works like *The Fire Next Time* and *Notes of a Native Son*, explore the intersections of race, sexuality, masculinity, and spiritual struggle, positioning him as a queer theorist avant la lettre. Baldwin's insistence on complexity—his refusal to separate identity categories or simplify human desire—has made him an enduring figure in both Black and queer literary traditions.

Audre Lorde (1934–1992)

A Black lesbian feminist, poet, and theorist, Audre Lorde challenged every axis of oppression—racism, sexism, homophobia, and classism—through her writing. Her work is intersectional in both form and content, fusing the personal with the political, the poetic with the theoretical. In her biomythography *Zami: A New Spelling of My Name* (1982), Lorde recounts her experiences of growing up as a Black lesbian in mid-20th-century America, creating a new genre that blends autobiography, myth, and theory.

Her essay collection *Sister Outsider* (1984) includes seminal texts like "The Uses of the Erotic" and "The Master's Tools Will Never Dismantle the Master's House," which articulate the power of marginalized identities as sources of knowledge and creative resistance. For Lorde, queerness was not a singular or isolated identity, but part of a larger matrix of embodied difference that demanded both literary recognition and political transformation.

Allen Ginsberg (1926–1997)

One of the leading figures of the Beat Generation, Allen Ginsberg was also one of the first openly gay poets of the 20th century. His landmark poem *Howl* (1956) is a declaration of queer eroticism, madness, spiritual searching, and cultural dissent. Dedicated to his lover Carl Solomon, "Howl" shocked literary audiences with its unfiltered celebration of homosexual desire and its condemnation of repressive social norms.

Ginsberg's work, which combines Whitmanesque expansiveness with modernist fragmentation and Beat spontaneity, refuses to divorce queer identity from the broader critiques of war, capitalism, censorship, and conformity. He was also an activist, advocating for LGBTQ+ rights, free speech, and psychedelic exploration. Ginsberg's poetry not only queered literary form but also publicly redefined what it meant to live and love outside the heterosexual norm.

Leslie Feinberg (1949–2014)

A pivotal figure in transgender and gender-nonconforming literature, Leslie Feinberg is best known for the semi-autobiographical novel *Stone Butch Blues* (1993). Set against the backdrop of working-class Buffalo, New York, the novel follows Jess Goldberg, a gender-nonconforming individual navigating the complexities of butch/femme lesbian culture, police violence, workplace discrimination, and medical pathologization.

Feinberg's work is notable for its grounded realism and emotional intimacy, offering a portrait of gender identity that is historically specific yet widely resonant. Stone Butch Blues is more than a coming-of-age novel—it is a document of survival, resistance, and radical visibility. The novel has become a foundational text in trans literature, queer theory, and working-class studies, and remains one of the most influential works of LGBTQ+ fiction ever written.

Literary Techniques and Themes

The emergence of feminist, LGBTQ+, and gender-nonconforming literature in the 20th century not only transformed the content of American literature but also revolutionized its form, style, and narrative strategies. These writers employed innovative literary techniques and thematic explorations to challenge dominant ideologies and create new spaces for marginalized voices. The resulting works were not merely political manifestos but complex artistic expressions that reflected the fluidity, fragmentation, and resistance at the heart of their subjects.

Below are the most salient literary techniques and recurring themes found in gender- and identity-focused literature:

Confessionalism: The Personal as Political

A defining technique across much feminist and queer literature, confessionalism blurs the line between autobiography and fiction. Inspired in part by poets like Sylvia Plath and Anne Sexton, this mode of writing foregrounds vulnerability, personal trauma, mental health, sexuality, and domestic experience, treating the interior self as a valid and essential subject of literature.

Confessional literature often resists traditional literary detachment, instead presenting intimate emotional realities that destabilize the notion of objective narrative. Works like Audre Lorde's *Zami: A New Spelling of My Name*, Leslie Feinberg's *Stone Butch Blues*, or Maya Angelou's autobiographical volumes exemplify this mode, asserting that truth is embedded in lived, embodied experience—especially for those historically silenced.

Body as Text: Inscription, Control, and Liberation

In feminist and queer literature, the body is more than a physical entity—it is a site of struggle, deeply inscribed by culture, ideology, and history. Writers explore how bodies—particularly those that are female, queer, trans, or racialized—are disciplined, policed, sexualized, and pathologized by societal norms.

At the same time, the body also becomes a source of empowerment. For instance, Gloria Anzaldúa's concept of the "mestiza consciousness" fuses spiritual, cultural, and sexual hybridity through bodily metaphor, while

Audre Lorde's essay "Uses of the Erotic" reclaims sensuality as a political and creative force. In such texts, the body writes back, asserting presence, agency, and multiplicity.

Nonlinear and Fragmented Structures

Many feminist and LGBTQ+ authors disrupt chronological and traditional narrative forms, using nonlinear, circular, or fragmented structures to reflect the discontinuities of identity, memory, and trauma. This stylistic choice mirrors the lived experiences of those whose lives do not conform to dominant societal scripts.

For example, Toni Morrison's *Beloved* is structured around flashbacks and spectral interruptions, destabilizing the temporal logic of realism to emphasize the persistence of historical trauma. Similarly, Jeanette Winterson's *Written on the Body* (though British) and Carson McCullers' *The Member of the Wedding* use fragmented or ambiguous perspectives to explore queer and gender-nonconforming subjectivities.

Intertextuality and Myth Revision

A powerful thematic and formal device in feminist and queer literature is the revision of classical, biblical, or canonical texts from a subversive perspective. These reimaginings serve to deconstruct patriarchal myths and reclaim agency for marginalized figures.

For example:

- Margaret Atwood's *The Penelopiad* (2005), although Canadian, rewrites the Odyssey from Penelope's point of view, challenging male heroism and revealing female silencing.
- Christa Wolf's *Cassandra* and Gayl Jones's *Corregidora* similarly use myth and history to question traditional gender roles.
- Queer authors often engage in intertextual critique, referencing dominant narratives only to invert, parody, or explode them, as seen in Allen Ginsberg's use of Whitman or Eileen Myles' repurposing of Catholic ritual and Americana.

Intersectionality: Multiple Axes of Identity

A defining theme of late 20th-century feminist and queer literature is intersectionality—a concept first articulated by legal scholar Kimberlé Crenshaw, but long explored in the works of authors like Audre Lorde, Gloria Anzaldúa, and Alice Walker. Intersectional texts examine how gender identity is never singular, but always mediated by race, class, nationality, sexuality, ability, and religion.

Literature grounded in intersectionality resists simplistic narratives of oppression or identity. Instead, it offers nuanced, layered depictions of lived experience, where privilege and marginalization intersect in complex ways. This approach also challenges the homogeneity of earlier feminist movements, insisting that liberation must be inclusive, contextual, and coalition-driven.

Shaping the Canon: Challenges and Achievements

For much of literary history, the canon of American literature was overwhelmingly white, male, and heteronormative—constructed around notions of "universal" experience that were in fact deeply exclusionary. Female, LGBTQ+, and gender-nonconforming authors were long relegated to the margins of academic discourse, their works dismissed as too personal, too political, or insufficiently "literary" by dominant critical standards. Yet beginning in the mid-20th century and accelerating in the 1970s and beyond, a growing movement of scholars, critics, and activists began to challenge the canon's exclusivity and redefine the boundaries of literary value and legitimacy.

This transformation was neither swift nor uncontested. It involved decades of resistance, scholarship, and advocacy, both inside and outside the academy. Today, the presence of feminist and queer authors in syllabi, anthologies, and major literary prizes reflects not only aesthetic recognition but political victory—the result of persistent efforts to ensure that literature reflects the diversity of human experience.

Exclusion from the Canon: A Historical Overview

For centuries, women and LGBTQ+ authors were excluded from mainstream literary discourse, often denied access to publication, criticism, and institutional validation. Even celebrated authors such as Emily Dickinson, Zora Neale Hurston, or Walt Whitman were, at various points, marginalized due to their gender, race, or perceived queerness. Many writers, particularly women, were forced to publish under male pseudonyms or anonymously to gain legitimacy.

This exclusion was not merely a matter of oversight but reflected structural biases: patriarchal academic institutions, male-dominated publishing industries, and critical paradigms that privileged male-centered narratives of heroism, individualism, and rationality. As a result, women's writing was often relegated to the realm of "domestic fiction" or "sentimentalism," while queer writing was pathologized, censored, or erased.

The Rise of Feminist Literary Criticism

The 1970s marked a turning point in the reclamation of marginalized literary voices, thanks to the rise of feminist literary criticism. Pioneering scholars such as Elaine Showalter, Sandra Gilbert, and Susan Gubar launched a sustained critique of the male-dominated canon and its interpretive frameworks.

- Elaine Showalter's concept of "gynocriticism" called for a distinct critical approach rooted in the experiences and traditions of women writers, rather than through the lens of male-defined standards.
- Gilbert and Gubar's seminal work, *The Madwoman in the Attic* (1979), examined how 19th-century women writers like Charlotte Brontë and Mary Shelley used fiction to challenge the constraints of patriarchal ideology, often through themes of madness, rebellion, and doubled selves.

These scholars emphasized the need to recover "lost" women writers, re-evaluate previously dismissed genres (such as diaries, letters, and domestic fiction), and interrogate how gender influences literary production and interpretation.

Queer Theory and LGBTQ+ Literary Inclusion

By the 1990s, the emergence of queer theory further expanded the boundaries of literary analysis. Scholars like Eve Kosofsky Sedgwick, Judith Butler, and Michael Warner argued that sexuality, like gender, was a cultural construct shaped by discourse and power, and that literature could serve as a site of subversion, resistance, and transformation.

Queer theory helped legitimize the study of LGBTQ+ authors, themes, and representations, not as niche or peripheral subjects but as central to understanding broader cultural dynamics. The works of writers like James Baldwin, Audre Lorde, Allen Ginsberg, Jean Genet, and Leslie Feinberg were brought into mainstream critical conversation, and sexuality became a recognized lens of literary inquiry alongside race, class, and gender.

Reshaping Institutions: From Margins to the Center

Over time, these critical interventions led to significant institutional changes. University curricula, once dominated by Eurocentric and patriarchal texts, began to incorporate diverse, intersectional voices. Literary anthologies, such as *The Norton Anthology of Literature by Women* or *This Bridge Called My Back*, provided platforms for previously marginalized writers and helped canonize their work for future generations.

Moreover, major literary awards and recognitions—including the Pulitzer Prize, National Book Award, and Nobel Prize—began honoring female and queer authors. Writers such as Toni Morrison, Alice Walker, Adrienne Rich, and Joyce Carol Oates became not only celebrated artists but symbols of literary legitimacy for underrepresented groups.

Ongoing Challenges and Future Directions

Despite these achievements, challenges remain. Representation in publishing remains unequal, with BIPOC, trans, and disabled writers still facing systemic barriers. Backlashes against so-called "identity politics" or "wokeness" continue to threaten the gains of inclusive literary scholarship. Furthermore, the commercial pressures of the literary marketplace can sometimes tokenize diverse voices without fully supporting structural change.

Nonetheless, the inclusion of feminist, queer, and intersectional perspectives has irrevocably altered the literary landscape. What was once peripheral is now central. The canon is no longer a static list but a dynamic, contested, and evolving space—open to revision, expansion, and critique.

Contemporary Voices and the Future

The enduring legacy of 20th-century feminist, queer, and gender-nonconforming literature is vibrantly alive in the work of contemporary authors who continue to challenge conventions, expand the boundaries of identity, and reimagine the possibilities of literature itself. These writers build upon a rich foundation of political resistance, personal testimony, and artistic innovation while responding to new realities—digital culture, trans visibility, intersectionality, trauma theory, and global migration.

Far from presenting a singular narrative, contemporary gender- and identity-focused literature embraces multiplicity, contradiction, and fluidity. It celebrates literature as a living, shape-shifting form that can accommodate the complexities of race, gender, class, and sexuality in our time. The following authors exemplify this new era of American letters.

Roxane Gay (b. 1974)

Author of *Bad Feminist* (2014) and *Hunger* (2017), Roxane Gay is among the most influential cultural critics and essayists of the 21st century. Her work engages deeply with intersectional feminism, body politics, trauma, and cultural critique, often blending memoir with literary analysis.

In *Bad Feminist*, Gay explores what it means to be an imperfect feminist navigating pop culture, politics, and academia. *Hunger* is a raw, vulnerable account of living in a fat body after sexual violence, challenging societal narratives around desire, control, and shame.

Gay's voice is distinctive for its honesty, clarity, and refusal to separate the personal from the political. Her writing has helped popularize a nuanced, accessible feminism that remains deeply grounded in lived experience.

Ocean Vuong (b. 1988)

Born in Vietnam and raised in the United States, Ocean Vuong is a poet, novelist, and essayist whose work explores the intersections of queerness, trauma, war, language, and diaspora. His debut novel, *On Earth We're Briefly Gorgeous* (2019), is an epistolary narrative written from a queer Vietnamese American son to his illiterate mother. The novel blurs genre—melding poetry and prose—and navigates themes of immigrant identity, toxic masculinity, and queer coming-of-age with lyrical grace.

Vuong's poetic style foregrounds fragmentation and tenderness, reflecting a generation shaped by both inherited and personal trauma, as well as a deep longing for connection across cultural and emotional boundaries.

Carmen Maria Machado (b. 1986)

With *Her Body and Other Parties* (2017) and *In the Dream House* (2019), Carmen Maria Machado has redefined genre, narrative, and feminist horror. Her work often merges science fiction, magical realism, gothic horror, and memoir, pushing readers to reconsider the boundaries of fiction and autobiography.

In the Dream House is a groundbreaking memoir of same-sex intimate partner abuse, written in a formally experimental style—each chapter assumes a different narrative lens (e.g., "Dream House as Noir," "Dream House as Stoner Comedy"). This kaleidoscopic approach deconstructs trauma narratives while addressing the lack of cultural models for queer abuse.

Machado's work is a potent example of how contemporary feminist and queer writers use form as content, highlighting how trauma, memory, and desire defy linear storytelling.

Torrey Peters (b. 1981)

Author of *Detransition, Baby* (2021), Torrey Peters became the first openly trans woman nominated for the Women's Prize for Fiction. Her novel is a provocative, deeply humane exploration of gender transition, parenthood, and chosen family. Peters tackles complex and controversial questions—about what it means to be a woman, to be a parent, to detransition, and to live with the legacies of past identities—through a narrative that balances wit, compassion, and philosophical depth.

In centering trans women's voices without sanitizing or simplifying their experiences, Peters signals a powerful shift in the literary landscape: one that values messiness, multiplicity, and radical empathy over normativity and closure.

Saidiya Hartman (b. 1961)

A scholar and creative writer, Saidiya Hartman's *Wayward Lives, Beautiful Experiments* (2019) blends archival research, literary experimentation, and historical imagination to reconstruct the lives of young Black women at the turn of the 20th century.

Hartman employs what she calls "critical fabulation"—a method that uses fiction to fill in the silences of the historical record, especially in cases where marginalized lives were ignored, misrepresented, or erased.

Her work confronts the violence of the archive, the limits of conventional historiography, and the need for reparative narrative practices. Hartman's prose is lyrical, radical, and deeply political, challenging literary and academic forms alike.

Emerging Trends and the Literary Horizon

Across the work of these authors and others, several new directions can be identified in 21st-century literature related to gender and identity:

- **Intersectional experimentation:** Writers refuse to isolate gender from race, class, disability, or cultural background. Instead, they embrace overlapping, often contradictory subject positions.
- **Genre fluidity:** Boundaries between fiction, nonfiction, memoir, criticism, poetry, and speculative fiction are increasingly porous, reflecting the fluidity of identity itself.
- **Queer futurism and trans aesthetics:** Literature explores what gender might become, not just what it has been—often imagining radically new futures and selves.
- **Digital narratives and activism:** Many of these writers are also active online and in media spaces, using platforms to foster communities and critique dominant cultural narratives.

Conclusion: Toward an Inclusive Literary Landscape

The evolution of gender and identity in 20th- and 21st-century American literature represents one of the most transformative developments in the field. What began as a struggle for recognition—by women, LGBTQ+ individuals, and gender-nonconforming writers—has become a full-scale reimagining of the literary canon, reshaping how stories are told, who gets to tell them, and what counts as literature in the first place.

This shift was not simply additive. The demand was not merely to include more women or queer voices in an unchanged canon, but to challenge the ideological, aesthetic, and epistemological structures that had historically excluded them. As a result, contemporary American literature has become a site of dynamic contestation and renewal, where questions of power, identity, and representation are central to both form and content.

Literature as Resistance, Literature as Reclamation

Throughout the 20th century, literature became a crucial mode of resistance for those whose identities and experiences had been marginalized by dominant culture. Feminist authors questioned patriarchal narratives of domesticity, desire, and madness. Queer writers reclaimed their own stories from silence, stigma, or subtext. Trans and gender-nonconforming authors exploded the binary frameworks that limited how the body, voice, and self could be represented.

What united these diverse movements was not a singular vision of identity, but a commitment to speaking truth to power, even when that truth was fragmented, painful, or incomplete. These writers insisted on the validity of lived experience—not as a private concern, but as a literary and political intervention. In doing so, they redefined literature as a space for multiplicity, ambiguity, and radical honesty.

Beyond Representation: Formal Innovation and Narrative Disruption

The expansion of literary voices also brought with it an expansion of form and technique. Confessionalism, nonlinear storytelling, myth revision, genre hybridity, vernacular experimentation, and intertextuality became tools for expressing the complexities of marginalized identities. The very shape of the text was often disrupted—mirroring the disruption of normative ideas about gender, sexuality, and selfhood.

For instance, Toni Morrison's fragmented temporal structures, Ocean Vuong's poetic prose, or Carmen Maria Machado's genre-defying memoir are not simply aesthetic choices—they are embodied acts of resistance against linear, universalizing, and heteronormative narratives. These authors insist that identity is not fixed, and therefore the stories we tell about identity must also remain fluid, hybrid, and open-ended.

The Mirror and the Map

This body of literature holds up a mirror to American society, revealing its failures: racism, sexism, homophobia, transphobia, and systemic erasure.

At the same time, it functions as a map—charting alternative paths forward, reimagining kinship and community, and modeling new ways of being in the world.

By centering the marginalized, feminist and queer literatures also decentralize the hegemonic gaze. They expose the limits of dominant narratives while offering spaces for healing, solidarity, and imaginative freedom. In this way, literature becomes not only a witness to suffering but also an agent of transformation.

Continuing the Work

Despite these advancements, the work of literary inclusion is far from complete. Canonical institutions—academic curricula, publishing houses, literary awards, and critical gatekeepers—still reflect enduring disparities in access and power. New waves of writers, particularly those who are trans, disabled, Indigenous, or from immigrant communities, continue to push against the boundaries of what is visible, valued, and legible in mainstream literary culture.

The future of American literature lies in its ability to remain responsive, reflexive, and radically inclusive—a space where questions of gender and identity are not side notes, but central threads in the ongoing tapestry of national storytelling.

Final Reflection

Gender and identity are not static categories—they are performative, contextual, and perpetually in flux. American literature, at its most vibrant, has mirrored this truth. In the voices of those once silenced, we find not only critique but creativity, not only dissent but vision. These authors have not simply asked to be read; they have demanded that we read differently—more widely, more critically, and more compassionately.

In doing so, they have not just expanded the literary landscape—they have redefined its very terrain.

8

Technology, War, and the Literary Imagination

Narrating the Age of Machines and Madness

Introduction: From Typewriters to Atomic Bombs

The 20th century was an era marked by contradiction: astonishing technological innovation coexisted with brutal warfare and unprecedented destruction. For American writers, this historical context presented not only new subjects to narrate but also new challenges in how to narrate. The language of the past—rooted in notions of progress, reason, and human mastery—often seemed inadequate in the face of mechanized slaughter, nuclear annihilation, and digital abstraction.

From the rhythmic clatter of the typewriter to the silent detonation of the atomic bomb, from the radio waves that connected nations to the surveillance networks that monitored them, the technological and military developments of the 20th century reshaped the aesthetic, ethical, and ontological frameworks of American literature. Writers were forced to ask: How do you represent a world in which machines outpace humans, where war is waged by unseen forces, and where reality itself is mediated by screens and codes?

Technology as Both Muse and Threat

Technology appeared in 20th-century American literature in dual and often contradictory forms. On one hand, it promised modernity, convenience, and progress—the automobile, the typewriter, the airplane, the television, and eventually the computer all transformed daily life. On the other, these same advancements were deeply implicated in alienation, mechanization, surveillance, and mass destruction.

Authors such as Don DeLillo, Thomas Pynchon, and Ray Bradbury dramatized this duality, portraying technology as both a symbol of human ingenuity and a harbinger of existential dread. In literature, the machine often became a metaphor: for the mechanized routines of modern life, for the dehumanization of industrial capitalism, or for the cold logic of bureaucratic and military systems.

War and the Fragmented Self

Equally influential were the century's global and domestic conflicts. The First and Second World Wars, the Korean and Vietnam Wars, and the Cold War's ever-present nuclear threat created a psychological and emotional terrain that demanded literary exploration. War produced not just physical destruction, but epistemological crisis—a breakdown of meaning, morality, and narrative coherence.

Writers like Ernest Hemingway, Kurt Vonnegut, and Tim O'Brien sought to depict war not merely as a political event but as a psychological rupture. Their works reveal fractured selves, unstable chronologies, and unreliable narration—all formal responses to the disorientation caused by violence. In doing so, they rejected the glorification of war found in earlier literature and replaced it with portraits of trauma, guilt, absurdity, and moral ambiguity.

Revolutions in Literary Form

The impact of technology and war on literature was not limited to content; it also transformed form and structure. The rise of modernist and postmodernist aesthetics—characterized by fragmentation, nonlinearity, irony, and self-reflexivity—was intimately tied to a world shaped by mass production, mechanical reproduction, and global warfare.

- Modernist writers like T.S. Eliot and William Faulkner experimented with stream-of-consciousness, polyphony, and narrative disjunction to reflect the fractured modern psyche.
- Postmodernists such as Pynchon and Burroughs used collage, pastiche, and metafiction to capture a world where meaning itself seemed to collapse under the weight of competing technologies and ideologies.
- Science fiction, long relegated to the margins, emerged as a literary laboratory for testing ethical, political, and existential questions raised by technology—from artificial intelligence to time travel to genetic engineering.

A Literature of Ethical Reckoning

Technology and war did not simply provide new literary motifs; they provoked deep ethical questions. What is the writer's responsibility in an age of genocide and atomic power? Can fiction bear witness to atrocity, or does it inevitably aestheticize suffering? Can language itself survive the assault of totalitarianism, propaganda, and digital noise?

These questions are central to the works of Elie Wiesel, Sylvia Plath, Norman Mailer, and Joan Didion, among others. Their writing interrogates the limits of representation, the complicity of the intellectual, and the possibility of redemption in a century defined by both cultural innovation and catastrophic violence.

The World Wars: A Fractured Worldview

The two World Wars of the 20th century redefined the human condition in literature. They shattered the Enlightenment ideals of reason, progress, and order, replacing them with disillusionment, existential crisis, and moral ambiguity. For American writers, especially those who experienced war firsthand, the battlefield became a crucible not only of violence but of narrative transformation. The literature that emerged was fragmented, introspective, and deeply skeptical of traditional heroic or patriotic storytelling.

World War I (1914–1918): The Birth of Disillusionment

Though the United States entered World War I relatively late (1917), the psychological and cultural aftermath of the conflict reverberated deeply across American letters. Many American writers—often expatriates—grappled with a sense of alienation, futility, and spiritual void, themes that defined the "Lost Generation".

Ernest Hemingway – A Farewell to Arms (1929)

Hemingway's terse, unadorned prose became emblematic of postwar realism. In A Farewell to Arms, he draws on his own service as an ambulance driver in Italy to craft a story of doomed love and existential despair. The war is not glorified; instead, it serves as a backdrop for emotional detachment, fatalism, and the collapse of romantic illusions. Hemingway's minimalist style—what he called the "iceberg theory"—reflects a world where meaning lies submerged and language cannot fully contain trauma.

John Dos Passos – U.S.A. Trilogy (1930–1936)

Dos Passos pioneered narrative experimentation as a means of conveying national disintegration. His U.S.A. *Trilogy*—comprised of *The 42nd Parallel*, 1919, and *The Big Money*—weaves together "newsreels," stream-of-consciousness "camera eye" passages, and biographical sketches to reflect a fragmented American consciousness. The trilogy critiques capitalism, war, and the loss of individual agency in a mechanized society. It presents World War I not as a unifying national cause but as a moment that fractures personal and collective identity.

Literary Impact

World War I catalyzed the emergence of modernism in American literature. Writers like Hemingway, Dos Passos, and Gertrude Stein rejected the romanticism and moral certainties of previous generations. Instead, they developed techniques—minimalism, non-linear narration, irony, fragmentation—that echoed the shattered landscapes and psyches left by mechanized warfare.

World War II (1939–1945): Confronting Genocide and Total War

Unlike the First World War, which was often depicted as a tragic mistake, World War II introduced a literature of conscience, atrocity, and existential absurdity. The Holocaust, the atomic bombings of Hiroshima and Nagasaki, and the rise of fascism brought the capacity for human evil and technological devastation into stark relief. Literature from this period often wrestled with guilt, survival, complicity, and the failure of rationality.

Norman Mailer – The Naked and the Dead (1948)

Written while Mailer was still in his twenties, this novel stands as one of the most influential American depictions of the war. Set in the Pacific Theater, it combines naturalistic detail with philosophical introspection, offering a psychologically rich portrayal of soldiers shaped by fear, class dynamics, and moral ambiguity. The novel departs from heroic or nationalist tropes, emphasizing instead the dehumanization of military life and the brutality of hierarchical systems.

Kurt Vonnegut – Slaughterhouse-Five (1969)

Vonnegut's surreal, genre-defying novel—part science fiction, part war memoir—is rooted in his experience as a prisoner of war during the firebombing of Dresden. The novel's protagonist, Billy Pilgrim, becomes "unstuck in time," a narrative strategy that mirrors the disorientation of trauma. With its recurring refrain "So it goes," the book offers a bleak, ironic commentary on death, war, and historical memory. *Slaughterhouse-Five* exemplifies postmodern responses to war: parodic, metafictional, and morally ambivalent.

Other Notable Figures

- Joseph Heller – *Catch-22* (1961): Satirizes the absurdity and circular logic of military bureaucracy.
- James Jones – *From Here to Eternity* (1951): Offers a gritty, pre-Pearl Harbor narrative that focuses on military repression and personal alienation.

The Evolution of the War Narrative

The literary legacy of the World Wars marked a decisive departure from the noble-war tradition of earlier American writing (e.g., Stephen Crane or Walt Whitman). Instead of courage and triumph, 20th-century war literature highlighted:

- The loss of individual agency in massive institutional systems.
- The collapse of moral certainty in the face of genocide and atomic warfare.
- The challenge of representing trauma, where traditional narrative structures often fell short.

Formally, this shift manifested in:

- Nonlinear storytelling
- Unreliable narrators
- Satire and irony
- Surrealism and science fiction tropes

These strategies allowed authors to critique not only the wars themselves but also the social systems, ideologies, and technologies that enabled them.

Cold War Anxiety and Dystopian Visions

In the aftermath of World War II, the United States found itself embroiled in a new kind of conflict—the Cold War, a decades-long ideological standoff with the Soviet Union that redefined the global order. Unlike conventional warfare, this conflict was marked by espionage, propaganda, arms races, nuclear brinkmanship, and an ever-present fear of annihilation. American literature in this period did not merely reflect the tensions of the era; it actively grappled with paranoia, surveillance, conformity, censorship, and existential dread, often through speculative and dystopian forms.

Literature as a Mirror of Cold War Paranoia

During the Cold War, the boundaries between fiction and political commentary became increasingly porous. Writers used allegory, satire, dystopia, and speculative fiction to explore a society gripped by fear, repression, and ideological orthodoxy. As the atomic bomb loomed over everyday life and McCarthyism silenced dissent, American authors turned to literature to express anxieties that could not be openly stated.

Ray Bradbury – *Fahrenheit 451* (1953)

Perhaps the most iconic dystopian novel of mid-century America, *Fahrenheit 451* imagines a future in which books are outlawed and "firemen" burn them. Bradbury's dystopia critiques not only government censorship but also the voluntary cultural descent into anti-intellectualism and distraction. The novel warns against the numbing effects of mass media, shallow entertainment, and technological pacification. Though written during the height of McCarthy-era repression, Bradbury's target is broader: the systemic suppression of thought and individuality. His spare yet lyrical prose evokes a world where knowledge is feared and history is erased.

Joseph Heller – *Catch-22* (1961)

A landmark work of postwar satire, Heller's *Catch-22* encapsulates the absurdity of bureaucratic logic and the psychological disintegration it causes. Set in World War II but published during the Cold War, the novel critiques the militarization of logic and language, where contradictory rules trap individuals in systems beyond their control. The titular "Catch-22" has become shorthand for circular, self-defeating reasoning—a critique of both wartime logic and Cold War ideology.

Heller's nonlinear narrative, absurd humor, and fragmented structure reflect the cultural disorientation of the Cold War era, particularly its skepticism toward authority and institutions. Catch-22 remains a profound meditation on freedom, autonomy, and the cost of survival under inhumane systems.

Arthur Miller – *The Crucible* (1953)

Written at the height of McCarthyism, Miller's The Crucible uses the 1692 Salem witch trials as an allegory for the Red Scare, when the U.S. government, through the House Un-American Activities Committee (HUAC), aggressively persecuted suspected communists. The play explores the mass psychology of fear, scapegoating, and the erosion of civil liberties. By drawing a parallel between the Puritanical hysteria of the 17th century and the political repression of his own time, Miller dramatized the dangers of ideological absolutism and moral panic.

Miller's tightly constructed drama is both historical and timeless, offering a cautionary tale about the fragility of truth in a climate of fear. The personal becomes political as characters sacrifice honesty and justice for self-preservation.

Philip K. Dick and Cold War Science Fiction

Philip K. Dick's prolific output in the 1950s and '60s exemplified Cold War psychological and philosophical anxieties, particularly concerning identity, reality, and state control. His novels—such as *The Man in the High Castle* (1962), which imagined an alternate reality where the Axis powers won WWII—used speculative fiction to interrogate authoritarianism, technological surveillance, and epistemological instability.

Dick's characters often suffer from paranoia and fragmented identity, reflecting the disorientation of a world saturated with propaganda, simulacra, and existential dread. His narratives resonate with the Cold War's disruption of certainty and the increasing blurring between truth and illusion.

Sylvia Plath and the Cold War Psyche

While not overtly political in the Cold War sense, Sylvia Plath's work—especially *The Bell Jar* (1963) and the poems in *Ariel*—captured the internalization of Cold War anxieties, particularly among women. Plath's exploration of mental illness, domestic alienation, and the pressure to conform can be read as a personal manifestation of larger societal tensions. In a world where nuclear threats, rigid gender roles, and cultural conformity prevailed, Plath's writing gave voice to the psychological toll of suppressed agency and systemic control.

John Hersey – *Hiroshima* (1946)

One of the earliest and most sobering literary responses to nuclear warfare, Hersey's *Hiroshima* combines journalistic detail with narrative prose to recount the stories of six survivors of the atomic bombing. By humanizing the victims and depicting the long-term devastation, Hersey challenged the American public to confront the moral consequences of technological power. The work stands as a stark, understated indictment of nuclear war and a call for ethical reflection in the atomic age.

Key Themes and Narrative Techniques

- **Dystopia and Surveillance:** Novels depict totalitarian regimes that control thought, memory, and expression (e.g., Bradbury, Dick).
- **Absurdism and Bureaucratic Irony:** Satirical approaches to the illogic of power structures (e.g., Heller).
- **Historical Allegory:** Use of past events to critique contemporary political repression (e.g., Miller).
- **Psychological Realism and Fragmentation:** Internal conflicts mirror societal instability (e.g., Plath).

Technology and the Machine Age

As the 20th century progressed, American literature found itself grappling with a new and increasingly pervasive force: technology. No longer confined to factories or battlefields, machines entered the intimate spaces of everyday life—from the living room television to the computer terminal. Alongside the rise of automation, digital culture, artificial intelligence, and biotechnology, literature began to reflect on the ways in which human identity, perception, and social experience were being transformed, fragmented, and sometimes obliterated by mechanized systems.

Unlike early industrial-era literature, which often expressed optimism or awe toward innovation, late 20th-century works frequently regarded technology with ambivalence or alarm. Writers began to explore how machines reshape not only the material world but also the structures of consciousness, language, and desire.

Don DeLillo – *White Noise* (1985)

One of the most influential postmodern novels of the late 20th century, DeLillo's *White Noise* critiques the hypermediated, consumer-driven, and anxiety-saturated culture of contemporary America. The novel's protagonist, Jack Gladney, is a professor of "Hitler Studies" living in a suburban world permeated by advertising jingles, toxic environmental disasters, and fear of death.

Technology in *White Noise* is not merely mechanical but **existential**—manifesting through media, pharmaceuticals, data collection, and invisible systems of control. The omnipresence of white noise itself—TV static, radio chatter, background hum—symbolizes the loss of authentic experience in an environment where simulation has replaced reality. DeLillo's prose is spare and ironic, and his critique of the digital spectacle and commodified fear resonates even more strongly in today's algorithmic age.

Thomas Pynchon – *Gravity's Rainbow* (1973)

In Pynchon's sprawling and cryptic novel, technology becomes a metaphor for both control and chaos. Set during and after World War II, *Gravity's Rainbow* is centered around the German V-2 rocket, which becomes a symbol of both technological triumph and existential despair. The novel explores themes of entropy, paranoia, sexual deviance, surveillance, and weaponized science.

Pynchon portrays a world in which human lives are dictated by vast, unknowable systems—corporations, governments, military-industrial complexes—creating an atmosphere of mechanical determinism and psychic fragmentation. Characters are swept up in equations, conspiracies, and feedback loops, with little hope of asserting free will.

The novel's nonlinear, encyclopedic style mimics the disruptive, nonlinear logic of machine systems, embedding scientific jargon, cultural references, and linguistic play. Pynchon anticipates the posthuman condition by questioning where the human ends and the machine begins, both materially and metaphysically.

Common Themes in Machine-Age Literature

The rise of the technological imagination in American literature led to a host of recurring themes that interrogated the relationship between humanity and its creations:

Loss of Authenticity in an Artificial World

As simulations and digital media replace direct experience, writers question what it means to live an "authentic" life. DeLillo's characters often float through environments structured more by media than by physical or emotional reality. Technology becomes a mediator between people and their world, and in doing so, erodes emotional depth and individual agency.

Surveillance, Control, and Systemic Alienation

Following the insights of Michel Foucault and extending Orwellian fears, many authors depict societies in which technology facilitates constant observation and behavioral manipulation. From government databases to corporate algorithms, machines serve not only as tools but as invisible architectures of control, often without moral accountability. In novels like *Gravity's Rainbow*, paranoia is not irrational—it is a survival mechanism in a world governed by hidden networks.

Machine vs. Human Consciousness

Technology is not merely external in this literature; it seeps into the psyche, altering how individuals think, feel, and remember. Some characters experience the world through computational metaphors or machinic logic. This raises profound philosophical questions: Can machines think? What separates human awareness from artificial intelligence? Does the increasing automation of life devalue the human soul—or merely redefine it?

Entropy, Fragmentation, and the Collapse of Narrative Order

Influenced by the Second Law of Thermodynamics, writers like Pynchon use entropy as a metaphor for the breakdown of meaning, coherence, and stability in both technological and narrative systems. In an age of infinite data and acceleration, stories unravel—mirroring the disintegrative effects of technology on cultural memory and human intimacy.

Other Notable Works and Authors

- William Gibson – *Neuromancer* (1984): Though not American, Gibson's cyberpunk classic heavily influenced American literary and cultural depictions of virtual reality, hacking, and artificial intelligence.

- Octavia Butler – *Parable of the Sower* (1993): Explores how technological collapse intersects with race, class, and ecological crisis.
- Philip K. Dick – *Do Androids Dream of Electric Sheep?* (1968): Questions the boundaries between humans and machines, emotion and programming, ethics and artificiality.

Cyberpunk and the Rise of Digital Futures

By the final decades of the 20th century, American literature found itself confronting an entirely new technological frontier: the digital. With the rise of personal computers, virtual reality, artificial intelligence, and the early internet, writers began imagining worlds in which digital technologies not only augmented reality but *redefined* it. The most powerful expression of this vision emerged in a literary subgenre known as cyberpunk.

Cyberpunk offered a gritty, dystopian vision of the near future, characterized by high-tech environments and low-life protagonists. The genre combined noir aesthetics with cutting-edge speculation, exploring themes of identity, surveillance, corporate dominance, cybernetic enhancement, and digital consciousness. While rooted in science fiction, cyberpunk deeply influenced the broader American literary imagination, especially in its cultural critique, fragmented style, and urban realism.

William Gibson and *Neuromancer* (1984)

The defining work of cyberpunk literature, *Neuromancer* by William Gibson, envisioned a future where cyberspace—Gibson's now-famous term—had become a tangible realm of digital experience. The novel follows Case, a washed-up hacker navigating a world of multinational conglomerates, cybernetic implants, artificial intelligences, and shadowy power brokers.

Though Canadian, Gibson's work has had a profound impact on American literary and cinematic culture, influencing films like *The Matrix*, shaping the aesthetics of digital dystopia, and blurring the lines between genre fiction and literary experimentation.

Key themes in *Neuromancer* include:

- **Disembodiment and virtual identity:** Characters jack into cyberspace, leaving behind their physical bodies and entering a world of pure information.
- **Corporate dystopia:** Governments are weak, and corporations wield unprecedented power, controlling lives and data with impunity.
- **Posthumanism:** The boundaries between humans and machines collapse, raising questions about consciousness, autonomy, and technological integration.

Gibson's dense, slang-infused prose style mimics the chaotic, data-saturated environment of his imagined future—an aesthetic that has become foundational in portraying digital modernity.

Cyberpunk Aesthetics and Literary Impact

Cyberpunk's influence goes beyond plot and setting. It also ushered in a distinct stylistic and thematic shift:

- **Urban Noir Environments:** Fictional futures are typically set in decaying mega-cities full of neon lights, ethnic enclaves, and techno-slums.
- **Technological Intimacy:** Devices are not distant machines but invasive, body-integrated tools—cybernetic limbs, neural interfaces, biotech augmentations.
- **Decentralized Narratives:** Many cyberpunk stories reject linear structure, instead mimicking the fragmentation of digital experience and algorithmic logic.
- **Digital Alienation:** Characters are often disconnected from community, lost in corporate systems, or struggling with simulated realities.

Afrofuturism: Race, Identity, and Speculative Technology

While early cyberpunk was often criticized for being white, male, and technocratic, African American writers like Octavia Butler and Samuel R. Delany began to reimagine speculative futures through the lens of Black identity, colonial history, and cultural hybridity. Their work challenged the default assumptions of the genre and introduced Afrofuturism—a movement that uses speculative fiction to explore the intersections of race, technology, and liberation.

Octavia Butler (1947–2006)

Butler's groundbreaking novels merged science fiction with African American history and feminist consciousness. In works like *Kindred* (1979), she explored time travel as a means to interrogate slavery and ancestry. In the *Parable* series (*Parable of the Sower* and *Parable of the Talents*), she imagined a near-future America wracked by ecological collapse, inequality, and fascism—only to offer spiritual and political visions of survival through community-building and adaptability.

Butler's protagonists are often Black women, biologically altered or telepathic, navigating hostile environments where identity, ethics, and evolution are in flux.

Samuel R. Delany (b. 1942)

An openly gay African American writer, Delany used speculative fiction to interrogate language, sexuality, and society. In *Dhalgren* (1975), he created a linguistically experimental and sexually fluid narrative set in a surreal, post-apocalyptic city. His earlier works, such as *Nova* and *Babel-17*, fused cyberpunk-like technological speculation with metaphysical and semiotic inquiry.

Delany's work defied binary categories of genre and identity, making him a forerunner of both postmodern science fiction and queer speculative literature.

Cyberpunk's Cultural Legacy

Cyberpunk did not remain confined to literature. Its vision of a networked, post-industrial dystopia permeated American culture—seen in everything from Hollywood films (*Blade Runner*, *The Matrix*) to video games (*Deus Ex*, *Cyberpunk 2077*), to fashion, art, and even hacker culture. It anticipated the real-life fusion of humans and machines, the commodification of data, and the ways in which digital reality can reshape our sense of self.

The genre's anti-heroic protagonists, jaded tone, and critique of capitalism also echo broader postmodern themes, making it a bridge between traditional science fiction and literary experimentation.

War, Trauma, and Narrative Innovation

The literature of war has long been a powerful medium through which authors confront violence, loss, and moral ambiguity. However, in the 20th century, particularly after Vietnam, literary responses to war evolved significantly in both form and tone, driven by the need to depict not just the external chaos of battle, but the internal disintegration of the self. Traditional linear narratives and heroic arcs no longer sufficed. Instead, writers turned to nonlinear storytelling, metafiction, and fragmented structures to convey the psychological wounds inflicted by warfare—not only on soldiers, but also on communities and future generations.

These narrative innovations mirrored the complexity of trauma, especially the kind associated with modern warfare: morally fraught, politically contested, and fought in environments where the enemy was often invisible and the objectives uncertain. From the jungles of Vietnam to the mesas of New Mexico, American writers used literary experimentation as a way to map trauma, memory, and the uncertain terrain of healing.

Tim O'Brien – *The Things They Carried* (1990)

Tim O'Brien's *The Things They Carried* is widely regarded as one of the most innovative and poignant literary works about the Vietnam War. Blurring the boundaries between memoir and fiction, the book consists of interlinked short stories that explore the physical and emotional burdens carried by American soldiers.

- The titular story details not only the literal items soldiers carry—guns, letters, keepsakes—but also the intangible weight of fear, guilt, love, and memory.
- The narrative frequently circles back on itself, revising and recontextualizing events, reflecting how trauma distorts and fragments memory.
- O'Brien frequently intrudes as both character and author, raising philosophical questions about truth in storytelling, the nature of fiction, and whether narrative can ever adequately convey trauma.

> *"A thing may happen and be a total lie; another thing may not happen and be truer than the truth."* – Tim O'Brien

O'Brien's work exemplifies metafiction as a tool for emotional truth, suggesting that storytelling—however constructed—is essential to processing trauma, even if it cannot offer resolution.

Leslie Marmon Silko – *Ceremony* (1977)

Leslie Marmon Silko's *Ceremony* tells the story of Tayo, a Laguna Pueblo WWII veteran struggling with post-traumatic stress disorder upon returning to a reservation plagued by poverty and cultural dislocation. Silko's narrative approach is deeply nonlinear and mythopoetic, blending personal trauma with tribal myths, oral tradition, and ritual healing.

- The novel shifts between prose and poetry, past and present, Western and Indigenous storytelling forms.
- Tayo's PTSD is not just a result of war, but of colonial trauma—the loss of land, language, and identity.
- Healing, in Silko's novel, comes not through medicine or therapy, but through ceremony, storytelling, and reconnection to ancestral ways.

Silko's integration of Native worldviews challenges dominant narratives of war trauma that center individual psychology. Instead, she presents trauma as communal and intergenerational, and healing as cultural reclamation.

Narrative Themes and Techniques

Authors responding to the trauma of war have employed a wide range of stylistic innovations to mirror the psychological and moral complexity of armed conflict:

Moral Ambiguity of Warfare

Unlike earlier war literature, which often portrayed combat as heroic or patriotic, 20th-century works from Vietnam and beyond underscore the conflicted, morally compromised nature of modern conflict. Soldiers grapple not with enemies alone, but with their own actions, the legitimacy of their mission, and the loss of innocence.

- In *The Things They Carried*, O'Brien meditates on killing and cowardice, showing how moral lines blur in combat.
- Silko questions the idea that Native Americans could serve a country that has oppressed them, raising the paradox of patriotism in the face of colonization.

Psychological Fragmentation (PTSD)

The fragmented consciousness of trauma victims is reflected in the form of these works. Flashbacks, dissociation, and unreliable narration become literary tools to depict how memory becomes fractured and nonlinear after intense emotional upheaval.

- Tayo's perception of time and self is destabilized, with past and present bleeding into each other.
- O'Brien revisits the same scenes with variations, creating a loop that mirrors the obsessive replaying of traumatic memories.

Intergenerational Trauma and Cultural Memory

Both war and colonization produce trauma that ripples across generations. Contemporary war narratives increasingly explore how the scars of violence are transmitted through family, community, and cultural inheritance.

- Silko's novel links Tayo's trauma to centuries of Indigenous suffering and resilience, emphasizing storytelling as both burden and balm.
- Later authors, including Viet Thanh Nguyen (*The Sympathizer*) and Ocean Vuong (*On Earth We're Briefly Gorgeous*), continue this tradition, showing how war trauma shapes diasporic and postcolonial identities.

The Literary Ethics of War and Progress

As the 20th century unfolded—with its massive technological leaps and unprecedented destruction—American writers became increasingly preoccupied with the moral contradictions embedded in modern "progress." The very forces that had once been celebrated for advancing civilization—science, technology, and rationalism—had also given rise to industrialized warfare, nuclear annihilation, environmental degradation, and mass surveillance. Literature, in response, became a crucial space for exploring the ethical costs of this trajectory.

American authors began to scrutinize the promises of modernity, interrogating whether technological advancement necessarily equated to human betterment. Could a society that built concentration camps, dropped atomic bombs, and created weapons of mass destruction still claim to be civilized? Could progress be considered ethical if it was divorced from empathy, conscience, and humanistic values?

The Atomic Bomb and the Ethics of Scientific Knowledge

The detonation of atomic bombs over Hiroshima and Nagasaki in 1945 marked a turning point in human history—and literary consciousness. No longer was war a matter of mere guns and trenches; it now carried the potential for total annihilation.

- John Hersey's *Hiroshima* (1946) was one of the first literary responses to nuclear warfare. Through the intimate stories of six survivors, Hersey humanized the abstract statistics of mass death, foregrounding the ethical implications of technological power unleashed without moral reflection.
- Kurt Vonnegut's *Cat's Cradle* (1963) satirizes blind scientific ambition through the fictional substance "Ice-Nine," which threatens to freeze the entire planet. Vonnegut's narrative underscores the disconnect between scientific discovery and ethical accountability, suggesting that knowledge without wisdom can become catastrophic.

"Science is magic that works," Vonnegut famously wrote—but *Cat's Cradle* questions what kind of "magic" humanity has unleashed.

The Holocaust, Dehumanization, and Mechanized Evil

The Holocaust, perhaps more than any other event, forced writers to grapple with the ethical collapse that can accompany bureaucratic and technological systems. It was not only about hatred—it was about systematic, efficient, and industrialized genocide.

- Though not American, **Primo Levi's memoirs** influenced American literature by demonstrating how **language, science, and progress** could be co-opted into serving **inhuman ends**.
- American authors like **Philip Roth** and **Bernard Malamud** explored the psychological and spiritual wreckage that followed the Holocaust, both for survivors and for the broader human conscience.

Literary responses asked a fundamental question: How could the nation that produced Goethe, Beethoven, and Einstein also engineer Auschwitz?

Artificial Intelligence, Surveillance, and the Machine Mind

As computers and AI began to shape the latter half of the 20th century, writers turned their attention to the ethical implications of artificial consciousness, autonomy, and the devaluation of human labor and thought.

- Philip K. Dick, in novels like *Do Androids Dream of Electric Sheep?* (1968), pondered what it means to be human. His work raised ethical dilemmas surrounding empathy, identity, and artificial life, asking whether machines could become more humane than their creators.
- Don DeLillo and Thomas Pynchon continued this thread, depicting societies in which humans are increasingly mechanized and disconnected, caught in systems of control they neither understand nor escape.

The specter of technology replacing or regulating humanity prompted reflection on how progress, when stripped of conscience, leads not to liberation but to existential and societal crisis.

Themes of Ethical Reckoning in Literature

Across these works, several recurring ethical concerns emerge:

- **The Value of Human Life:** Can technological development truly be called progress if it comes at the cost of millions of lives—or the cheapening of life itself? Writers question whether modern society values efficiency over humanity.
- **The Cost of Industrialization:** Industrial-scale warfare, environmental devastation, and the alienation of labor raise doubts about whether industrial and technological "advancements" have improved the human condition—or only made destruction more efficient.
- **The Erosion of Empathy and Spirituality:** In hyper-rational, technologically saturated societies, many writers explore the loss of spiritual depth, human connection, and ethical grounding. The disconnection between moral intuition and scientific capability becomes a central concern.

Blending Genres: The Literary Fallout

The devastation of global conflict and the disorienting pace of technological change left a permanent imprint on the literary imagination of the 20th century. As traditional narrative structures failed to capture the surreal and morally ambiguous realities of the postwar world, writers began to blur, fracture, and reconfigure literary form. The result was an era of genre experimentation and boundary dissolution, where memoir merged with fiction, science fiction absorbed realism, and the novel became both a story and a self-aware critique of storytelling itself.

This aesthetic fragmentation was not merely stylistic—it was a direct response to a world where conventional truths had become suspect. Literature, once grounded in realism or idealism, began to reflect chaos, uncertainty, and rupture through innovative genre-blending.

Hybrid Genres: Reconstructing Form in the Ruins

Postwar literature witnessed the rise of hybrid genres—cross-pollinations of narrative forms that could better represent the contradictions and complexities of the age.

- Science fiction merged with realism, as in Kurt Vonnegut's *Slaughterhouse-Five* (1969), which recounts the real bombing of Dresden through the fantastical lens of time travel and alien abduction. The juxtaposition emphasizes the absurdity of war and the inadequacy of conventional realism in depicting trauma.
- Memoir and fiction intertwined, most notably in Tim O'Brien's *The Things They Carried* (1990), where autobiographical war recollections are deliberately blurred with invention. This creates an emotional truth that transcends factual accuracy, forcing readers to question the nature of storytelling, memory, and history.
- Dystopian allegory fused with political critique, as in Ray Bradbury's *Fahrenheit 451* (1953), which combined speculative fiction, psychological drama, and philosophical reflection to explore censorship and conformity in a media-dominated society.

By refusing to remain within fixed genres, these works carved out new literary terrains—expanding the boundaries of what fiction could be and do.

Metafiction and Unreliable Narrators: Narrating Uncertainty

The instability of the postwar world was matched by a literary turn toward narrative self-consciousness. Many authors used metafiction—stories that comment on their own construction—to highlight the limits of representation and the subjective nature of truth.

- In Thomas Pynchon's *The Crying of Lot 49* (1966), the protagonist's quest for meaning becomes a parody of interpretation itself, with plotlines spiraling into ambiguity and endless digressions. The novel openly resists resolution, mirroring a world where systems of power remain opaque and meaning elusive.

- Don DeLillo, in works like *White Noise* (1985), constructs narrators who are immersed in simulation and media spectacle, distanced from reality and often unreliable in their perceptions. Their fragmented consciousness echoes the disintegration of shared narratives in the postmodern age.

Unreliable narrators became emblematic of a broader epistemological crisis: in a world shaped by propaganda, surveillance, and trauma, how can anyone claim to speak truthfully?

Irony and Black Humor: Coping with the Absurd

Another signature feature of postwar literature is its embrace of irony, satire, and black humor—not merely as stylistic flourishes, but as psychic survival tools.

- Joseph Heller's *Catch-22* (1961) coined a term that came to define bureaucratic absurdity and circular logic. Its humor is savage, surreal, and rooted in the tragic recognition that war renders reason obsolete.
- Sylvia Plath's *The Bell Jar* (1963), though deeply serious in its portrayal of mental illness and gender oppression, uses irony to critique societal expectations and the performativity of sanity.
- In Philip K. Dick's paranoid science fiction, such as *Ubik* (1969), absurdity and unreliability become metaphors for technological disorientation and existential instability.

For many writers, laughter in the face of horror was not escapism but resistance—a way of reclaiming agency in a world where logic and morality had collapsed.

Mirroring a Fractured World: Form Reflecting Content

The blending of genres and narrative experimentation was not simply a reaction to stylistic trends; it was a mimetic strategy. In a fragmented world, only a fragmented form could do justice to the experience.

- The narrative disjunction in war literature often mirrors post-traumatic consciousness, where time is nonlinear, memory is unreliable, and identity is unstable.
- The fusion of genres allowed authors to capture both the banality and extremity of modern life, from boardrooms to battlefields, televisions to trenches.
- The playfulness of these texts, often undercut by bleakness, embodied the absurdity of existence in the atomic age.

Conclusion: Writing in the Shadow of Power

The 20th century stands as one of the most paradoxical eras in human history—an age of extraordinary technological achievement shadowed by apocalyptic violence and existential uncertainty. For American writers, this contradiction provided both material and mandate: to narrate, to question, and, most importantly, to bear witness to the moral and psychological costs of modernity.

From the muddy trenches of World War I to the bombed-out cities of Hiroshima and Dresden, from Cold War paranoia to the unsettling intimacy of digital surveillance, literature evolved as a vital space where technology and war were not merely documented, but deeply interrogated. Writers became the conscience of a culture hurtling toward progress without pause, often asking uncomfortable questions: What is the value of life in an age of mechanized death? Can humanity survive its own inventions? Where does the soul reside in a world of simulation, mass destruction, and bureaucratic inhumanity?

A Century of Invention and Invasion

This chapter has traced how American literature responded to a century in which power—military, technological, ideological—was both celebrated and feared. The weapons of war, the tools of surveillance, and the omnipresence of screens and machines became not only plot devices but metaphors for deeper anxieties about autonomy, identity, and truth. Authors such as Vonnegut, O'Brien, Pynchon, DeLillo, Silko, and Bradbury did not merely describe a world in crisis—they experimented with language and form to mirror that crisis in the very structure of their works.

Their novels, poems, and plays often eschewed traditional realism, instead embracing nonlinearity, fragmentation, metafiction, and hybrid genres to reflect the disintegration of trust in political institutions, objective truth, and even the coherence of the self.

Literature as Resistance and Reckoning

The literature of war and technology does not present easy answers. Rather, it wrestles with contradiction, embodying the tension between awe and terror, power and fragility, progress and devastation. It critiques the cost of empire, the machinery of death, and the ethical erosion wrought by consumerism, automation, and virtuality.

Importantly, these literary works resist the normalization of violence and the abstraction of human suffering. By focusing on the individual psyche, collective trauma, and cultural memory, they preserve what machines and wars often erase: empathy, reflection, and the messiness of lived experience.

The Role of the Writer in the Machine Age

In the shadow of technological and military power, American writers redefined the role of literature itself. It was no longer merely a mirror to society but a radical tool of interrogation—a way to deconstruct myths of heroism, rationality, and moral certainty. Literature became a space where dissent could flourish, where voices displaced by war or silenced by authority could speak with urgency and invention.

The writer, then, is not a passive observer but an active resistor—a chronicler of chaos, a critic of control, and a curator of human complexity. The act of writing became, in itself, a form of political and ethical engagement.

Legacy and Continuing Relevance

Though the 20th century has passed, the questions raised by its literature remain more relevant than ever. In an era of artificial intelligence, drone warfare, climate disaster, and algorithmic bias, the entanglement of technology and power continues to reshape our realities. The literary imagination—sharpened by decades of war and wonder—remains a crucial tool for navigating this ongoing terrain.

These works remind us that even in the face of overwhelming systems, stories matter. They help us remember, critique, and envision alternatives. They give shape to grief, provide language to protest, and offer space for healing and imagination.

9

The Immigrant Experience and Multicultural Voices

Many Tongues, One Nation: Rewriting the American Dream

Introduction: The Mosaic of American Identity

The United States has long cultivated its image as a land of immigrants—a nation forged through the dreams, labor, and resilience of people from across the globe. Traditionally characterized by the "melting pot" metaphor, which implies the blending of cultures into a singular American identity, contemporary scholars and writers argue that this concept erases the complexity and diversity of immigrant experiences. A more nuanced and respectful metaphor is that of a "mosaic"—a composition of distinct yet interconnected pieces, each retaining its unique shape and color while contributing to a larger, more inclusive national narrative.

Throughout the 20th century, immigrant voices gained increasing prominence in American literature. Writers who were either immigrants themselves or born to immigrant parents began to reshape literary traditions by injecting fresh idioms, multilingual sensibilities, hybrid identities, and global perspectives into their works. These authors expanded the thematic and stylistic range of American literature, engaging deeply with questions of identity, displacement, memory, and cultural legacy. Their stories emerged not merely as reflections of cultural difference but as interrogations of what it means to be American. As these literary contributions deepened and diversified the national canon, they prompted a rethinking of American identity itself—no longer fixed and singular, but plural, contested, and ever-evolving.

Literature as a Space of Belonging and Resistance

Immigrant literature has served as a critical medium for expressing the emotional, psychological, and cultural struggles of migration. Whether portraying families from Mexico settling in Chicago, refugees from Haiti resettling in Miami, or Chinese American girls navigating generational divides in California, these stories often reveal the dissonance between the longing for opportunity and the pain of cultural dislocation. Authors use fiction, poetry, drama, and memoir to render the intricate layers of immigrant life: the nostalgia for a lost homeland, the trauma of forced exile, the frustration of navigating racism and xenophobia, and the precarious balance between assimilation and cultural preservation.

Crucially, immigrant narratives do more than document hardship; they resist cultural erasure and redefine the contours of American identity. Writers such as Maxine Hong Kingston (*The Woman Warrior*), Sandra Cisneros (*The House on Mango Street*), Jhumpa Lahiri (*Interpreter of Maladies*), and Edwidge Danticat (*Breath, Eyes, Memory*) provide multifaceted portrayals of women navigating bicultural realities, often challenging patriarchal structures within both their ethnic communities and the broader American society. Through their works, these authors reclaim space in a literary landscape that historically excluded or misrepresented them. Their literature becomes a form of cultural activism, foregrounding voices that have too often been silenced or stereotyped.

These narratives also confront and complicate the myth of the American Dream. While immigrant characters often aspire to success and stability, their journeys reveal the barriers posed by systemic racism, class inequality, and gender bias. The dream, in their telling, is not universally accessible—it is filtered through structures of power that privilege some while excluding others. In this way, immigrant literature becomes not only a vehicle of storytelling but a site of resistance—challenging dominant ideologies and reimagining national ideals from the perspective of those historically left at the margins.

From Margin to Center: Shifting the Canon

The latter half of the 20th century witnessed a paradigm shift in American literature. Once confined to "ethnic" or "minority" literature shelves, the works of immigrant writers began to claim central space in mainstream literary discourse. This shift was propelled not only by critical acclaim and prestigious literary awards but also by the growing recognition of multiculturalism in academic curricula. Universities increasingly integrated immigrant narratives into their syllabi, acknowledging that these stories were essential—not supplementary—to understanding the American experience.

This transformation also coincided with larger socio-political changes: the Civil Rights Movement, the Immigration and Nationality Act of 1965, and the rise of global migration in the postcolonial world. As immigration patterns diversified, so too did the literary voices that emerged. Authors of Asian American, Latinx, African, Arab, Caribbean, Jewish, and mixed-heritage backgrounds brought with them new storytelling traditions, languages, and historical frameworks that enriched the American literary canon.

Importantly, these writers did not simply add multicultural flavors to a dominant tradition—they redefined the tradition itself. Works by Chang-rae Lee (*Native Speaker*), Julia Alvarez (*How the García Girls Lost Their Accents*), and Mohsin Hamid (*The Reluctant Fundamentalist*) illustrate the tensions between personal identity and political context, exploring how immigrant experiences are shaped by broader histories of colonialism, war, and displacement. By centering the lives of immigrants, these authors disrupted the normative, white-centric narrative of American life and created a more expansive and accurate reflection of the nation.

A Global America

As America's demographic landscape continues to diversify, its literature reflects an increasingly globalized identity. The 20th century saw the rise of transnational narratives that transcend the traditional binary of "homeland vs. host country." Writers like Chimamanda Ngozi Adichie (*Americanah*) explore how migration reconfigures one's sense of self, especially in the context of race and gender. Adichie's protagonist, for instance, confronts the complexities of being a Black woman in America versus Nigeria, navigating social expectations, political consciousness, and cultural dissonance.

Similarly, the literature of the Caribbean diaspora, represented by writers like Edwidge Danticat and Jamaica Kincaid, offers poignant explorations of memory, exile, and intergenerational trauma. Their works often blur the lines between autobiography and fiction, giving voice to the psychological scars of colonial violence and forced migration.

Asian American authors such as Amy Tan, Viet Thanh Nguyen, and Ocean Vuong explore how inherited trauma, war memory, and intergenerational silence shape the identities of second-generation immigrants. Their stories grapple with the legacy of U.S. imperialism in Asia and the emotional toll it takes on immigrant families living in America.

The Latinx literary tradition, too, has grown in both breadth and depth. From the magical realism of Rudolfo Anaya to the contemporary urban poetry of Elizabeth Acevedo, Latinx writers have chronicled the borderland identities, language politics, and resilience of Latin American immigrants and their descendants. These stories offer a vibrant counter-narrative to mainstream depictions of Latinx communities, centering complexity, agency, and cultural pride.

The American Dream

In the tapestry of American literature, immigrant voices are no longer fringe threads—they are integral strands shaping the entire design. These writers have expanded not just what stories get told, but how they are told: introducing hybrid forms, non-linear narratives, and multilingual expressions that reflect the realities of displacement and diaspora. They have shown that the American Dream is not a static promise, but a contested idea—reshaped with every generation that arrives on its shores.

Through their work, immigrant and multicultural authors demand that we rethink national identity—not as a singular, monolithic truth, but as a collection of lived experiences, each with its own history, struggle, and hope. In doing so, they remind us that America's strength lies not in uniformity, but in the mosaic of many voices, many dreams, and many homes.

Early Immigrant Voices and Cultural Hybridity

The early decades of the 20th century witnessed a significant rise in literary expression from America's immigrant communities, particularly those arriving from Eastern Europe, Southern Europe, Asia, and the Caribbean. These writers, many of whom were first-generation Americans or immigrants themselves, grappled with the realities of economic hardship, cultural dislocation, and the brutal pressures of assimilation. Their literature reflects a powerful dual consciousness—an internal conflict between loyalty to one's cultural heritage and the overwhelming demand to conform to American norms and values. This negotiation of identity became a central theme in early immigrant literature, paving the way for more expansive explorations of hybridity, resistance, and belonging in later decades.

At a time when mainstream American literature largely centered on Anglo-American narratives, early immigrant writers disrupted dominant literary frameworks by foregrounding experiences shaped by linguistic difference, religious identity, labor exploitation, and racial exclusion. Their characters often found themselves trapped between two worlds—never fully accepted by the dominant culture, yet increasingly estranged from their roots. The literature of this period served as a vital site for exploring the pain of displacement, the yearning for dignity, and the search for meaning in an alien environment.

Anzia Yezierska: Jewish Immigrant Womanhood and Cultural Conflict

One of the most prominent voices from this era was **Anzia Yezierska**, a Polish-Jewish immigrant who chronicled the lives of Jewish women in the Lower East Side of New York. Her semi-autobiographical novel *Bread Givers* (1925) stands as a landmark in early immigrant literature, portraying the tension between Jewish orthodoxy and American secularism through the story of Sara Smolinsky, a young woman determined to forge her own path in a patriarchal and traditionalist community.

Yezierska's work is significant not only for its depiction of immigrant life but also for its feminist undertones. Sara's struggle to pursue education, independence, and romantic autonomy in the face of her father's religious rigidity reflects a broader conflict between old-world values and new-world aspirations. Yezierska does not romanticize either side of this conflict. Instead, she portrays cultural hybridity as a painful yet necessary process—a form of survival that entails both loss and transformation.

Language plays a crucial role in Yezierska's work. Her characters often speak in a hybridized form of English inflected with Yiddish idioms, mirroring the real-life struggles of immigrants navigating linguistic alienation. Through this stylistic choice, Yezierska foregrounds the authenticity of immigrant voices and challenges the hegemony of standard English as the sole vehicle of literary expression.

Carlos Bulosan: Race, Labor, and Resistance in the Filipino American Experience

While Yezierska wrote from the vantage point of Jewish immigrant life in the urban Northeast, Carlos Bulosan brought to American literature the voice of the Filipino migrant laborer in the rural West. His semi-autobiographical work *America Is in the Heart* (1946) chronicles his journey from poverty in the Philippines to a life of racial violence, economic exploitation, and political awakening in the United States. Published in the aftermath of World War II, the book is both a personal narrative and a political testament to the resilience of immigrant laborers of color.

Bulosan's depiction of America is striking in its ambivalence. On one hand, he expresses an almost mythic hope in the ideals of democracy, justice, and equality. On the other, he lays bare the brutal realities of migrant life—unpaid labor, lynching, police brutality, and systemic racism. His America is not a promised land, but a contested space in which hope and despair coexist.

What sets Bulosan apart is his ability to situate the Filipino American experience within the broader context of imperialism, migration, and class struggle. His work challenges the notion of a singular American identity and introduces a distinctly transnational perspective. Like Yezierska, Bulosan engages with hybridity—not just cultural, but political—bridging the gap between homeland and host land, colonizer and colonized, idealism and disillusionment.

Legacy and Literary Foundations

Together, writers like Yezierska and Bulosan laid the foundational stones of immigrant literature in the United States. They were among the first to give literary form to the emotional and social costs of migration, while also asserting the legitimacy of immigrant voices in shaping the national narrative. Their stories exposed the contradictions within the American Dream and redefined notions of citizenship, belonging, and cultural identity.

Moreover, their work influenced the evolution of literary multiculturalism, inspiring later generations of writers to further explore the complexities of bicultural life. Contemporary authors such as Jhumpa Lahiri, Sandra Cisneros, and Viet Thanh Nguyen build upon the themes first articulated by Yezierska and Bulosan—navigating generational conflict, reclaiming marginalized histories, and interrogating the structures of power that continue to shape immigrant life in America.

In a broader sense, these early 20th-century immigrant voices made it possible to imagine American literature not as a homogeneous tradition, but as a dynamic and evolving dialogue among many cultures. They demonstrated that to be American is not to shed one's past, but to remake identity through the entanglement of memory, struggle, and aspiration.

Asian American Voices

Asian American literature emerged as a powerful force in the American literary landscape in the post–World War II period, gaining significant recognition by the 1970s and continuing to evolve in richness and diversity through the 21st century. While early representations of Asian Americans in U.S. culture were often steeped in orientalist stereotypes or complete erasure, a growing cohort of Asian American writers began to reclaim their narratives—articulating the complexities of identity, cultural hybridity, and racial belonging.

The term "Asian American" itself is politically charged, encompassing a broad and heterogeneous group that includes Chinese, Japanese, Korean, Filipino, Indian, Vietnamese, and other diasporas from across the Asian continent. Despite the internal diversity of this label, many Asian American literary works share common thematic threads: the intergenerational conflict between immigrant parents and American-born children, the burden of cultural memory, the trauma of displacement, and the struggle to negotiate bicultural identities within a racially stratified society.

This literature often responds to, and pushes back against, both dominant American narratives and mainstream Asian cultural expectations. It creates space for exploring experiences that are neither entirely Asian nor entirely American, but rather shaped by the friction and fusion of both worlds.

Maxine Hong Kingston: Myth, Memory, and Identity

Maxine Hong Kingston's *The Woman Warrior: Memoirs of a Girlhood Among Ghosts* (1976) is a seminal text in Asian American literature, blending autobiography, Chinese folklore, and speculative narrative. Kingston's work defies easy categorization, purposefully blurring the lines between memoir and fiction to reflect the fragmented, contradictory nature of diasporic identity. In *The Woman Warrior*, she recounts her childhood as a Chinese American girl growing up in California, haunted by the "ghosts" of both American society and Chinese tradition.

A central theme in Kingston's work is the silencing of women in patriarchal culture. The book's narrator wrestles with the stories told (and untold) by her mother and aunties—legends of women warriors, fallen daughters, and ancestral shame. Through storytelling, Kingston reclaims silenced histories and questions the authority of inherited traditions. Her innovative narrative structure mirrors the psychological experience of bicultural life: fragmented, nonlinear, and mythically charged. By merging Chinese oral tradition with American feminist thought, Kingston constructs a literary identity that is defiantly hybrid and unapologetically personal.

Amy Tan: Generational Dialogue and Cultural Translation

Amy Tan's *The Joy Luck Club* (1989) is another landmark in Asian American literature, widely read and taught for its portrayal of Chinese American mother-daughter relationships. Structured as interwoven vignettes, the novel gives voice to four Chinese immigrant mothers and their American-born daughters, tracing the miscommunications and cultural clashes that arise from their divergent life experiences.

Tan's exploration of generational conflict is both emotionally resonant and culturally specific. The mothers, shaped by war, loss, and survival in China, often view their American daughters as willfully ignorant of their heritage and suffering. The daughters, raised in the United States, struggle to understand the unspoken traumas their mothers carry and often reject what they see as controlling or outdated values. Through these parallel narratives, Tan reveals the painful yet poignant ways in which family, culture, and identity are transmitted—and sometimes lost—across generations.

The novel also engages with the concept of translation—not only linguistic but emotional and cultural. Tan illustrates how meaning is altered in transit, how stories shift depending on who tells them, and how memory itself becomes a contested terrain. *The Joy Luck Club* remains a deeply moving exploration of diaspora, memory, and the fragile ties that bind immigrant families.

Jhumpa Lahiri: Quiet Displacement and Subtle Longing

Although Lahiri's heritage is South Asian, her inclusion in discussions of Asian American literature underscores the expanding scope of the term. Her Pulitzer Prize–winning debut, *Interpreter of Maladies* (1999), is a collection of short stories that delicately explores the lives of Indian immigrants and their children navigating everyday life in the United States and abroad. Her prose is understated, lyrical, and imbued with a deep sense of emotional restraint—echoing the quiet dislocation of her characters.

Lahiri's work often centers on themes of loneliness, alienation, and the ache of cultural disconnection. Characters struggle to bridge the cultural chasm between India and America, often feeling unmoored from both. In stories such as "Mrs. Sen's," the loss of language and foodways becomes symbolic of a broader disorientation in a foreign land. Her fiction foregrounds the subtle moments of longing and estrangement that define the diasporic experience—not dramatic confrontations, but slow, aching realizations of otherness.

Lahiri also explores the idea of home—not as a fixed location, but as an evolving, sometimes elusive concept shaped by emotion, memory, and longing. Through her meticulous prose, she elevates the ordinary immigrant experience into profound meditations on identity and place.

Core Themes in Asian American Literature

The "Model Minority" Myth

Asian American writers frequently grapple with the "model minority" stereotype—the perception that Asians are high-achieving, obedient, and economically successful. This myth erases the internal diversity of Asian communities, downplays histories of discrimination, and pits Asian Americans against other marginalized groups. Literature has become a site for deconstructing this myth and exposing its psychological toll, particularly on second-generation youth who feel pressured to conform to impossible standards of perfection.

Language Loss and Cultural Memory

Many Asian American works address the gradual erosion of native languages across generations. This loss is not merely linguistic but symbolic of deeper estrangements from cultural heritage. Writers portray how language serves as a bridge between generations—and how its loss creates emotional and epistemological gaps that are difficult to mend.

East-West Generational Gaps

A recurring theme is the generational divide between immigrant parents and their American-born children. While the former often cling to cultural customs, discipline, and survivalist instincts, the latter are shaped by American ideals of individualism, freedom, and self-expression. This generational tension becomes a crucible for identity formation, as characters try to honor their parents' sacrifices while forging their own paths.

Asian American literature is not a monolith but a vibrant, evolving field that reflects the multiplicity of experiences within the Asian diaspora. From the myth-infused memoirs of Maxine Hong Kingston to the emotional landscapes of Amy Tan and the understated elegance of Jhumpa Lahiri, these writers have challenged simplistic notions of assimilation and redefined the contours of American identity. Their works offer deeply personal yet politically resonant insights into how culture, memory, and identity are negotiated across generations and geographies.

As these voices continue to grow in number and diversity—incorporating queer, refugee, working-class, and multiracial perspectives—the Asian American literary tradition affirms its central role in shaping a more inclusive and truthful American narrative.

Latino and Chicano/a Literature

Latino and Chicano/a literature has emerged as one of the most vibrant and politically resonant traditions within American letters, reflecting a rich tapestry of cultural experience rooted in migration, colonialism, resistance, and community. While "Latino" (or Latinx) is often used as an umbrella term for people of Latin American descent in the U.S., "Chicano/a" specifically refers to Mexican Americans, particularly those who affirm a political and cultural identity shaped by the Chicano Movement of the 1960s and 1970s. Together, these intersecting traditions foreground the complexities of bicultural identity, the legacy of colonial histories, and the enduring struggle for justice, language rights, and visibility in American society.

Latinx and Chicano/a writers write from and about the "borderlands"—not only the geographic U.S.-Mexico border, but also metaphorical and psychological spaces where two (or more) cultures collide. Their literature often resists assimilationist narratives, instead embracing hybridity, mestizaje (cultural mixing), and linguistic fusion, especially through the use of Spanglish, code-switching, and bilingual storytelling. The result is a literary tradition that is not only aesthetically innovative but also deeply rooted in social and political consciousness.

Rudolfo Anaya: Myth, Spirituality, and Identity in the Chicano Southwest

Rudolfo Anaya's *Bless Me, Ultima* (1972) is widely considered the foundational novel of Chicano literature. Set in New Mexico during World War II, the novel follows Antonio Márez, a young boy caught between conflicting spiritual and cultural forces—Catholicism, Indigenous spirituality, and the mystical teachings of a curandera (healer) named Ultima. Through this coming-of-age narrative, Anaya explores themes of moral awakening, cultural inheritance, and the search for identity within a hybridized Chicano world.

Anaya's writing draws heavily on Mexican American folklore, oral traditions, and magical realism, presenting a world where the mystical and the mundane coexist. *Bless Me, Ultima* challenges the dominance of Eurocentric literary forms by embedding Indigenous knowledge and Chicano worldviews into its narrative structure. The novel is also notable for its affirmation of the land—not merely as a setting but as a living presence that shapes cultural memory and identity.

Sandra Cisneros: Gender, Language, and Urban Latina Identity

Sandra Cisneros's *The House on Mango Street* (1984) brought Chicana literature to a broader audience through its poetic and accessible style. Told through a series of interconnected vignettes, the novel follows Esperanza Cordero, a young Latina girl growing up in a working-class neighborhood of Chicago. Through Esperanza's eyes, readers witness the daily struggles of women in her community—poverty, domestic violence, and cultural expectations—alongside her dreams of self-definition and escape.

Cisneros's prose blends lyrical imagery with raw realism, capturing both the beauty and the hardship of barrio life. One of her most significant contributions lies in the portrayal of Latina girlhood and the way it is shaped by intersecting forces of class, gender, and ethnicity. Esperanza's desire for a room of her own—both literal and metaphorical—symbolizes a larger yearning for autonomy and creative freedom in a world that often silences women.

The House on Mango Street also engages in linguistic innovation, incorporating Spanish words and idioms that reflect the speaker's bicultural reality. In doing so, Cisneros challenges the monolingual assumptions of American literature and affirms the legitimacy of Spanglish as a mode of artistic expression.

Julia Alvarez: Exile, Memory, and the Dominican-American Experience

Julia Alvarez's *How the García Girls Lost Their Accents* (1991) is a landmark novel in Dominican American literature. Structured in reverse chronological order, the novel traces the lives of four sisters who immigrate to the United States from the Dominican Republic after their father becomes entangled in political resistance. The narrative moves back and forth in time and across borders, capturing the fluid and fragmented nature of diasporic memory.

Alvarez's writing deals with the trauma of exile, the disorientation of cultural dislocation, and the challenges of assimilation. The García girls grapple with the loss of language, shifting gender roles, and the need to reinvent themselves in an unfamiliar society. In many ways, Alvarez's work embodies the psychological borderlands of immigrant life—spaces where identity is constantly being negotiated and redefined.

Her use of English infused with Spanish syntax, idioms, and rhythms reflects the fractured experience of living between cultures. Rather than present assimilation as a simple or desirable process, Alvarez portrays it as fraught, painful, and often incomplete. Her novel speaks to the resilience of immigrant families and the enduring ties to homeland that persist despite geographic separation.

Recurring Themes in Latino and Chicano/a Literature

Hybridity and Spanglish

Language in Latinx and Chicano/a literature is more than a tool for communication—it is a marker of identity, a site of resistance, and a cultural archive. Writers often use Spanglish and code-switching to reflect the lived linguistic realities of their communities. This hybrid language challenges dominant norms and affirms the legitimacy of bilingual expression as a vehicle for literature. It also mirrors the cultural fusion inherent in the Latinx experience—where identities are not divided but layered and interwoven.

Familia and Faith

Family, or familia, is a central motif in Latinx and Chicano/a writing, often depicted as both a source of strength and a site of tension. Traditional family roles, especially those involving gender, are frequently scrutinized and reimagined by writers like Cisneros and Alvarez. Religious faith—especially Catholicism—also plays a prominent role, sometimes reinforcing cultural continuity, and at other times conflicting with personal desires or modern values.

Geographic and Psychological Borderlands

The borderland is both a literal and symbolic space in these narratives. Physically, it refers to the U.S.-Mexico border and the contested terrain of migration and belonging. Psychologically, it represents the inner conflict of living between cultures, languages, and expectations. Writers like Gloria Anzaldúa (whose *Borderlands/La Frontera* is foundational, though not listed above) have theorized this space as one of possibility, pain, and transformation—a third space where new identities can be forged.

9.5 African Immigrant and Afro-Caribbean Voices

By the late 20th century, the contributions of African immigrant and Afro-Caribbean writers profoundly reshaped American literature by introducing transnational, diasporic, and postcolonial perspectives that interrogate identity, migration, and belonging in nuanced ways. Unlike earlier African American narratives rooted in the legacy of slavery and the civil rights struggle, these writers offered new frameworks that centered on voluntary migration, exile, and the cultural hybridity of those navigating life between multiple homelands.

A key figure in this literary movement is Edwidge Danticat, whose acclaimed debut novel *Breath, Eyes, Memory* (1994) explores the psychological and generational trauma experienced by Haitian women within and outside Haiti. Set between Haiti and the United States, the novel delves into themes such as sexual violence, mother-daughter relationships, silence, and the resilience of memory. Danticat's lyrical prose captures the tension between Haitian cultural heritage and American expectations, making her work a seminal text in Afro-Caribbean American literature.

Another important voice is Chimamanda Ngozi Adichie, a Nigerian author who, though primarily associated with African literature, plays a crucial role in the diasporic discourse through her novel *Americanah* (2013). The novel follows a young Nigerian woman's journey to the U.S. for higher education, where she encounters the racial complexities of America—an experience unfamiliar from her life in Nigeria. Adichie unpacks the contradictions of race and class, identity and love, and critiques how the American racial landscape forces immigrants to navigate a new sense of "Blackness" that often erases cultural specificity. Her work provides a lens into the immigrant condition that is simultaneously deeply personal and widely political.

These writers—and others such as Jamaica Kincaid, Caryl Phillips, and Teju Cole—question and redefine rigid notions of African American identity by presenting the Black experience as layered and diverse. They foreground intra-racial complexities, such as colorism, cultural alienation, and the tensions between African immigrants and African Americans, drawing attention to the plurality of Black voices and lived experiences. This reconfiguration of Black identity challenges the binary constructs often perpetuated by mainstream discourse and brings attention to the multiplicity within the African diaspora.

Furthermore, the themes of postcolonial dislocation, gendered trauma, migration under duress, and nostalgia for a fractured homeland recur prominently in their works. These narratives resonate with readers not only as stories of loss and longing but also as celebrations of resilience, cultural fusion, and survival.

In reshaping the American literary canon, African immigrant and Afro-Caribbean writers assert their presence within a broader narrative of multicultural America. Their contributions emphasize that to understand contemporary American identity, one must also grapple with the legacy of colonialism, the effects of global migration, and the evolving meanings of race, language, and nationality in an interconnected world.

Middle Eastern and Arab American Writers

Middle Eastern and Arab American writers began gaining significant literary recognition in the United States particularly in the late 20th and early 21st centuries, with a marked increase in visibility after the events of September 11, 2001. The post-9/11 sociopolitical landscape forced a re-examination of Arab and Muslim identities in America, as issues of race, religion, foreign policy, and national belonging came under intense public and media scrutiny. Writers from these communities found themselves at the crossroads of cultural representation and resistance, often working to dismantle orientalist stereotypes, confront Islamophobia, and explore the complexities of hybrid identity.

One of the most internationally recognized voices in this space is Khaled Hosseini, whose debut novel *The Kite Runner* (2003) brought Afghan-American narratives to a global audience. Though more broadly a diasporic and post-conflict novel than one centered purely on American life, it profoundly shaped how readers engaged with Middle Eastern stories. Set against the backdrop of Afghanistan's turbulent history, the novel addresses themes of personal guilt, betrayal, immigration, and the long shadow of trauma. In portraying the journey of its protagonist from Kabul to California, *The Kite Runner* invites readers to reckon with how geopolitical upheaval intersects with personal identity, memory, and redemption.

In the American context, authors like Randa Jarrar, Diana Abu-Jaber, and Mona Simpson have contributed vital narratives that reflect the lived realities of Arab Americans navigating both invisibility and hypervisibility.

Randa Jarrar, in *A Map of Home* (2008), presents a coming-of-age story filled with humor and grit, depicting a Palestinian-Egyptian girl growing up in Kuwait, Egypt, and eventually the United States. Jarrar's writing boldly explores sexuality, family dynamics, and cultural dislocation, resisting stereotypical portrayals of Arab women and instead foregrounding agency and complexity.

Diana Abu-Jaber, in works such as *Crescent* (2003) and *The Language of Baklava* (2005), blends fiction and memoir to explore Arab American identity, often through the lens of food, memory, and love. Her characters navigate bicultural existence, caught between Arab traditions and American modernity, longing and belonging. Her nuanced approach avoids monolithic portrayals and instead captures the layered negotiations of identity many Arab Americans face.

Mona Simpson, though often associated with broader American literary traditions, also grapples with themes of familial estrangement, dual cultural identity, and personal reinvention. As a writer of Syrian descent, her work adds a quieter but nonetheless significant voice to the conversation around Middle Eastern heritage in American life.

Thematically, these authors often address:

- The post-9/11 experience, marked by racial profiling, surveillance, and a redefinition of "Americanness" for Muslim and Arab individuals.
- Diaspora and dual identity, particularly the tension between cultural preservation and assimilation.
- Gendered identity, with many female authors challenging patriarchal structures within both their cultural communities and the broader American context.
- Narrative reclamation, as they strive to tell their own stories in contrast to the narratives often imposed by media and politics.

Overall, Middle Eastern and Arab American literature serves both as a mirror and a critique—reflecting the internal lives and external pressures experienced by these communities, while also confronting the reductive narratives that have historically dominated American portrayals of the Middle East. These writers contribute significantly to the rich tapestry of American multicultural literature by asserting a presence that is both uniquely their own and integrally American.

Common Literary Strategies and Themes

Immigrant and diasporic literature in America frequently employs a rich array of literary strategies to articulate the hybrid, multifaceted realities of migration, displacement, and cultural negotiation. These techniques are not just stylistic choices—they serve as powerful tools to challenge dominant narratives, preserve cultural memory, and articulate the internal tensions that define the immigrant experience.

One prominent strategy is code-switching and multilingual dialogue, where authors seamlessly integrate words, phrases, or entire passages from their native languages into English texts. This technique mirrors the linguistic reality of many immigrant communities, who navigate between languages in everyday life. It also resists the homogenization of culture by asserting the legitimacy and presence of non-English languages within American literature. By doing so, writers not only preserve the sound and rhythm of their heritage tongues but also emphasize that American identity is inherently multilingual and multicultural. Authors like Junot Díaz (*The Brief Wondrous Life of Oscar Wao*) and Sandra Cisneros (*The House on Mango Street*) are noted for their strategic and often playful use of Spanglish, which reinforces cultural authenticity and deepens thematic resonance.

Magical realism and folklore are also central strategies, especially in literature from Latinx, African, and South Asian traditions. By weaving the mystical, mythical, and ancestral into contemporary narratives, authors not only pay homage to cultural storytelling traditions but also push back against the dominance of Western realist modes. In Rudolfo Anaya's *Bless Me, Ultima*, for instance, indigenous spirituality and mythic figures blend with Catholic iconography to create a unique literary voice that bridges cultures. Similarly, Maxine Hong Kingston's *The Woman Warrior* incorporates Chinese legend and ghost stories to articulate the complexities of growing up Chinese-American. These elements allow writers to express the fluidity of memory, history, and truth in immigrant life, where the spiritual and the material often coexist.

Intergenerational conflict is another recurring theme, often reflecting the emotional and ideological gap between first-generation immigrants and their American-born children. The older generation may cling to the values, customs, and traumas of the homeland, while the younger generation seeks to assimilate into American society—leading to tensions over identity, gender roles, education, and freedom. This conflict becomes a lens through which larger questions of cultural preservation versus adaptation are explored. Works like Amy Tan's *The Joy Luck Club* or Jhumpa Lahiri's *The Namesake* poignantly portray how these familial tensions reflect broader diasporic anxieties.

Perhaps the most pervasive theme across immigrant literature is the exploration of home and exile. Whether through voluntary migration or forced displacement, characters often find themselves suspended between worlds—yearning for a homeland that may no longer exist as remembered, while struggling to find acceptance in a new land that treats them as outsiders. This in-betweenness creates a sense of psychic exile, where belonging is elusive and identity becomes a constantly shifting construct. The idea of "home" transcends physical geography, becoming instead a symbolic space of memory, language, relationships, and self-definition.

Taken together, these literary strategies and themes illuminate the layered and often paradoxical experience of being "American" while also being something else—Mexican, Chinese, Nigerian, Palestinian, Indian, Filipino, or Dominican. Through these narratives, immigrant writers enrich the American literary canon by foregrounding the voices, values, and visions that have long been marginalized or silenced. They transform the landscape of national identity, reminding readers that American literature is, at its heart, a literature of movement, transformation, and multiplicity.

9.8 From Margin to Center: Critical Reception and Academic Inclusion

In the broader trajectory of American literature, the inclusion of multicultural voices marks one of the most transformative developments of the late 20th and early 21st centuries. What was once viewed as peripheral or niche—literature by and about immigrants, people of color, and diasporic communities—gradually moved toward the center of both critical discourse and academic curricula. This shift did not occur overnight; it was the result of decades of activism, scholarship, and literary excellence that challenged the canon's narrow definition of what constituted "American" literature.

The 1980s and 1990s were pivotal decades in this evolution. During this period, institutions of higher learning began to recognize the need to diversify the study of literature to reflect the reality of America's multicultural society. This led to the institutionalization of Ethnic Studies, Asian American Studies, Chicano/a Studies, African American Studies, and Native American Studies programs in colleges and universities across the United States. These programs not only legitimized the study of marginalized literatures but also created academic frameworks for analyzing race, identity, colonialism, diaspora, and power.

The publication of inclusive anthologies—particularly *The Heath Anthology of American Literature*—was instrumental in reshaping curricula. Unlike traditional anthologies that focused almost exclusively on white, male, and Euro-American authors, The Heath Anthology sought to present a more representative cross-section of American voices, including Native American oral traditions, African American spirituals, immigrant narratives, and works by women and queer authors. These anthologies challenged the long-standing primacy of the Norton Anthology and expanded what students read in American literature courses.

However, the shift from margin to center was not without complications. As multicultural literature gained popularity, concerns emerged about tokenism—the inclusion of a few diverse voices as a symbolic gesture rather than a meaningful integration of multicultural perspectives. Authors from minority backgrounds were sometimes treated as representatives of their entire culture rather than as individual artists with distinct voices and aesthetics. This kind of essentialism risked flattening complex identities into easily digestible stereotypes for mainstream consumption.

Another persistent debate revolves around authenticity. Who gets to tell whose story? Can a writer from outside a particular culture authentically portray its experiences? Questions of voice, representation, and positionality have become central to literary criticism. The issue of cultural appropriation—especially when white authors profit from or misrepresent marginalized cultures—has sparked intense discussions in both literary circles and the public sphere. These debates underscore the need for responsible storytelling and the importance of lived experience in narrative authority.

Despite these challenges, the rise of multicultural literature has enriched the American literary landscape, offering a more inclusive and accurate reflection of the nation's complex social fabric. It has also reshaped literary criticism itself, prompting the development of new theoretical frameworks such as postcolonial theory, critical race theory, diaspora studies, and intersectional feminism. These approaches have allowed critics to better engage with the layered meanings and historical contexts embedded in multicultural texts.

In sum, the movement of multicultural literature from the margins to the center represents more than a curricular update—it is a profound reimagining of what American literature is and who gets to define it. While debates around tokenism, authenticity, and appropriation persist, they reflect a healthy, ongoing negotiation about voice, power, and inclusion. Through this discourse, American literature continues to evolve into a more democratic and pluralistic space, one where diverse stories are not only heard but valued on their own terms.

Contemporary Voices and Global Outlook

The contemporary landscape of American literature is characterized by a rich, polyphonic chorus of voices that reflect the ongoing evolution of national and global identities. Building upon the foundations laid by earlier generations of immigrant and multicultural writers, today's authors engage deeply with the themes of globalization, transnational migration, postcolonialism, and intersectionality. Rather than focusing solely on assimilation into a dominant American culture, these writers emphasize cultural negotiation, hybridity, and resistance—constructing narratives that defy binary categories and fixed definitions of identity.

Writers like Ocean Vuong, whose lyrical novel *On Earth We're Briefly Gorgeous* (2019) reimagines the immigrant narrative through a queer, Vietnamese American lens, exemplify this shift. Vuong's work blends poetry, trauma, memory, and intergenerational pain in a narrative that is at once intensely personal and politically resonant. His writing interrogates the legacy of war, masculinity, language, and silence, showing how personal history intersects with national violence.

Kali Fajardo-Anstine, author of *Sabrina & Corina* (2019), brings to light the voices of Indigenous Latina women in the American West, challenging dominant narratives of both Latinx and Native American identity. Her stories often dwell in the everyday experiences of women facing cultural erasure, gendered expectations, and socio-economic hardship, all while celebrating the beauty and resilience of community.

Similarly, Xochitl Gonzalez (*Olga Dies Dreaming*, 2022) crafts narratives that merge political critique with cultural satire. Set against the backdrop of Puerto Rican identity, diaspora politics, and gentrification in Brooklyn, Gonzalez's work critiques systemic inequities while illustrating the nuances of ambition, cultural loyalty, and family.

Héctor Tobar, known for *The Tattooed Soldier* and *Deep Down Dark*, continues to explore the Latinx diaspora, often focusing on working-class immigrant lives, political upheaval, and transborder realities. His journalism background enriches his fiction with a grounded, empathetic perspective on human displacement and resilience.

Tommy Orange, whose novel *There There* (2018) electrified the literary scene, offers a powerful redefinition of Native American identity in urban contexts. By centering Native characters in contemporary Oakland, Orange dismantles stereotypical portrayals of Indigenous life and foregrounds themes of historical trauma, cultural survival, and urban alienation.

These and other contemporary authors are marked by formal innovation as much as thematic complexity. Many experiment with structure, voice, and language, incorporating multilingualism, fragmented narrative forms, epistolary elements, and hybrid genres. Their work is not just about telling stories, but about reshaping how stories are told and whose voices are heard.

A defining feature of contemporary multicultural literature is its global consciousness. These writers often inhabit multiple cultural spaces simultaneously, engaging with diasporic, cosmopolitan, and postnational frameworks. Their narratives traverse borders—both literal and metaphorical—and resonate with readers across geographies. Whether depicting the transgenerational effects of colonialism, the fluidity of gender and sexuality, or the impact of climate change and displacement, today's literature reflects a world increasingly interconnected yet fraught with inequality and fragmentation.

Furthermore, the digital era and increased transnational migration have fostered a literature that is inherently intersectional. Contemporary writers grapple not only with race and ethnicity but also with gender, class, queerness, ability, and religion, crafting layered identities that mirror the complexities of lived experience. Literature now serves as a space where these intersecting identities can be explored, affirmed, and contested.

In essence, contemporary multicultural American literature is no longer centered on the idea of "becoming American" in the traditional sense. Instead, it is concerned with challenging, expanding, and redefining what "American" means. Writers now assert their right to occupy space, not through assimilation, but through *reclamation* and *reinvention*. Through this dynamic, contemporary voices contribute to a vibrant, inclusive, and ever-evolving literary tradition that mirrors the multiplicity of modern life.

Conclusion: Many Americas, One Voice

The literary contributions of immigrants and their descendants have not merely added to American literature—they have fundamentally redefined it. Through fiction, poetry, memoir, drama, and hybrid forms, these voices have reclaimed narrative authority, offered counter-histories, and articulated identities too often silenced or stereotyped by dominant cultural narratives. Far from existing at the margins, immigrant and multicultural writers now form an essential core of what American literature is and what it aspires to be.

The immigrant experience is not monolithic; it encompasses a vast and diverse range of histories, languages, spiritualities, and worldviews. Whether shaped by forced displacement, political exile, voluntary migration, or generational legacy, these experiences reflect resilience, adaptation, resistance, and a deep yearning for belonging. Writers across ethnicities and cultural traditions—Latinx, Asian American, Arab American, African immigrant, Afro-Caribbean, and Indigenous voices—have illustrated that there are indeed many "Americas". Each story offers a different lens, grounded in specific geographies, memories, and struggles, yet tied together by the shared act of storytelling as a means of survival and affirmation.

In literature, these writers have expanded the boundaries of language and genre. They blend Spanglish, Creole, Taglish, Arabic idioms, Yoruba chants, and Vietnamese proverbs into English narratives, not as ornamental flourishes but as integral parts of character, history, and worldview. This multilingualism challenges the supremacy of English and affirms the reality of hybrid identities. Through magical realism, speculative fiction, oral tradition, and diasporic aesthetics, they challenge Western literary norms and enrich American letters with global sensibilities.

Critically, these writers have also reshaped national identity. They have pushed back against narrow definitions of Americanness, insisting that citizenship and cultural legitimacy are not tied to whiteness, assimilation, or erasure of ancestral roots. By centering experiences of borderlands, intergenerational trauma, gendered oppression, and racialized exclusion, their work calls into question the very myths upon which the nation has been built.

Moreover, immigrant literature is not merely reactive—it is visionary. It dares to imagine plural futures, inclusive communities, and transformed systems of power. Authors like Ocean Vuong, Tommy Orange, Edwidge Danticat, Sandra Cisneros, and Mohsin Hamid are not only chroniclers of injustice but architects of possibility. Their works offer blueprints for empathy, cross-cultural dialogue, and global solidarity.

In classrooms, bookstores, and critical scholarship, the inclusion of immigrant voices has prompted a rethinking of the canon itself. Once relegated to Ethnic Studies syllabi or "diversity" showcases, these works are now widely recognized for their literary innovation and philosophical depth. However, challenges remain—tokenism, cultural appropriation, publishing inequities, and backlash against multicultural education continue to test the endurance of these gains.

Ultimately, the literature of immigration reminds us that American identity is fluid, contested, and always in the making. It teaches us that the nation is not a fixed geography but a space of storytelling, negotiation, and reclamation. The phrase "Many Americas, One Voice" encapsulates not a forced unity but a shared commitment to dialogue, dignity, and truth-telling. In the polyphony of immigrant narratives, we hear the evolving heartbeat of a nation—one that carries its contradictions, its dreams, and its deep, enduring humanity in every word.

10

Literature and the American Dream: Illusions, Realities, and Revisions

Decoding the Promise of a Nation through Fiction

Introduction: The Mythos of Opportunity

The American Dream—rooted in ideals of liberty, self-determination, and economic prosperity—has served as one of the most potent myths in shaping both national identity and individual aspiration. From the Puritan work ethic to the Horatio Alger success story, the Dream has offered generations of Americans—and immigrants drawn to the nation's shores—a vision of upward mobility grounded in meritocracy and perseverance. However, as literature from the 20th century onward reveals, the reality of this dream is often far more complex.

American fiction, poetry, and drama have continually explored the tension between promise and reality, exposing the exclusions, contradictions, and emotional costs embedded within the Dream. For some characters, it offers hope and motivation; for others, it becomes a source of psychological torment, material disappointment, or moral decay. Writers have used narrative to interrogate who truly has access to the Dream—and who is systematically denied it because of race, class, gender, ethnicity, or circumstance.

Across genres and movements, from realism to postmodernism, from the Harlem Renaissance to contemporary immigrant literature, authors have taken up the Dream as a cultural text to be deconstructed. Some reveal its cracks through tragic character arcs and shattered illusions; others reimagine or reclaim it in more inclusive and intersectional ways. Whether by celebrating the Dream's enduring power or exposing its failures, American literature has consistently illuminated the sociopolitical machinery behind the myth.

This chapter examines the literary evolution of the American Dream, tracing how different voices—canonical and marginalized—have responded to its shifting contours. From F. Scott Fitzgerald's *The Great Gatsby* and Arthur Miller's *Death of a Salesman* to Toni Morrison's *Song of Solomon* and Jhumpa Lahiri's *The Namesake*, we will analyze how authors map the Dream's allure and costs across time, geography, and identity. These texts prompt us to ask: Is the Dream still viable? Has it become a relic of national nostalgia? Or can it be transformed into a more equitable and inclusive vision?

In doing so, we uncover not only the literary significance of the American Dream but also its role as a mirror to the American psyche—an evolving symbol of ambition, contradiction, and national self-examination.

The Dream in Early 20th Century Realism

The early decades of the 20th century saw the rise of American Realism—a literary movement that rejected romantic idealism and instead sought to portray life with uncompromising honesty. Within this framework, many writers took on the myth of the American Dream, not to celebrate it, but to expose its contradictions, inequalities, and failures. The optimism associated with self-made success was tempered by portrayals of social immobility, industrial exploitation, and the crushing weight of systemic forces.

One of the most searing critiques came from Theodore Dreiser in *An American Tragedy* (1925), a novel that follows Clyde Griffiths, a young man from a poor religious background who aspires to wealth and social prestige. Clyde's ambition—rooted in the very essence of the Dream—ultimately leads him down a dark path marked by moral compromise, manipulation, and tragedy. Dreiser presents the American Dream not as an empowering ideal but as a force that can corrupt, disillusion, and destroy. Clyde's downfall reflects the perils of a society obsessed with status and success, where upward mobility is less about virtue and more about calculated transgressions.

Similarly, Upton Sinclair's *The Jungle* (1906) provides a blistering exposé of the meatpacking industry and the exploitation of immigrant laborers in Chicago. The novel's protagonist, Jurgis Rudkus, arrives in America full of hope, believing in the promise that hard work will yield a better life. Instead, he encounters unrelenting poverty, dangerous working conditions, and systemic oppression. The Dream, for Sinclair, becomes a cruel illusion designed to pacify the masses while preserving the wealth of the elite. His work catalyzed public outrage and legislative reform, but its literary legacy remains in how starkly it dismantles the Dream's perceived attainability for immigrants and the working class.

These realist narratives underscore that the American Dream is not a universal pathway, but a conditional and often unreachable ideal.

In the world these authors depict, class barriers are entrenched, labor is dehumanizing, and success is tainted by moral compromise. Capitalism, rather than being an engine of opportunity, is portrayed as a force that distorts ambition, replacing integrity with survivalism and empathy with self-interest.

Moreover, the protagonists in these stories are rarely villains in the traditional sense—they are victims of social and economic systems that place the Dream just out of reach. Realist literature thus challenges readers to reconsider the fairness and inclusiveness of the American promise, revealing how easily it can become a mirage for those without privilege, education, or power.

Through the works of Dreiser, Sinclair, and their contemporaries, the early 20th-century realist tradition laid the foundation for future literary interrogations of the American Dream—insisting that for all its promise, it is often compromised by inequality, industrial exploitation, and a rigid class hierarchy.

The Great Gatsby and the Dream's Disillusionment

F. Scott Fitzgerald's *The Great Gatsby* (1925) has endured as one of the most incisive and haunting critiques of the American Dream. Set during the opulence and excess of the Roaring Twenties, the novel tells the story of Jay Gatsby, a mysterious millionaire who seemingly embodies the promise of upward mobility, only to reveal the emptiness at the heart of his ambition. Through its lyrical prose and tragic arc, Fitzgerald's novel dissects the American Dream—not just as a personal goal, but as a national myth distorted by materialism and social stratification.

At first glance, Gatsby appears to be the epitome of success: a man who has risen from humble beginnings to unimaginable wealth. Yet, his fortune is revealed to be the product of dubious dealings, and his extravagant lifestyle is in service of a single, unattainable dream—winning back Daisy Buchanan, a woman from the aristocratic class who embodies for Gatsby both romantic and social aspiration. His grand parties and golden aura are, in fact, performances meant to attract Daisy's attention and validate his transformation. But as the narrative unfolds, it becomes clear that Gatsby's dream is not only unfulfilled but fundamentally flawed.

Fitzgerald masterfully uses Gatsby's quest to critique the moral decay hidden beneath the glittering surface of American prosperity. The novel's central message lies in its portrayal of the American Dream as corrupted by materialism: what once may have symbolized hard work and self-made success has become a shallow chase for wealth and status. The Buchanans—Daisy and her husband Tom—represent the entrenched, indifferent upper class, insulated from consequences and untouched by Gatsby's desperation. Their carelessness and moral emptiness reveal a society where wealth shields the powerful, while outsiders like Gatsby remain forever excluded, no matter how hard they strive.

Importantly, Fitzgerald suggests that the Dream's failure is not simply a result of individual missteps, but is rooted in the systemic inequalities of class. Gatsby may have money, but he lacks the social pedigree that grants true access to elite circles. The green light at the end of Daisy's dock—Gatsby's guiding star—is a potent symbol of hope, yet it is always just out of reach, mirroring the elusive nature of the Dream itself.

The novel's narrator, Nick Carraway, provides a sobering perspective in the book's famous closing lines, observing how "we beat on, boats against the current, borne back ceaselessly into the past." This reflection encapsulates Fitzgerald's view that the American Dream is haunted by nostalgia, a longing for a past that never truly existed. The belief that one can reinvent oneself and overcome all barriers is shown to be both seductive and self-deluding.

Ultimately, *The Great Gatsby* reveals the American Dream not as a unifying national ethos, but as a dangerous illusion—one that promises fulfillment but often delivers disillusionment. Fitzgerald mourns not only Gatsby's personal failure, but the spiritual emptiness of a society that has replaced idealism with greed, and authenticity with performance. In doing so, he creates a timeless critique of a dream that, for many, remains just that: a dream, shimmering and unreachable across the water.

Depression-Era Literature and Broken Promises

The Great Depression of the 1930s marked a profound rupture in the American consciousness, exposing the fragility of the economic foundations upon which the American Dream rested. Unemployment soared, banks failed, and millions of Americans faced homelessness and hunger—conditions that forced a reevaluation of the nation's ideals of prosperity, meritocracy, and self-determination. Literature of this era became a powerful vehicle for social critique, turning a sharp lens on the myth of universal opportunity and foregrounding the voices of the dispossessed. Authors such as John Steinbeck and Richard Wright emerged as leading figures who unflinchingly examined the grim realities of American life for the working class and racial minorities.

John Steinbeck's *The Grapes of Wrath* (1939) stands as one of the most iconic literary responses to the collapse of the American Dream. The novel traces the journey of the Joad family, tenant farmers from Oklahoma forced off their land during the Dust Bowl. Driven westward by hope and desperation, they head to California, lured by the promise of plentiful work and a better future. However, upon arrival, they find a brutal labor system riddled with exploitation, corruption, and violence. Rather than encountering a land of opportunity, the Joads discover a place where human dignity is stripped away in the face of economic hardship. Through the Joads' experience, Steinbeck critiques the capitalist structures that prioritize profit over people and reveals how the Dream is systematically denied to the most vulnerable.

In *The Grapes of Wrath*, Steinbeck blends naturalistic detail with lyrical prose and collective narration to emphasize solidarity, resilience, and moral outrage. The novel's final scenes—particularly the image of a young woman nursing a starving man—embody a radical reimagining of hope, not as individual success but as communal survival and compassion. The work calls into question whether the American Dream is truly viable for all, or only for those already holding power and privilege.

Similarly, Richard Wright's *Native Son* (1940) presents a searing indictment of the structural racism and economic disenfranchisement that shape the lives of African Americans. Set in segregated Chicago, the novel follows Bigger Thomas, a young Black man whose life is circumscribed by poverty, fear, and lack of opportunity. His eventual descent into violence and incarceration is not portrayed as an isolated moral failing but as the product of a society that has systematically denied him humanity. Wright uses *Native Son* to challenge the racial blind spots of the American Dream, exposing how Black Americans are excluded from its promises and cast as threats within the dominant white imagination.

Wright's portrayal of Bigger is deliberately uncomfortable, forcing readers to confront the psychological and social consequences of oppression. Through a mix of realism and psychological introspection, the novel lays bare the dynamics of invisibility and criminalization that plague African American life. It is a story not just of one man's downfall, but of a nation's failure to live up to its own ideals of liberty and justice.

Both Steinbeck and Wright, in different but complementary ways, highlight how economic depression, racial segregation, and geographic displacement fracture the myth of the Dream. Their works give voice to the disenfranchised and insist that literature has a moral obligation to bear witness to suffering. Far from celebrating the Dream, Depression-era literature interrogates it, revealing the profound inequalities that determine who gets to dream—and who does not.

In this context, the American Dream is no longer an aspirational horizon but a crumbling facade, propped up by myths of meritocracy while millions struggle in the shadows. These authors laid the groundwork for a more inclusive and critical literary tradition, one that seeks not just to reflect the nation's ideals, but to hold them accountable.

Post-War Consumerism and the Hollow Dream

The post-World War II era brought a renewed sense of optimism to the United States. With the economy booming, suburban neighborhoods rapidly expanding, and consumer goods flooding the market, the American Dream seemed more attainable than ever before. Homeownership, upward mobility, and nuclear family ideals were widely promoted through advertising, education, and government policy. Yet beneath this surface of affluence and conformity, many writers began to uncover the emotional, psychological, and spiritual costs of this rebranded Dream. Literature of the late 1940s through the 1960s increasingly portrayed the Dream not as a source of fulfillment, but as a mechanism of repression, alienation, and despair.

Arthur Miller's *Death of a Salesman* (1949) serves as a seminal critique of postwar consumerism and its impact on the individual psyche. The protagonist, Willy Loman, is a traveling salesman whose identity is inextricably tied to capitalist ideals—success, likability, and material wealth. Yet Willy's inability to achieve these benchmarks plunges him into delusion and ultimately suicide. The play deconstructs the Dream by illustrating how it fosters self-deception, unrealistic expectations, and emotional isolation. Through shifting timelines, dreamlike monologues, and tense family interactions, Miller emphasizes the tragic dissonance between the Dream's promise and its human cost. Willy is not just a man who fails the Dream; he is a man whom the Dream has failed, destroyed by a society that equates worth with wealth.

Beyond Miller, other postwar authors similarly explored the dark undercurrents of American affluence. John Cheever's short stories, often set in the affluent suburbs, subtly expose the fragility of domestic stability and the hollowness of middle-class values. In works like *The Swimmer* and *The Enormous Radio*, Cheever uses surreal and ironic elements to illustrate how suburban life, while outwardly idyllic, conceals deep emotional emptiness, marital discord, and identity crises. Characters drink excessively, lie to their spouses, and question their life choices—all within the neatly trimmed hedges of postwar suburbia.

Sylvia Plath, writing from a more personal and psychological vantage point, offers a gendered critique of the Dream. In her novel *The Bell Jar* (1963) and many of her poems, Plath reveals the immense pressure placed on women to conform to ideals of domesticity, beauty, and passivity. Her protagonist Esther Greenwood experiences a mental breakdown not in spite of having opportunities, but because the societal expectations feel stifling and inauthentic. The so-called Dream offers her no real autonomy or creative freedom. For Plath and many postwar women, the Dream wasn't exclusionary in the same overt way it was for minorities—it was claustrophobically inclusive, expecting conformity to a narrow model of success and femininity.

This period also saw the rise of existential themes in American literature, reflecting broader philosophical concerns about meaning, identity, and alienation. Writers like Saul Bellow, J.D. Salinger, and Richard Yates presented protagonists who, despite living in materially comfortable circumstances, struggled with a sense of disconnection from themselves and society. Their works point to a subtle but significant shift: the American Dream was no longer just an economic or social narrative—it had become deeply psychological, shaping how people understood their worth, purpose, and identity.

By the 1960s, literature had begun to reject the Dream's facade of universal prosperity and happiness. Instead, writers exposed the mental health crises, moral compromises, and emotional toll that accompanied a life spent chasing status, conformity, and consumer goods. In this sense, the postwar Dream was not a guiding light but a haunting specter—one that lured Americans into suburban homes and corporate jobs, only to leave them questioning their place in the world.

Thus, postwar literature marks a turning point in the evolution of the American Dream narrative. It signals a shift from external struggles (poverty, race, class) to internal battles—a reckoning with the self in a world that prizes appearance over authenticity and material success over emotional truth. The Dream, once a national aspiration, had become a source of personal disillusionment, setting the stage for the radical literary critiques of the 1960s and beyond.

The American Dream and Minoritized Perspectives

While the American Dream is often touted as a universal promise—where hard work, determination, and talent lead to upward mobility—minoritized writers have long contested this vision. For many African Americans, immigrants, women, Indigenous peoples, and other marginalized communities, the traditional Dream has proven either inaccessible or illusory. Rather than a pathway to equality, it has historically reinforced social hierarchies and systemic barriers. As a result, writers from these communities have reimagined or rejected the Dream altogether, offering alternate visions rooted in cultural survival, resistance, and the pursuit of dignity and justice.

James Baldwin stands as one of the most forceful critics of the American Dream. In essays such as *The Fire Next Time* (1963) and *Notes of a Native Son* (1955), Baldwin dismantles the illusion that America offers equal opportunity to all. He argues that the Dream is sustained by a denial of the country's racial history and by the exploitation of Black lives. For Baldwin, the American Dream is not only inaccessible to Black Americans—it is actively constructed on their subjugation. He writes, "I am terrified at the moral apathy, the death of the heart... which is happening in my country." Baldwin does not seek inclusion into the Dream; rather, he demands a fundamental rethinking of what America is and whom it serves. His work asserts that true liberation lies not in assimilation, but in radical honesty, love, and mutual accountability.

Other writers, like Sandra Cisneros, Maxine Hong Kingston, and Joy Harjo, challenge the American Dream from the perspectives of Latinx, Asian American, and Indigenous experiences, respectively. In *The House on Mango Street* (1984), Cisneros portrays a young Chicana girl navigating the challenges of poverty, gender, and cultural identity in a Chicago barrio. Esperanza, the narrator, does not aspire to the Dream in its capitalist form—wealth, suburban life, or white approval—but dreams instead of a home that represents freedom, creative expression, and personal autonomy. The novel deconstructs the Dream from the inside, revealing how working-class immigrant families are systemically excluded from its benefits, yet still nurture dreams of transformation grounded in community and storytelling.

Maxine Hong Kingston's memoir *The Woman Warrior* (1976) blends myth, history, and personal experience to interrogate the expectations placed on Chinese American women. For Kingston, the Dream is entangled with cultural silences and familial obligations. Her narrative does not follow a traditional rags-to-riches arc; instead, it examines the psychological and cultural costs of assimilation. The book resists the binary of success versus failure, offering a more complex meditation on identity, heritage, and voice.

Joy Harjo, the first Native American U.S. Poet Laureate, offers a completely different lens. Her poetry centers Indigenous worldviews, where dreams are not about material gain but about survival, spiritual harmony, and ancestral connection. In poems like "She Had Some Horses" and "Remember," Harjo evokes a Dream that predates colonization and capitalism—a dream rooted in land, memory, and healing. For Indigenous peoples, the American Dream has historically represented displacement, genocide, and forced assimilation. Harjo's work reclaims narrative space, asserting that Indigenous dreams are not part of the American Dream—they are an act of resistance against it.

Across these authors, a common thread emerges: the critique of a Dream that centers whiteness, patriarchy, and capitalism. Instead of chasing wealth or upward mobility, these writers envision dreams of liberation, cultural affirmation, and emotional truth. They expose the American Dream's exclusions and failures, while simultaneously crafting alternative dreams that reflect their communities' values and histories.

In doing so, they reframe the national myth not as a shared destination, but as a contested terrain—one where the struggle for justice, recognition, and self-definition continues. By decentering the dominant narrative, they force a reckoning with the Dream's limits and invite us to imagine new futures, where freedom is not defined by material success but by authenticity, solidarity, and storytelling.

The Dream in Postmodern and Contemporary Literature

As the 20th century gave way to the 21st, the American Dream—once heralded as a promise of progress, freedom, and prosperity—became a target of deep literary interrogation. Postmodern and contemporary authors often approach the Dream not as a guiding ideal, but as a cultural fiction—constructed, commercialized, and ultimately corrosive. With irony, fragmentation, and metafictional techniques, they reveal the disintegration of national myths in an age of consumerism, inequality, and historical reckoning. The American Dream in this context becomes less a beacon of hope and more a symbol of alienation, exploitation, and delusion.

In Don DeLillo's *White Noise* (1985), the Dream is filtered through the static of media saturation, consumer culture, and suburban banality. DeLillo's protagonist, Jack Gladney, is a professor of "Hitler Studies" living in a world inundated by shopping malls, fast food, and pharmaceutical fixes. The novel satirizes the middle-class pursuit of comfort and safety, showing how American life has become defined not by self-realization but by fear—of death, of insignificance, of entropy. The Dream, in DeLillo's vision, is no longer about striving but about *distracting oneself from meaninglessness.* Through absurdity and existential dread, the novel critiques the emptiness of modern American aspirations.

Similarly, Bret Easton Ellis's *American Psycho* (1991) presents a disturbing portrayal of the Dream's descent into moral and psychological decay. Patrick Bateman, the novel's wealthy Wall Street banker and serial killer, embodies the apex of capitalist success—wealthy, powerful, and meticulously groomed. Yet beneath his polished surface lies a void: he is emotionally numb, socially disengaged, and violently psychotic. Ellis uses hyperbole and satire to critique the commodification of identity, where appearance trumps substance and status replaces empathy. The American

Dream, in this novel, has become a grotesque parody—where humanity is sacrificed at the altar of materialism and narcissism.

In contrast, Colson Whitehead offers a revisionist approach to the American Dream by excavating the historical foundations of American inequality. His Pulitzer Prize-winning novel *The Underground Railroad* (2016) reimagines slavery-era America through speculative fiction, turning the metaphorical railroad into a literal subterranean network. By combining historical brutality with fantastical elements, Whitehead forces readers to confront the nation's foundational violence. In *The Nickel Boys* (2019), based on a real reform school in Florida, he explores the abuse and erasure of Black youth in the Jim Crow South. Both novels dismantle the myth that America is inherently a land of opportunity. Instead, they expose how the Dream has been systematically denied to Black Americans, replaced with state-sanctioned terror and false narratives of progress.

Contemporary literature further expands the critique of the Dream through voices that explore immigration, diaspora, gender, and precarity. Authors like Jhumpa Lahiri, Chimamanda Ngozi Adichie, and Ocean Vuong examine how the promise of America collides with cultural dislocation, generational trauma, and economic instability. Their characters often grapple with *dual consciousness*—torn between the ideals of the Dream and the realities of exclusion or displacement. In Vuong's *On Earth We're Briefly Gorgeous* (2019), the narrator—a queer Vietnamese immigrant—writes a letter to his illiterate mother, unpacking the violence, silence, and resilience that define their American experience. For Vuong, the Dream is not about assimilation or triumph, but about bearing witness, surviving grief, and finding language for one's pain.

Thus, in postmodern and contemporary literature, the American Dream is less a unifying national ethos than a contested and fractured myth. It is portrayed as:

- Empty and consumer-driven, as seen in DeLillo and Ellis;
- Historically violent and racially unjust, as illustrated by Whitehead;
- Emotionally complex and culturally fraught, as explored by diasporic and queer writers.

These authors refuse to romanticize the Dream. Instead, they expose its contradictions, unravel its false promises, and often replace it with dreams of *truth-telling, survival, and healing.* The modern literary landscape suggests that the American Dream, if it is to survive at all, must be radically redefined—not as a ladder of material success, but as a shared commitment to justice, inclusion, and human dignity.

Reimagining the Dream in the 21st Century

In the 21st century, the American Dream has not disappeared, but it has evolved into something far more pluralistic, contested, and reflective of the country's deep social contradictions. Contemporary writers are not merely critiquing the traditional Dream—they are actively reimagining it. No longer confined to the narrow ideals of upward mobility, homeownership, and white-picket-fence prosperity, the Dream now encompasses justice, visibility, cultural survival, and healing. Literature has become a powerful space where this redefinition unfolds—especially through the voices of those long excluded from dominant narratives.

In Angie Thomas's *The Hate U Give* (2017), the Dream is reframed through the lens of racial justice and youth activism. The novel follows Starr Carter, a Black teenager who witnesses the police killing of her unarmed friend. As Starr navigates the worlds of her underprivileged neighborhood and her elite private school, Thomas exposes the systemic racism that undermines the very foundation of equality and opportunity. Yet amid grief and rage, the novel is ultimately hopeful: it envisions a new kind of Dream—one shaped by solidarity, truth-telling, and the courage to demand change. Here, resistance becomes a form of aspiration, and young people are cast not just as dreamers but as agents of transformation.

Similarly, Ocean Vuong's *On Earth We're Briefly Gorgeous* (2019) reimagines the Dream as an intensely personal and poetic journey. The novel takes the form of a letter from a Vietnamese American son to his illiterate mother, blending memoir, fiction, and lyrical prose to explore trauma, queerness, language, and love. Vuong dismantles the conventional Dream of success by showing how immigrant life is saturated with both pain and beauty, survival and silence. The narrator's identity is complex and intersectional—queer, poor, brown, a refugee—and yet, through storytelling, he claims space, visibility, and voice. In Vuong's vision, the Dream is not about assimilation or wealth, but about *the freedom to speak, to be, to remember*.

In Tommy Orange's *There There* (2018), the American Dream is interrogated from an urban Native American perspective. The novel weaves together the stories of twelve Native characters in Oakland, California, culminating in a powwow that serves as both a cultural gathering and a site of confrontation. Orange addresses the legacies of displacement, addiction, generational trauma, and erasure. His characters struggle to reclaim identity in a society that often denies their existence. Yet the novel also celebrates resilience, continuity, and community—a quiet but profound assertion that Native people are still here, dreaming their own futures. The Dream here is not about becoming American, but about resisting disappearance and embracing a complex, sovereign selfhood.

Together, these works assert that the American Dream must be decolonized, de-gendered, and democratized. The newer literary voices call for:

- **Truth over myth:** Acknowledging America's violent and unjust pasts is essential to envisioning a better future.
- **Plurality over uniformity:** There is no single Dream—only overlapping dreams shaped by culture, race, sexuality, geography, and history.
- **Resilience over consumption:** Success is no longer measured in material terms alone, but in the ability to persist, create, and redefine oneself.

Rather than rejecting the Dream outright, 21st-century authors rewrite it on their own terms. Their narratives serve as blueprints for a future in which the Dream can be reclaimed—not by erasing difference, but by embracing it. The Dream survives not as a promise delivered from above, but as a struggle enacted from below—by the marginalized, the young, the silenced—who insist that they, too, belong in the American story.

Conclusion: Dreams Deferred, Dreams Reclaimed

The evolution of the American Dream in 20th- and 21st-century literature reflects not a singular, unified belief, but a contested cultural narrative—one that has been shaped, challenged, and reimagined by each generation of writers. Far from being a fixed ideal, the Dream is a dynamic and malleable concept, responding to changing socio-economic realities, political tensions, and the deepening complexity of American identity.

Throughout the century, literature has served as both a mirror and a critique of the Dream's promises and failures. In the works of Theodore Dreiser, Upton Sinclair, and F. Scott Fitzgerald, we see early warnings that ambition and opportunity are often undermined by class, corruption, and illusion. During the Great Depression, authors like Steinbeck and Richard Wright stripped the Dream of its romanticism, showing it to be unattainable for the poor and racially marginalized. After World War II, the renewed consumerist Dream, rooted in suburban comfort and capitalist productivity, was unmasked by writers like Arthur Miller, Sylvia Plath, and John Cheever, who revealed the psychological and emotional costs of hollow success.

As the century progressed, writers from minoritized communities stepped forward to revise the narrative entirely. James Baldwin, Maxine Hong Kingston, Sandra Cisneros, and others insisted that the Dream had never been inclusive. For them, the very foundation of the American Dream was built on exclusions—racial, gendered, economic, and cultural. Their work did more than critique; it offered alternative dreams—dreams rooted in freedom, self-expression, justice, and cultural survival.

By the end of the 20th century and into the 21st, literature embraced postmodern deconstruction and diverse reimaginings. Authors such as Don DeLillo, Bret Easton Ellis, Colson Whitehead, Angie Thomas, and Ocean Vuong approach the Dream with irony, pain, and invention. Their work suggests that while the Dream may be broken or deferred, it is not entirely lost. Instead, it is reclaimed and rewritten—often in the voices of those once denied its promise.

Ultimately, the literature of the American Dream tells us not what America *is*, but what it *aspires to be*—and how far it has fallen short. Writers have revealed that the Dream is neither a lie nor a truth, but a battleground. It must be fought for through honesty, inclusion, and imaginative reinvention. Whether through disillusionment or hope, literature teaches us that the Dream's survival depends not on wealth or power, but on storytelling itself—the ability to envision something better, more just, and more real.

In this way, dreams deferred become dreams reclaimed—not by forgetting the past, but by confronting it. The American Dream may be elusive, but it remains a potent symbol of struggle, resilience, and the possibility of transformation.

Conclusion

Enduring Echoes – The Literature That Changed a Nation

As we reflect upon the literary journey of 20th-century America, we encounter not merely a collection of texts but a profound chronicle of transformation—social, political, cultural, and psychological. This was a century in which literature did not merely mirror reality; it interrogated it, reframed it, and, at times, reimagined it entirely. In doing so, American literature became a vital site of national self-examination—one that illuminated both the triumphs and traumas of a complex, often divided society.

Throughout the century, literature functioned as a cultural compass, guiding generations through the turbulence of war, economic collapse, migration, civil rights movements, and sweeping technological change. Writers engaged these upheavals not with passivity but with fierce creativity and moral urgency. From the fragmented consciousness of T.S. Eliot's The Waste Land to the mythic introspection of Toni Morrison's Beloved, from the biting critique of Arthur Miller's Death of a Salesman to the poetic protest of Langston Hughes—each literary voice added to an expanding tapestry that sought to capture, challenge, and sometimes heal the American spirit.

The American Dream—once idealized as a promise of prosperity, equality, and self-made success—was repeatedly deconstructed, questioned, and rewritten. No longer a one-size-fits-all narrative, it became instead a contested terrain—one shaped by race, gender, class, sexuality, and geography. For many, the Dream remained elusive, a mirage obscured by systemic inequality and historical erasure. Literature gave form to these silences and fractures, rendering visible the invisible, and audible the unheard.

Equally significant was the emergence of minoritized voices that disrupted traditional literary canons. African American, Native American, Latinx, Asian American, queer, immigrant, and working-class writers redefined the very essence of American literature. Authors such as James Baldwin, Sandra Cisneros, Maxine Hong Kingston, and Sherman Alexie wrote not from the margins, but from lived experience, demanding recognition, reparation, and representation. Their works carved space for alternate dreams—of survival, selfhood, community, and cultural continuity.

The recurring motifs of alienation, dislocation, trauma, identity, and resilience speak not just to individual experiences but to collective reckonings. Literature became both a repository of memory and a catalyst for change, capable of evoking empathy and inspiring action. Through fiction, poetry, drama, and memoir, writers invited readers to grapple with the nation's deepest contradictions—between promise and practice, idealism and injustice, unity and fragmentation.

As we move further into the 21st century, the legacy of 20th-century American literature remains vibrantly alive. Contemporary writers like Colson Whitehead, Ocean Vuong, Tommy Orange, and Angie Thomas continue this tradition of truth-telling and imaginative resistance. They stand on the shoulders of literary ancestors while forging new paths that reflect our pluralistic, digitized, and often polarized age. Their work affirms that literature is not static but evolutionary—a dialogue between past and present, memory and imagination.

In the final analysis, the enduring power of 20th-century American literature lies not only in its stylistic innovation or thematic range but in its moral courage and emotional resonance. These works are not mere historical artifacts; they are living texts—breathing, questioning, provoking. They ask us to read not just with our eyes, but with our conscience.

Let us therefore carry forward this legacy of engagement and empathy. Let us continue to read deeply, think critically, and listen attentively to the myriad voices that compose the American story. For in doing so, we honor the enduring echoes of a literary tradition that did more than change a nation—it revealed its soul.

Appendixes

Appendix A: Literary Timeline – Key Moments in 20th Century American Literature

Year	Event / Publication
1906	**Upton Sinclair** publishes *The Jungle* – a landmark muckraking novel that exposes the appalling conditions of the meatpacking industry and sparks food safety reforms.
1913	**Willa Cather** releases *O Pioneers!* – the first in her Great Plains trilogy, celebrating pioneer resilience while challenging romanticized frontier myths.
1915	**T.S. Eliot** publishes "The Love Song of J. Alfred Prufrock" – introducing a fragmented, modernist voice that grapples with alienation, indecision, and cultural disintegration.
1922	*The Waste Land* by **T.S. Eliot** and *Ulysses* by **James Joyce** signal the peak of literary modernism, blending myth, stream of consciousness, and linguistic experimentation.
1925	**F. Scott Fitzgerald**'s *The Great Gatsby* critiques the hollowness of the American Dream amid the Jazz Age's glittering excess.
1926	**Langston Hughes** publishes *The Weary Blues* – a seminal poetry collection of the Harlem Renaissance, fusing jazz rhythms with racial consciousness.
1937	**Zora Neale Hurston**'s *Their Eyes Were Watching God* foregrounds the interior life and struggles of an African American woman in the South, now a classic of Black feminist literature.
1939	**John Steinbeck** publishes *The Grapes of Wrath*, chronicling the Dust Bowl migration and exposing class struggle during the Great Depression.
1940	**Richard Wright**'s *Native Son* offers a harrowing exploration of race, poverty, and systemic injustice in urban America.
1949	**Arthur Miller**'s *Death of a Salesman* interrogates capitalist ideals and personal failure, becoming a cornerstone of American drama.
1951	**J.D. Salinger** releases *The Catcher in the Rye*, capturing adolescent disillusionment and alienation in postwar America.
1953	**Ray Bradbury** publishes *Fahrenheit 451*, a dystopian critique of censorship, conformity, and anti-intellectualism in the Cold War era.
1957	**Jack Kerouac**'s *On the Road* defines the restless spirit of the Beat Generation, celebrating spontaneity, rebellion, and spiritual searching.

Year	Event / Publication
1960	**Harper Lee**'s *To Kill a Mockingbird* becomes a landmark novel confronting racial injustice in the Jim Crow South.
1965	**Sylvia Plath**'s *Ariel* is published posthumously, marking a major moment in confessional poetry and feminist literary expression.
1967	**S.E. Hinton** publishes *The Outsiders*, credited with launching modern Young Adult fiction through its depiction of teenage class conflict.
1970	**Toni Morrison** debuts with *The Bluest Eye*, examining internalized racism and beauty standards within the Black community.
1972	**Rudolfo Anaya**'s *Bless Me, Ultima* pioneers Chicano literature, blending folklore, spirituality, and cultural identity.
1974	**Octavia E. Butler** releases *Patternmaster*, launching her legacy as a foundational figure in Afrofuturism and speculative fiction.
1976	**Maxine Hong Kingston** publishes *The Woman Warrior*, a hybrid memoir that explores Chinese-American female identity and ancestral mythology.
1982	**Alice Walker**'s *The Color Purple* wins the Pulitzer Prize, powerfully depicting the resilience of Black women in the American South.
1985	**Margaret Atwood** (Canadian-American context) publishes *The Handmaid's Tale*, a dystopian feminist classic increasingly relevant in contemporary discourse.
1987	**Toni Morrison**'s *Beloved* reclaims the narrative of slavery through historical fiction imbued with magical realism and emotional depth.
1989	**Amy Tan** publishes *The Joy Luck Club*, capturing the generational and cultural tensions between Chinese immigrant mothers and their American-born daughters.
1993	**Toni Morrison** becomes the first African American woman to win the Nobel Prize in Literature, honoring her literary legacy and cultural influence.
1996	**David Foster Wallace** releases *Infinite Jest*, a sprawling postmodern novel examining addiction, entertainment, and late-capitalist malaise.
1999	**Jhumpa Lahiri**'s *Interpreter of Maladies* wins the Pulitzer Prize, bringing Indian-American immigrant experiences into the literary mainstream.
2001	Post-9/11 literature begins to emerge, with authors like **Don DeLillo** (*Falling Man*) and **Jonathan Safran Foer** (*Extremely Loud & Incredibly Close*) grappling with trauma, grief, and global politics.
2003	**Edward P. Jones**'s *The Known World* wins the Pulitzer, offering a complex narrative about African American slaveholders in the antebellum South.
2009	**Colson Whitehead**'s *Sag Harbor* explores Black middle-class adolescence and memory; he would later win Pulitzers for *The Underground Railroad* (2016) and *The Nickel Boys* (2019).

Year	Event / Publication
2010s	Rise of intersectional narratives from voices like **Chimamanda Ngozi Adichie**, **Jesmyn Ward**, **Roxane Gay**, and **Tommy Orange**, reflecting themes of race, gender, trauma, and indigeneity.
2020s	Literature responds to the pandemic, Black Lives Matter, and political polarization. Works by **Ocean Vuong**, **Angie Thomas**, **Clint Smith**, and others redefine the American literary imagination for a new generation.

Appendix B: Glossary of Key Literary Terms and Movements

Term	Definition
Modernism	A groundbreaking literary and artistic movement that emerged in the early 20th century, characterized by a conscious break from traditional narrative structures, linear time, and realism. Modernist works often employ fragmentation, stream-of-consciousness, and symbolism to reflect disillusionment with modern society and the chaos of the post–World War I era. Notable figures include T.S. Eliot, Virginia Woolf, and James Joyce.
Postmodernism	A literary and cultural movement that arose in the mid-to-late 20th century as a reaction to modernism. Marked by irony, intertextuality, metafiction, pastiche, and skepticism toward objective truth or grand narratives, postmodern literature often blurs the boundaries between fiction and reality. Key writers include Thomas Pynchon, Don DeLillo, and Margaret Atwood.
Harlem Renaissance	A vibrant cultural, intellectual, and artistic movement during the 1920s and 1930s, centered in Harlem, New York. It marked a flourishing of African American literature, music, and art that celebrated Black identity, creativity, and resistance to racism. Luminaries include Langston Hughes, Zora Neale Hurston, and Claude McKay.
Beat Generation	A literary and cultural movement of the 1950s that rejected mainstream American values, materialism, and conformity. Embracing spontaneity, Eastern philosophies, jazz rhythms, and drug experimentation, Beat writers like Jack Kerouac, Allen Ginsberg, and William S. Burroughs influenced the counterculture of the 1960s.
Stream of Consciousness	A narrative technique used to depict the continuous, often chaotic flow of a character's thoughts, feelings, and sensory impressions. This method seeks to portray inner experience with immediacy and psychological depth. Prominent examples can be found in the works of Virginia Woolf, James Joyce, and William Faulkner.

Term	Definition
Magical Realism	A literary mode in which fantastical or supernatural elements are integrated seamlessly into a realistic setting, treated as normal by the characters. Often associated with Latin American literature, it is used to explore complex social, cultural, or historical realities. Key authors include Gabriel García Márquez, Isabel Allende, and Toni Morrison.
Metafiction	Fiction that self-consciously draws attention to its own artificiality or construction. It often breaks the "fourth wall," comments on the act of storytelling, and challenges conventional notions of narrative truth. Metafiction is a hallmark of postmodern literature.
Diaspora	A term commonly used in literary studies to describe works that reflect the experiences of individuals or communities who have been displaced from their homeland. Diasporic literature often explores themes of cultural identity, exile, assimilation, memory, and transnational belonging.
Bildungsroman	A literary genre focused on the psychological, moral, and emotional development of the protagonist, typically from youth to maturity. The term originates from German literature and is often translated as "coming-of-age novel." Classic examples include *Jane Eyre* and *The Catcher in the Rye*.
Revisionist History	In literature, this refers to works that challenge dominant historical narratives by presenting events from alternative or marginalized perspectives. Such texts aim to recover suppressed voices, question official histories, and reframe cultural memory—often seen in postcolonial, feminist, and African American literature.

Appendix C: Key Author Profiles

1. **Toni Morrison (1931–2019):** A towering figure in American literature, Toni Morrison was awarded both the Nobel Prize in Literature and the Pulitzer Prize for her profound explorations of African American life. Her novels—such as *Beloved*, *The Bluest Eye*, and *Song of Solomon*—examine the complexities of memory, generational trauma, motherhood, and Black identity. Morrison's lyrical prose and unapologetic focus on the interior lives of Black women redefined the American literary canon and gave voice to historically marginalized experiences.
2. **F. Scott Fitzgerald (1896–1940):** Often regarded as the literary chronicler of the Jazz Age, F. Scott Fitzgerald captured the extravagance, disillusionment, and moral decay of 1920s America. Best known for

The Great Gatsby and *Tender Is the Night*, his work explores themes of the American Dream, romantic illusion, wealth, and the emptiness of material success. Fitzgerald's tragic characters and lyrical style underscore the fragility of aspiration and the decadence of a generation.

3. **Langston Hughes (1902–1967):** A central voice of the Harlem Renaissance, Langston Hughes was a poet, novelist, and essayist whose work celebrated African American culture, music, and everyday life. His collections, including *The Weary Blues* and *Montage of a Dream Deferred*, blend blues rhythms with incisive commentary on race and injustice. Hughes championed the dignity and resilience of Black communities while pushing for racial equality through art.
4. **Sylvia Plath (1932–1963):** Known for her haunting introspection and poetic brilliance, Sylvia Plath remains one of the most influential voices in confessional literature. Her semi-autobiographical novel *The Bell Jar* and posthumously published poetry collection *Ariel* delve into mental illness, identity, feminism, and the desire for self-liberation. Plath's stark imagery and emotional intensity have made her a powerful symbol of artistic struggle and psychological depth.
5. **Ralph Ellison (1914–1994):** Ralph Ellison's seminal novel *Invisible Man* stands as a landmark in American literature, addressing the psychological and social invisibility faced by African Americans. Through his protagonist's journey, Ellison explores themes of race, individuality, identity, and existential alienation in a racially stratified society. His work blends modernist technique with sharp sociopolitical critique.
6. **Maxine Hong Kingston (b. 1940):** A pioneer of Asian American literature, Maxine Hong Kingston is best known for *The Woman Warrior* and *China Men*. Blending memoir, folklore, and fiction, her work addresses issues of cultural hybridity, gender roles, immigration, and the complexities of storytelling across generations. Kingston's voice has helped redefine narratives of the Chinese American experience and broader diasporic identities.
7. **Jack Kerouac (1922–1969):** As a leading figure of the Beat Generation, Jack Kerouac's spontaneous prose and countercultural ethos shaped mid-20th-century American literature. His iconic novel *On the Road* celebrates freedom, spiritual quest, and rebellion against societal norms. Kerouac's rhythmic style and emphasis on personal experience, travel, and nonconformity embody the restless spirit of postwar youth.
8. **Sandra Cisneros (b. 1954):** An influential Chicana author, Sandra Cisneros is celebrated for her lyrical and intimate portrayals of working-class Latino life. Her most famous work, *The House on Mango*

Street, is a coming-of-age novel written in vignettes that explore gender, ethnicity, neighborhood life, and the aspirations of a young Latina girl. Cisneros's voice bridges the personal and the political, highlighting the intersections of culture, language, and identity.

9. **James Baldwin (1924–1987):** James Baldwin was a searing moral voice in American literature and civil rights. His novels and essays—such as *Go Tell It on the Mountain* and *The Fire Next Time*—probe issues of race, sexuality, religion, and alienation with unflinching honesty. Baldwin's eloquence and emotional depth, combined with his activist commitment, make him one of the most enduring voices in the fight for justice and understanding in American letters.
10. **Jhumpa Lahiri (b. 1967):** A Pulitzer Prize-winning author, Jhumpa Lahiri explores the intricacies of diasporic identity, family, and cultural dislocation. Her works, including *Interpreter of Maladies* and *The Namesake*, delve into the emotional landscapes of Indian American immigrants, tracing their efforts to navigate dual identities, language, and generational tension. Lahiri's elegant prose captures both the beauty and loneliness of the in-between spaces her characters inhabit.

Appendix D: Suggested Further Readings

I. Foundational Works of 20th Century American Literature

- **F. Scott Fitzgerald – *The Great Gatsby* (1925)**: A classic critique of the American Dream during the Jazz Age.
- **William Faulkner – *The Sound and the Fury* (1929)**: A stream-of-consciousness masterpiece exploring Southern identity and decay.
- **Ernest Hemingway – *The Sun Also Rises* (1926):** A postwar novel that captures the disillusionment of the "Lost Generation."
- **Toni Morrison – *Beloved* (1987)**: A poetic novel about slavery's haunting legacy, memory, and motherhood.
- **Ralph Ellison – *Invisible Man* (1952):** A powerful exploration of Black identity and social invisibility in mid-century America.

II. Key Texts of Major Literary Movements

Modernism

- **T.S. Eliot – *The Waste Land* (1922)**: A dense, allusive poem that encapsulates the disillusionment of post-WWI Europe.
- **Ezra Pound – *Cantos* (1915–1962):** A sprawling, ambitious poetic work embodying modernist innovation and complexity.

Harlem Renaissance

- **Zora Neale Hurston – *Their Eyes Were Watching God* (1937):** A vital portrayal of Black womanhood and autonomy.
- **Langston Hughes – *Selected Poems* (1959):** A comprehensive introduction to Hughes's lyrical celebration of African American life.

Beat Generation

- **Allen Ginsberg – *Howl and Other Poems* (1956):** A rebellious and energetic challenge to mid-century conservatism.
- **Jack Kerouac – *On the Road* (1957):** A defining text of youthful rebellion and spiritual exploration.

III. Diverse Voices in American Literature

- **Maxine Hong Kingston – *The Woman Warrior* (1976):** A blend of memoir and myth that reflects on Chinese American female identity.
- **James Baldwin – *Giovanni's Room* (1956):** A groundbreaking exploration of same-sex love and alienation.
- **Sandra Cisneros – *Woman Hollering Creek and Other Stories* (1991):** A mosaic of Chicana experiences, gender roles, and cultural tension.
- **Jhumpa Lahiri – *Unaccustomed Earth* (2008):** Short stories that portray the subtle emotional landscapes of immigrants and their descendants.

IV. Theoretical and Critical Frameworks

- **Harold Bloom – *The Western Canon* (1994):** A provocative defense of traditional literary values and enduring works.
- **bell hooks – *Ain't I a Woman: Black Women and Feminism* (1981):** A foundational feminist text examining intersections of race, gender, and class.
- **Edward Said – *Culture and Imperialism* (1993):** Offers postcolonial insights into literature's entanglement with empire.
- **Leslie Fiedler – *Love and Death in the American Novel* (1960):** A seminal critical work examining American myth and literary identity.

V. Autobiographies, Memoirs, and Nonfiction Influences

- **Richard Wright – *Black Boy* (1945):** A searing autobiography of race, resistance, and self-education in the Jim Crow South.
- **Maya Angelou – *I Know Why the Caged Bird Sings* (1969):** A lyrical memoir of trauma, resilience, and Black womanhood.
- **Barack Obama – *Dreams from My Father* (1995):** A personal narrative exploring race, family, and American identity in the late 20th century.